Contested Commodities

Contested Commodities

Margaret Jane Radin

Harvard University Press

Cambridge, Massachusetts
London, England
1996

Six lines from "Description without Place," from Wallace Stevens, *Collected Poems*, copyright 1945 by Wallace Stevens; reprinted by permission of Alfred A. Knopf, Inc., and Faber and Faber Ltd.

Library of Congress Cataloging-in-Publication Data

Radin, Margaret Jane.
    Contested commodities / Margaret Jane Radin.
      p. cm.
    Includes index.
    ISBN 0-674-16697-3 (alk. paper)
    1. Commercial products—Social aspects. 2. Marketing—Social aspects. I. Title.
HM211.R33 1996
 306.3—dc20   95-51051
              CIP

For Amadea and Wayland

Acknowledgments

Although he probably doesn't realize it, Alan Schwartz provided a stimulus for this book. Conversations with him in the mid-1980s, when we were both teaching at the University of Southern California Law Center, made me see that my reevaluation of the personality theory of property necessitated a reevaluation of the question of alienability. During that process, nurtured by USC's extraordinary collegiality, I came to realize that commodification was the key issue. For his good questions I thank Scott Altman, the student editor of my article "Market-Inalienability," which served as the embryo of this book.

Friends and colleagues too numerous to name have contributed to the project since then, both informally and at lectures, workshops, and colloquia. Thanks at least to Anita Allen, Lori Andrews, C. Edwin Baker, John H. Bogart, Richard Craswell, Barbara Herman, Richard Posner, David A. J. Richards, Alan Ryan, Larry Sager, William H. Simon, Cass Sunstein, Richard Warner, and Catharine Wells.

I am grateful to Thomas C. Grey, who read an earlier version of the manuscript and offered insightful suggestions; to Don Herzog, who made wonderful comments on almost every page; and to readers for Harvard University Press, whose thoughtful assessments helped me to improve the manuscript. I also thank all my former students who provided research assistance: Sarah Dennison-Leonard, Wesley Felix, Chad Atkins, and particularly Brendan P. Cullen, Norman W. Spaulding III, and Madhavi Sunder.

I am grateful to Stanford Law School for providing summer research funds and a great deal of noncommodified support. Paul Brest, our dean, has been wonderfully supportive in many ways, as have many of my colleagues, especially Janet Cooper Alexander, Barbara Fried, Janet E. Halley, and Kathleen M. Sullivan.

Special thanks to Christopher L. Hamlin for helping me find courage to face questions I can't answer.

Earlier versions of portions of this book appeared in the following articles, and permission to reprint is gratefully acknowledged: "Reconsidering Personhood," 74 *Oregon Law Review* (forthcoming); "A Deweyan Perspective on the Economic Theory of Democracy," 11 *Constitutional Commentary* 530 (1994–95); "Compensation and Commensurability," 43 *Duke Law Journal* 56 (1994); "Reflections on Objectification," 65 *Southern California Law Review* 341 (1991); "The Pragmatist and the Feminist," 63 *Southern California Law Review* 1699 (1990); "Justice and the Market Domain," in *Markets and Justice* (ed. J. Chapman and J. Pennock 1989); "Market-Inalienability," 100 *Harvard Law Review* 1849 (1987).

Contents

Preface

The contemporary arena of moral and political debate is full of painful and puzzling controversies about what things can properly be bought and sold: babies? sexual services? kidneys and corneas? environmental pollution permits? These things are contested commodities. They challenge us to try to understand the appropriate scope of the market. This book presents a pragmatic philosophical and legal approach to thinking about some of our contested commodities—those that are related to persons and the nature of human life.

It is now customary for scholars in many fields to borrow the sociologists' concept of "social construction" to denote the way social practice creates the meaning of the interactions and events in which we participate. In exploring the meaning of our market transactions, I am investigating one kind of social construction.

The ungainly word "commodification" denotes a particular social construction of things people value, their social construction as commodities. Commodification refers to the social process by which something comes to be apprehended as a commodity, as well as to the state of affairs once the process has taken place. "Contested commodification"—the focus of this book—refers to instances in which we experience personal and social conflict about the process and the result.

The word "commodity," as I use it, is a conception embedded in modern market society. There are other ways of understanding the word "commodity" that are outside the culture of the market society or that antedate its historical era. But in this book I am concerned with the connotations of something's being treated as a commodity against the background of our contemporary common understanding of organized markets.

Although there are affinities between my use of the term "commodity" and Marx's, I do not adopt the notion, which some derive from Marx, that commodification is always wrong. Nor do I find, as many Marxists would, that commodified understandings of social interactions cannot coexist with noncommodified ones.

Instead I believe there can be coexistent commodified and noncommodified understandings of various aspects of social life. The questions I believe need to be asked are in what instances there actually is such coexistence, and whether that coexistence is unstable, threatening to decay into a monolithic structure of commodification.

These questions arise from the pragmatic methodology I favor. This book reflects a pragmatist's take on the social meaning(s) of market trading and of the attendant notions of property entitlements alienable through freedom of contract. True to the pragmatic spirit, the explorations in this book are relatively retail rather than wholesale—sticking fairly close to the details of context and not engaging in a search for a grand theory. In my view, no one theory is suitable for all cases of contested commodification.

Meaning—and attendant normative evaluation—is the aim of these explorations. Thus, I consider not only actual buying and selling but also thoughts couched in terms of buying and selling—the conception of things as suitable for trade. I consider market discourse and its role in commodification as a worldview.

Considering commodification as a worldview involves confronting one influential strand of contemporary economic analysis. The Chicago school of economics tends to conceive of everything people may value as a scarce commodity with a price. Economic journals are full of studies treating as market commodities aspects of life and love that the rest of us are used to thinking of as noneconomic. Policy analysts ask us to make monetized tradeoffs about the length and quality of life in order to allocate health care resources; they ask us to value life in dollars in order to find out the "right" level of occupational safety risk. Is anything wrong with reasoning that way? If there are realms of social life that are or should be off-limits to the market, how should we delineate those realms, and what kind of analysis could we use in them? What (if anything) is wrong with commodification of everything?

Because these questions ask about the appropriate relationship of particular things to the market, it looks as if we need a normative theory about the appropriate social role of the market to answer it. Theories about the role of the market can be imagined as ordered on a continuum stretching from universal noncommodification (nothing in markets) to universal commodification (everything in markets). On this continuum, Karl Marx's theory can represent the theoretical pole of universal noncommodification. The views of Gary Becker, a Nobel laureate who applies economic analysis to family life, and of Judge Richard Posner, author of an economic theory of sex, can be seen as close to the opposite theoretical pole. In this book I explore the theoretical poles, but I find matters too complex to be captured adequately by one of these wholesale theories.

If both theoretical poles are inadequate, what is in the middle? A traditional middle way has been a kind of market compartmentalization. Many theorists in the liberal political tradition see a normatively appropriate but limited realm for commodification coexisting with one or more nonmarket realms. They partition the social world into markets and politics, markets and rights, markets and families, and so on. For a compartmentalizer, the crucial question is how to conceive of the permissible scope of the market. An acceptable answer would solve problems of contested commodification. Nevertheless, I argue that traditional liberal compartmentalization is at best oversimplified and cannot lead to the kind of answer envisioned. Worse, it may tempt us to overlook the ways in which market and nonmarket conceptualizations of social interactions can and do coexist, and it fails to give us a theoretical handle on how to evaluate these cultural crosscurrents.

I want to argue for a different kind of middle way. In this book I develop a notion of incomplete commodification that I hope will help us deal better with the complexities of commodification as we experience it. These complexities include the plurality of meanings of any particular interaction, the dynamic nature of these meanings (their instability), and the possible effects (good or ill) in the world of either promoting or trying to forestall a commodified understanding of something that we have previously valued in a noneconomic way. I give no wholesale argument that commodified understandings—market conceptualizations—are bad no matter where and how they occur. Instead I try to work through these complexities with respect to a number of salient issues, among them prostitution, baby-selling, and tort compensation for pain and suffering. I consider the ramifications of understanding free expression as a laissez-faire market-place of ideas, and of understanding democracy as merely a species of economics.

This book is one of many possible pictures one might draw, with a particular collection of shapes portrayed, many others omitted, and some lucky accidents. It seems to me in retrospect that trying to write about commodification more systematically would be like trying to write a systematic treatise on life as we know and live it.

Thus the theory of description matters most.
It is the theory of the word for those

For whom the word is the making of the world,
The buzzing world and lisping firmament.

It is a world of words to the end of it,
In which nothing solid is its solid self.

Wallace Stevens
"Description without Place"

1

Commodification as a Worldview

Literal and Metaphorical Markets

In a literal market, things are exchanged for money under certain social conditions. Sellers deliver goods to buyers; buyers deliver money to sellers. We participate in this practice every day, and we take those social conditions for granted. There's nothing strange about taking a Coke from the shelf and handing the store clerk money in return.

In a metaphorical market, social interactions that do not involve actually handing over money for goods are talked about as if they did. When Nobel prize–winning economist Gary Becker writes of family interactions, of love, marriage, and birth, as market transactions,[1] the market is metaphorical. This theoretical practice, unlike our habitual participation in literal markets, seems very strange to many people. Lovers and family members do not conceive of their own actions as trades, nor do they collect money from one another when they receive benefits from one another.

As a theoretical practice, the market metaphor is not necessarily intended to reflect people's actual understandings of themselves, their relationships, and activities, but rather to make accurate predictions. Nevertheless, it will be revealing, I believe, to investigate the implications of the divergence between the terms of the model and people's actual understandings; and this investigation will occupy much of this book.

Commodification as I understand it elides literal and metaphorical markets. In one sense, there cannot be any sharp divide between the literal and the metaphorical, because there is no sharp divide between action and discourse—between the nature of a transaction and the conceptual scheme or discursive framework in which we understand it. But neoclassical economic theorists, especially those of the Chicago school, elide literal and metaphorical markets in a much more straightforward sense. The writings of these economic theorists can be understood to reflect a methodological archetype that I will call universal commodification. This is the methodology that undergirds conceiving of love, marriage, and birth as market transactions.

Universal Commodification

Our investigation of contested commodification must begin with an understanding of the archetype in which commodification is uncontested. As an archetype, universal commodification is oversimplified, a caricature. It is my attempt to gather together and boil down fragments that are part of a certain way of thinking and of talking. The archetype is useful for analysis, although it does not—and could not[2]—fully describe the complexities of the real world or real people. I present here a more or less intuitive overview of its contours, which can serve as a basis of exploration in the next several chapters.

The archetype of universal commodification presents a one-dimensional world of value. From the perspective of universal commodification, all things desired or valued—from personal attributes to good government—are commodities. Anything that some people are willing to sell and that others are willing to buy can and should in principle be the subject of free market exchange. All social interactions are conceived of as free market exchanges. For example, when John gives his bicycle to Mary, he exchanges the bicycle, which he values at $100, for a feeling of generosity, which he values at $150. In the terms of universal commodification, the person is conceived of as both a commodity-holder and a commodity-trader. The person is a commodity-holder: universal commodification describes in monetary terms all things of value to the person—including personal attributes, relationships, and religious and philosophical commitments. In the framework of universal commodification, the functions of government, wisdom, a healthful environment, and the right to bear children are all commodities. The person is also a commodity-trader: all these things are assumed in principle to be alienable; they are capable of being exchanged for money; and freedom is defined as free trade of all things.

In universal commodification, the value of a commodity (from the social point of view) is defined as its exchange value, often referred to as market value, when it is traded in a laissez-faire market—or hypothetically traded in a hypothetical laissez-faire market. Valuation in terms of dollars implies that all commodities are fungible and commensurable—capable of being reduced to money without changing in value, and completely interchangeable with every other commodity in terms of exchange value. (Commensurability is central to commodification, and I return to it below.)

Universal commodification takes into account that people may value their commodities "subjectively" at a sum other than the market price, but the value is still assumed to be a price. From the individual point of view, the value of a commodity is defined as either the sum of money the holder will accept in order to relinquish it, or the sum of money the potential holder will pay in order to acquire it. The simplest version of universal commodification tends to presume that individual value is equivalent to exchange value. When possible divergence is acknowledged, exchange value is often called "objective" value and individual value is often called "subjective" value.[3]

Most legal academics are familiar with this economistic conception of life, because "law and economics" has been a prominent intellectual paradigm in law school teaching since the 1970s. Many of the writings of Gary Becker and of Judge Richard Posner, formerly a law professor, call readily to mind the archetype of universal commodification.

In his discussion of the criteria for an appropriate property regime in *Economic Analysis of Law*, Posner assumes that everything people value is (or should be) ownable and salable.[4] Posner's criteria are "universality," "exclusivity," and "transferability." He argues that "if every valuable (meaning scarce as well as desired) resource were owned by someone (universality), if ownership connoted the unqualified power to exclude everybody else from using the resource (exclusivity) as well as to use it oneself, and if ownership rights were freely transferable, or as lawyers say alienable (transferability), value would be maximized."[5] The only limitation Posner places on this claim that everything valuable should be alienable property is that it must be qualified by the costs of implementing such a system.

These arguments may seem abstract, but Posner and Becker show the depth (and courage) of their convictions by applying this analysis to people's desire for, and relationships with, children. In a 1978 article coauthored with Elisabeth Landes, Posner explored the advantages of a free market in babies. He considered "the possibility of taking some tentative and reversible steps toward a free baby market in order to determine experimentally the social costs and benefits of using the market in this area."[6] He speculated that the poor may actually do better in a free baby market than under present adoption law, because "[p]eople who might flunk the agencies' criteria on economic grounds might, in a free market with low prices, be able to adopt children, just as poor people are able to buy color television sets."[7]

Gary Becker, like Posner, unflinchingly employs the market model to analyze the desire for children. In straightforwardly speaking of children as a commodity, Posner and Becker are using the vocabulary I call market rhetoric. In doing so they extend the market, metaphorically at least, beyond what we are conventionally comfortable with. But how close do they come to the archetype of universal commodification? Do they want to extend the market to everything?

Yes, insofar as they adhere to characteristic neoclassical economic methodology, particularly as that methodology is applied by practitioners of law and economics. The methodology universalizes the market, both literally (to the extent possible, absent market failure) and metaphorically. The tendency toward universalization of metaphorical markets can be seen, for example, in Posner's definition of "value" in terms of money[8] and in his conception of justice as a good with a price.[9]

Many practitioners of law and economics define economics globally. In Posner's words, it is "the science of rational choice" in a world of scarce resources. Its task is "to explore the implications of assuming that man is a rational maximizer of his ends in life, his satisfactions—what we shall call his 'self-interest.' "[10] Unlike many other practitioners of the genre, Posner goes all the way; he applies his analysis to human sexuality. In *Sex and Reason*, he argues that sexual orientation and behavior can be explained in terms of the "reason" of economics: sexual actors are simply seeking to satisfy their preferences in such a way as to achieve the largest difference between benefits and costs.[11]

Universal commodification, in conceiving of the person as a commodity-trader, implies a certain view of human freedom. Market trading and its outcomes represent individual freedom and the ideal for individuals and society. Unrestricted choice about what goods to trade represents individual freedom, and maximizing individual gains from trade represents the individual's ideal. In keeping with its conception of the person as a commodity-trader, universal commodification also implies a certain view of political life. All social and political interactions are conceived of as exchanges for monetizable gains. Politics reduces to "rent seeking" by logrolling selfish individuals or groups, in which those individuals or groups vie to capture social wealth for themselves. The social ideal reduces to efficiency.[12]

Efficiency is pursued through the market methodology of cost-benefit analysis. Cost-benefit analysis evaluates human actions and social outcomes in terms of actual or hypothetical gains from trade, measured in money. In seeking efficiency through market methodology, universal commodification posits the laissez-faire market as the rule. Laissez-faire is presumptively efficient because it is a system of voluntary transfers. In the framework of universal commodification, voluntary transfers are presumed to maximize gains from trade, and all human interactions are characterizable as trades. Because freedom is defined as free choices of the person seen as trader, laissez-faire also presumptively expresses freedom.

The presumptive efficiency and presumptive freedom of laissez-faire suggest that the philosophical commitments of theorists whose views evoke universal commodification may be either utilitarian or libertarian. Many (probably most) law-and-economics theorists are utilitarians.[13] Some theorists whose views tend toward universal commodification see themselves as libertarians. If their reasoning is pressed, though, the ethic that drives their analysis seems to be wealth or welfare maximization.[14]

Later I will be exploring the philosophical implications of commodification—its theories of freedom, personhood, and politics—in more detail. For now, it is worth noting that the archetype I characterize as universal commodification is different from mere consequentialism or mere utilitarianism.

Consequentialism is a very broad label for the idea of identifying right and wrong by results; of course it is possible to do this without making monetization or market trading central to the scheme. Although some utilitarians may endorse universal commodification, others do not go all the way to its theoretical pure form, in which all values can be expressed in dollars. Amartya Sen, a prominent economist and social theorist, defines individual and aggregate social value as welfare maximization without supposing utility to be intrinsically characterizable in money terms and without supposing interpersonal comparisons to be possible.[15] This type of utilitarianism diverges to some extent from the characteristic reductionism of the market metaphor: that all values may be translated into—reduced to—money and readily (numerically) compared.[16] (Later, in Chapter 8, I will consider whether stopping short of expressing all value in dollars saves a theoretical practice from the implications of commodification.)

Finally, as I will discuss in more detail later, universal commodification implies extreme objectification. Commodities are socially constructed as objects separate from the self and social relations. Universal commodification assimilates personal attributes, relations, and desired states of affairs to the realm of objects by assuming that all human attributes are possessions bearing a value characterizable in money terms, and by implying that all these possessions can and should be separable from persons to be exchanged through the free market.

Market Rhetoric

Universal commodification is a conceptual scheme, a worldview. The language in which this conceptual scheme is couched is the rhetoric of the market: supply, demand, price, opportunity costs, production functions, and so on. By market rhetoric I mean the discourse in which we conceive of and speak of something as if it were a commodity subject to market exchange. I will sometimes speak of market rhetoric as the discourse of commodification, or as commodification in rhetoric.

Hobbes conceived of the value of a person in market rhetoric: "the Value or WORTH of a man, is as of all other things, his Price; that is to say, so much as would be given for the use of his Power."[17] In Hobbes's conception, everything about a person that others need, desire, or value is a possession that is priced. The Hobbesian person fits into the archetype of universal commodification. The Hobbesian conception of the political order likewise conceives of politics in market rhetoric. Modern Hobbesians view political activity as fully describable in terms of "rent seeking" by those who can achieve monetary gain from the capture of portions of Leviathan's power.[18]

Here is a sample of market rhetoric from Gary Becker: "Children are usually not purchased but are self-produced by each family, using market goods and services and the own time of parents, especially of mothers. Since the cost of own time and household production functions differs among families, the total cost of producing and rearing children also differs." Continuing in market rhetoric, Becker explains something about what governs people's desire for children: "The demand for children would depend on the relative price of children and full income. An increase in the relative price of children . . . reduces the demand for children and increases the demand for other commodities (if real income is held constant)." Speculating further about why people want this commodity (children), Becker notes that

> [t]he net cost of children is reduced if they contribute to family income by performing household chores, working in the family business, or working in the marketplace. Then an increase in the "earning" potential of children would increase the demand for children. Indeed, I believe that farm families have had more children mainly because children have been considerably more productive on farms than in cities.[19]

For one who is willing to conceive of everything (corneas for transplant, sexuality, babies for adoption) in market rhetoric, the only explanation for why some things might be held out of the market is market failure: free riders and holdouts, administrative costs, information costs, and so on. Judge Posner, for example, apparently considers a ban on selling oneself into slavery to be justified by information costs.[20] Finding no apparent market failures that would suggest noncommodification of children, he suggests that a free market in babies would be a good idea.[21] Becker, noting that baby-selling is forbidden by most societies, states that "it is easy to forbid what would be uncommon," and goes on to reason that baby-selling would be uncommon because "[o]ne could postulate a 'taste for [one's] own children' which is no less (and no more) profound than postulating a taste for good food or for any other commodity entering utility functions."22

Should market rhetoric trouble us? Perhaps you think this economics talk is just a silly metaphor, and nothing to pose a serious social worry. Economics talk does sometimes elicit giggles, but the giggles cover people's discomfort. I think the reason people are uncomfortable about market rhetoric is that it does tend to crystallize a social worry—the worry about inappropriate commodification.

The worry about inappropriate commodification is complex in a number of ways. An important complexity I will explore later is that commodification worries seem to occur only in conjunction with other worries about social wrongs, in particular about subordination and maldistribution of wealth. Cases of contested commodification in the real world are "mixed" and not "pure." When we worry about baby-selling or kidney-selling, for example, concerns about commodification are mixed up with concerns about the effects of poverty, sexism, and racism on the would-be sellers, as well as concerns about harm to innocent third parties (the babies who are sold).

Although the "pure" case of troublesome commodification seems to be only hypothetical, I do not think that means commodification is insignificant and only the other concerns (subordination, maldistribution, third-party effects) deserve attention. My view is that in our culture commodification is intertwined with those other concerns at a deep level, and I will attempt to plumb some of those depths in this book.

Commensurability and Reductionism

Universal commodification implies that all value can be expressed in terms of price. For those who believe value is not unitary in this way, commodification "reduces" all values to sums of money. Commodification is a reductionist conceptual scheme. Sums of money, in turn, can be compared consistently in a linear way. Commodification is thus also a conceptual scheme that is committed to commensurability of value.

Jeremy Bentham confidently argued, "Of two individuals he who is the richer is the happier or has the greater chance of being so. This is a fact proved by the experience of all the world."23 For anyone committed to a commodified conceptual scheme, and thereby committed to commensurability of value, there is no mystery about which of two items is more valuable; it is the one with the higher price tag. Furthermore, for any two items, one of them must be more valuable than the other, or else the two must be equal in value. Moreover, transitivity holds: if A is more valuable than B and B is more valuable than C, then A is more valuable than C. Commodification thus implies a strong form of value commensurability.

In this book I deny that all values are commensurable in this way. This denial is central to my critiques of universal commodification: it cannot capture—and may debase—the way humans value things important to human personhood. So something must be said here about what it means to be committed instead to value incommensurability. This is a murky subject, and I mean to keep the discussion brief.

I believe by and large that philosophical argument, such as it is, cannot force those who are committed to commensurability to change their minds.[24] There aren't any knock-down logical arguments that compel people to recognize incommensurability. (At least I haven't found any, and don't know how such an argument might be structured.) Those who are committed to commensurability can always—from their point of view—"translate" value incommensurabilities into their conceptual scheme. (See Chapter 8.) Rather, I want to show that many of us do have implicit unrecognized commitments to incommensurability. I want to make them explicit and show why incommensurability is important, and how it connects up with questions of contested commodification like sale of reproductive services.

Philosophers have puzzled over a problem named "incommensurability" in various contexts. In each of them, the problem is whether incommensurability exists. Although it goes by the same name, I am not sure to what extent incommensurability is usefully regarded as the same problem in all contexts. One context is a debate over relativism.[25] There a commitment to the existence of incommensurability signifies a commitment to radical untranslatability between different cultural groups or different historical periods. That commitment supports relativism. If the language, conventions, and forms of life of one group cannot be made at all intelligible in terms of the language, conventions, and forms of life of another, then it is thought that there is nothing to be said about which practices are better. They are incommensurable.

Another context, which appears to be subsumed by the broader debate about relativism, is a debate about Kuhnian paradigms in the philosophy of science. Thomas Kuhn argued that successive paradigms are incommensurable, inhabiting different worldviews, such that statements in one cannot be translated into statements in the other.[26] He thought it "illusive in principle"[27] to suppose that successive paradigms are coming closer and closer to some fixed reality existing independent of any paradigm. When his critics taxed him with relativism, he denied it by saying that paradigms could be judged better or worse by their success at puzzle-solving, and that it was characteristic of later paradigms to be better at puzzle-solving.[28]

Donald Davidson argued forcefully against the possibility of incommensurability, understood as radical untranslatability between cultural groups or historical periods.[29] Hilary Putnam did the same thing for the Kuhnian subcategory.[30] I cannot do justice here to these elegant and complex arguments, but their core is simple: The notion that we would be able to know such incommensurability when we saw it, much less proceed to talk about it, is conceptually incoherent. If we couldn't make intelligible *anything* that some other group of human beings does, we would have no basis for identifying them as human beings in the first place.

Another context in which an argument about incommensurability comes up is debates in ethics about whether values can be summed. This is the kind of incommensurability I think relevant to the questions about commodification I am exploring.[31] This notion of incommensurability is a broad strategy for attacking utilitarianism.[32]

It appears that a utilitarian injunction to maximize the sum of values implies either a reductionist or a scalar claim, or both. The reductionist claim is that there is one "stuff" of value to which all other values can be reduced, and this "stuff" is what we sum when we maximize. The scalar claim is that all values and packages of values can be arrayed in order from least valuable to most valuable on a continuous curve, so that we can maximize value by picking the highest package on the curve.

The notion of incommensurability, in arguments about ethics, is meant to deny one or both of these claims. If incommensurability is put forward to deny the reductionist claim, then the claim that values are incommensurable means that there is no "stuff" that we can substitute equivalent amounts of when we try to sum values. If incommensurability is put forward to deny the scalar claim, then the claim that values are incommensurable means that there is no scale along which all values can be arrayed in order so that for any value or package of values we can say definitively that it has more or less value than some other.

Either of these claims can be made partial. It need not be the case that either all values are reducible or scalable, or none are. A utilitarian may claim that many values reduce to some "stuff" even if not all of them do; an opponent may claim that a few values may reduce to some "stuff" but most of them do not. A utilitarian may claim that many values can be arrayed on a scale, or on a number of scales, even if pockets of incommensurability exist; an opponent may claim that some values can be arrayed on a scale or scales but that there are large or significant areas of incommensurability.

This last debate, about the extent or significance of incommensurability, seems to come down to deeply held conflicting intuitions. Some writers, such as James Griffin,[33] find that incommensurability is not an important problem. Others, for example Joseph Raz,[34] find that it is. Much of their disagreement seems to amount to different intuitions about how to characterize certain kinds of commonplace actions and interactions. In particular, how do we interpret the evidence of an actor's choices? May we infer commensurability to the extent that the actor actually does choose one thing over the other? (Should choices between values be read as "trade-offs"?)

In an example patterned on one of Raz's, suppose that a man is faced with the choice whether to take a job in a distant city that pays $100,000 more than his present job, but if he takes it he will forgo the company of his spouse.[35] If he takes the job, are we entitled to infer that he values the company of his spouse less than he values $100,000? This is to infer commensurability. It assumes the two values can be placed on the same scale, from which we can read off that one thing is more valuable than the other. Company is "traded off" for dollars. Those who make the inference find the language of revealed preference apposite. By making the "trade-off" of his spouse's company in return for $100,000, the man "reveals" that the dollar value he places on his spouse's company is less than $100,000.

Writers like Griffin think the inference of commensurability is obviously correct:[36] if we see people making choices among things they value, there must be a scale on which those things can be arrayed. But writers like Raz think the inference is an obvious non sequitur:[37] from the fact of choice nothing about the commensurability of values can be inferred. The nature of an action, its meaning, is simply the conventional understanding of it, and people in our culture do not conceive of these kinds of choices as "trades."

Many people think choices like this "must" imply commensurability, and many think the fact of choice implies nothing at all about commensurability. The intuitions prove stubborn; there do not seem to be arguments that change people's minds about this. People seem to be deeply committed to values' being orderly in this way, or deeply committed to their not being so. My own intuitions are with Raz. Someone who says there "must" be a scale, "behind" or "underlying" people's choices, is like one of Wittgenstein's interlocutors who says there "must" be something common to all games.[38] There is no "must" about it—unless our socially shared understanding of these choices (whoever "we" might be in this context) includes such a "must." The meaning of choices is how they are socially understood. There is no mysterious something that "underlies" such conventions of language and practice.

That people's intuitions are stubbornly diverse about how to interpret actions that could be read as "trades" carries through, I think, to a conflicted response to market rhetoric such as Posner's or Becker's. Those who readily read human actions as "trades" are unfazed by market rhetoric. They are genuinely mystified by the gut feelings of horror and dismay such rhetoric arouses in those who do not read human actions as "trades."

Linking Actual Trades and Market Rhetoric

There are narrow and broad senses of commodification. Commodification in the narrowest sense describes events in literal laissez-faire markets, in which material goods and economic services are literally bought and sold. This narrow, literal sense of commodification flows into broader senses. One way it does this is through the ideology that anchors such literal laissez-faire markets. As I will review in Chapter 3, much of the history of liberal thought involves the philosophical elaboration of the underpinning of the laissez-faire market: private property plus free contract.

A broad understanding of commodification encompasses market rhetoric. In market rhetoric, the discourse of commodification, one conceives of human attributes (properties of persons) as fungible owned objects (the property of persons).[39] One conceives of human interactions as "sales" with "prices" even where no money literally changes hands. Private property plus free contract covers the universe of human voluntary interaction. Thus, in the passage quoted earlier, Becker referred to children as a commodity with a price and a demand function. In discussing the possibility of a market in babies, Becker posited a limited scope for that market on the ground that parents would try to unload their "lemon" children, keeping the superior children for themselves, if "buyers were not readily able to determine quality." And he assumed that "all children in the same family have the same quality" in deriving the utility function that "distinguishes the quality of children from other commodities."[40] In his discussion of the effect of the decline in the infant mortality rate, he considered children as fungible commodities; in a decision about how many grown children are desired, one child is perfectly substitutable for another.

Insofar as Becker was not engaging in any literal transactions involving children or even advocating that children be literally bought and sold, his market rhetoric reflects the broad or metaphorical sense of commodification but not its narrow or literal sense. My discussion of the archetype of universal commodification has assumed that the two senses are connected. But just how? The nature of the connection is a complex issue that will recur in many guises in this book.

The reason people are troubled by "mere" market rhetoric, when applied in ways they think inappropriate, is that they think it will be contagious and will lead to literal commodification. They think that someone who thinks like Becker or Posner will end up advocating that indeed we should exchange children for money.[41] They think that the rhetoric will proliferate of its own accord, and that one advocate will encourage others. They think that if enough people conceive of children in market rhetoric and advocate that we exchange children for money, then literal buying and selling of children will result.

Of course, if market rhetoric took over the world to such an extent that there was no other way available to us in which to conceive of children, then there would be no reason left to avoid trading them as commodities. In such a world the prediction that such a trade would spring up would no doubt be accurate, and in that world we might no longer have the conceptual tools to be worried about it. But our world is more complex. Market and nonmarket conceptualizations of various interactions seem often to coexist as opposing rhetorical crosscurrents.

In this book I take a pragmatic view: the likelihood that pervasive use of market rhetoric will result in literal markets must be evaluated contextually. Because of the coexisting crosscurrents of nonmarket conceptualization, I believe that most of the time Chicago-style market rhetoric does not of itself operate to bring on literal markets. How the rhetoric might proliferate, and how it might be connected with the advent of literal markets are both issues that need investigation.

But even if there is no slippery slope inevitably linking metaphorical with literal markets, I think it is important to realize that metaphorical markets cannot be placed beyond the scope of concern by defining them as "mere" discourse as opposed to action. The reason that people are troubled by literal commodification is not divorced from "mere" commodification in rhetoric. That money travels from John to Jane, and a child travels from Jane to John, isn't evil in itself, outside of our conceptualization of the interaction. Simply put, there is no sharp distinction between the nature of an interaction and the terms in which we conceive of it. (This point will be elaborated in Chapter 6.) Whenever we can perceive a harm to persons, our perception is mediated through a conceptual structure or structures; conceptualization makes it possible for us to see harm as harm.

Nevertheless, identifying the salient conceptual structure connected with our perception of a relationship as bad or harmful is not always simple. Slavery is wrong. But is the conceptual structure connected with our ability to see the wrongness primarily a concept of freedom? or a concept of power? Or is the concept of commodification the salient one? Or are they interdependent? Not all cultures where slavery is present connect it with property and markets. But American slaveholding did. As I will argue in Chapter 11, in our culture the conceptual structures of (un)freedom, disempowerment, and commodification are linked. Indeed, in our culture echoes of the buying and selling that characterized slavery contribute to the way we problematize baby-selling.[42]

Where commodification is the appropriate conceptual structure to identify as implicated in the wrongness of an interaction, the wrongness is not separate from the market rhetoric in which we conceive of the interaction. So, if literal commodification of persons is worse than "mere" commodification of them in rhetoric, the reason it is worse is not that (in some unexplained sense) it treats people in a way unworthy of their status as persons in "action" rather than just in "thought." Instead, as I will argue in Chapter 12, the reason literal commodification is worse—if it is—would have to be a finding that it tends even more strongly than "mere" commodification in rhetoric to undermine personhood by engendering inferior understandings—conceptualizations—of what a person is. These inferior conceptualizations that are evoked are the reason we are able to understand the "actual" bad treatment (for example, the exchange of dollars for a child) as bad.

I will have more to say in Chapter 10 on how we might think about baby-selling. Before returning to that and other specific instances of contested commodification, I want to consider some of the structural and historical features both of commodification and of an opposing worldview I call noncommodification. One of the earmarks of commodification, perhaps its central one, is that of *sale;* so commodification is undercut when things are thought of as, or declared to be, not capable of sale. Thus I turn first, in the next chapter, to nonsalability, which I call market-inalienability.

2

Market-Inalienability

Commodities are sold, or alienated. Alienability is important to commodification, and inalienability is important to probing its limits. An initial difficulty is that inalienability is not sharply defined. In order to explore the relationship that links inalienability and the impulse to limit commodification, I must first try to clarify its meaning(s). Then I must lay out a standard economic view of inalienability, the transaction cost model.

Sorting Out the Varieties of Inalienability

Some say that inalienability negates any loss or waiver of a right, entitlement, or attribute; some say that it negates voluntary transfer; some stake out positions between these two.[1] The traditional meanings of inalienability do have a common core: the notion of alienation as a separation of something—an entitlement, right, or attribute—from its holder. (The traditional conception of alienation as separation of objects from persons is related to the traditional subject/object dichotomy, which I discuss in Chapter 3. In what follows, I shall often refer generally to whatever is inalienable as a "thing." This is a necessary shorthand, although it does present the danger of an unwanted connotation of "objectness.")

16

Inalienability negates the possibility of separation. Meanings proliferate because the separation that constitutes alienation can be either voluntary or involuntary; thus the entitlement, right, or attribute may end up in the hands of another holder or may simply be lost or extinguished. Any particular entitlement, right, or attribute may be subject to one or more forms of inalienability.

In one important set of meanings, inalienability is ascribed to an entitlement, right, or attribute that cannot be lost or extinguished. Basic human rights, whatever their content, are of this type. If preclusion of involuntary loss is the point, "inalienable" may mean nonforfeitable or noncancelable; if preclusion of voluntary loss is the point, "inalienable" may mean nonwaivable or nonrelinquishable. ("Waiver" is ambiguous. I use it to refer to permanent abrogation of an entitlement, right, or attribute; but it may also refer to merely temporary abrogation. "Nonforfeitability" is also ambiguous. I use it to refer to an entitlement, right, or attribute that cannot be involuntarily negated, such as certain civil rights; but it may also refer to things that cannot be involuntarily transferred to the state without compensation.)

In another important set of meanings, inalienability is ascribed to an entitlement, right, or attribute that cannot be voluntarily transferred from one holder to another. "Inalienable" in these uses may mean nongivable, nonsalable, or completely nontransferable. If something is nontransferable, the holder cannot designate a successor holder. Something that is inalienable in this sense need not be inalienable in the broader senses detailed above. That is, something that is nontransferable might still be forfeited, canceled, relinquished, waived, or perhaps involuntarily transferred to the government or its designates.

As the two categories of meanings suggest, each of four broad categories of separability might be negated by a corresponding form of inalienability: involuntary extinguishment (cancellation, forfeiture of civil rights); voluntary extinguishment (waiver, abandonment); involuntary transfer (condemnation, adverse possession); and voluntary transfer (gift, sale). Except in special cases, however, the negation of involuntary transfer is not likely to be conceived of as inalienability; for example, we do not consider the prevention of theft an inalienability.

In addition, there are other variables that are sometimes significant for understanding inalienabilities. The most important of them are: the state's role in the interaction (whether the state is the instrument of involuntary loss or the recipient of involuntary transfer); the nature of the holder of an inalienable right, entitlement, or attribute (whether the holder is a person or group, and whether the person has an official capacity or the group has special normative significance); and the availability of compensation.

These and other variables can be thought either to create a larger matrix or to delineate subcategories in the four broad categories I mentioned. The taxonomy is not central to my argument here. The type of inalienability I will be exploring, market-inalienability, is a normatively important subcategory of my fourth category, inalienabilities that negate voluntary transfer. It is a subcategory delineated by the distinction between monetary exchanges and other voluntary transfers. Rather than analyze the entire four-celled matrix of possibilities generated by the two categories of meanings (voluntary versus involuntary; transfer versus loss or extinction), I will want to zero in on market-inalienability.

Nontransferability and Market-Inalienability

Nongivability and nonsalability are subsets of nontransferability. If something is inalienable by gift, it might be transferred by sale.[2] This category is not very important in our practice; few things can be sold but not given away.[3] On the other hand, if something is inalienable by sale, it might be transferred by gift.[4] This category is very important in our practice. In precluding sales but not gifts, market-inalienability places some things outside the marketplace but not outside the realm of social intercourse. People may interact in such a way as to share or transfer these things, but they are not for sale.

The first thing to notice about market-inalienability is that it negates a central element of traditional property rights. Many would say that the question of inalienable property is a contradiction in terms; it is at least a confrontation to be explored. Traditional property rights are alienable in all senses except that of cancellation. If I own something, I may transfer it either by gift or by sale; I may abandon or destroy it; I may waive or relinquish my claim to it; and I may forfeit it. The fact that traditional property rights cannot be canceled is usually not by itself considered inalienability. Yet it is helpful to think of noncancelability as inalienability in order to see the scope of the concept. Indeed, the "inalienable right to property" in the liberal political tradition may just mean that alienable property rights are noncancelable. (It may mean other things as well, for example, that the right of the autonomous individual to be a property holder is both nonrelinquishable and noncancelable.)

Market-inalienability is a particular species of nontransferability. It differs from the nontransferability that characterizes many nontraditional property rights—entitlements of the regulatory and welfare state—that are not for sale but not to be given away either. Examples are entitlements to social security and welfare benefits, and many kinds of licenses. I think of these as status-inalienabilities because they rigidify possession, constraining or precluding change, signifying some strong form of inseparability from the holder. Forms of status-inalienability could range from prohibition of voluntary transfers among private parties to prohibition of any kind of loss.

Market-inalienability also differs from the inalienability of other things, like voting rights, that seem to be moral or political duties related to a community's normative life; they are subject to broader inalienabilities that preclude loss as well as transfer. Nontransferable rights that at the same time may implicate affirmative duties fall into a category I think of as community-inalienability. Examples are the right (duty) to vote in political elections and the right (duty) to become educated. Rights of this kind not only may not be lost through change of hands, extinguishment, or cancellation, but also *ought* to be exercised. Although community-inalienability is a convenient label for these rights that are simultaneously duties, the more communitarian one's views about the nature of the person and the nature of social life, the more all justifiable inalienabilities will be related to community. It may turn out that market-inalienability is related to community (in what sense will need to be explored), but nevertheless, things that are not for sale need not be directly related to community in the way that voting rights are.

What is important to notice about market-inalienability in this regard is that, unlike the inalienabilities attaching to welfare entitlements or to political duties, market-inalienability does not render something inseparable from the person. Rather, it specifies that market trading may not be used as a social mechanism of separation. "Not for sale" does not necessarily mean not to be detached.

Market-inalienability should also be distinguished from the inalienability of things that are made nontransferable in order to implement a prohibition. Some things are deemed socially unacceptable to possess, give, or sell. Their existence is denounced completely by the social order. Heroin is in this class; alcoholic beverages passed into and out of it. The inalienability of things in this class is subsidiary to a social attempt to obliterate them. It is illegal to sell heroin only because we want no one to have anything to do with heroin. Producing heroin, possessing heroin, and giving away heroin are prohibited too. Inalienabilities incident to prohibitions can be labeled prohibition-inalienabilities to distinguish them from other kinds. Unlike prohibition-inalienability, market-inalienability does not signify that something is social anathema. "Not for sale" does not necessarily mean not to be countenanced. Preclusion of sales often coexists with encouragement of gifts. For example, the market-inalienability of human organs does not preclude—and, indeed, may seek to foster—transfer from one individual to another by gift.[5]

Noncommodification and Market-Inalienability

Market-inalienability is a focus of this book because it often represents an attempt to prevent commodification, or at least expresses an aspiration for noncommodification. By making something nonsalable we proclaim that it should not be conceived of or treated as a commodity. When something is noncommodifiable, market trading is a disallowed form of social organization and allocation. We place that thing beyond supply and demand pricing, brokerage and arbitrage, advertising and marketing, stockpiling, speculation, and valuation in terms of the opportunity cost of production.

Market-inalienability poses more than a binary choice whether something should be wholly inside or outside the market, completely commodified or completely noncommodified. Some things are completely commodified—deemed suitable for trade in a laissez-faire market. Others are completely noncommodified—removed from the market altogether. In my view, however, many things can be usefully understood as incompletely commodified—neither fully commodified nor fully removed from the market. Given the possibility of incomplete commodification, we may decide that some things are or should be market-inalienable only to a degree, or only in some aspects. Things that are incompletely commodified do not fully exhibit the typical indicia of traditional property and contract. For example, things that are subject to price controls are incompletely commodified because freedom to set prices is part of the traditional understanding of property and contract.[6] (I discuss incomplete commodification in Chapters 7 and 8.)

An understanding of the pros and cons of market-inalienability might give us a handle on the deeply contested issues of commodification that confront us. What are some of the things whose commodification is contested? Infants and children, human reproduction, sperm, eggs, embryos, blood, human organs, human sexuality, human pain, human labor. Should we pay market salaries to college athletes? Should we allocate artificial organs or kidney dialysis through a market regime? Should we place a monetary equivalent on a spouse's professional degree or homemaker services in a divorce? Should we award money damages for pain and suffering in tort actions?

These issues inhabit the domain of contested commodification, the arena of struggle over what things are suitable for market, both literally and metaphorically. The commodification debate is larger still, however, because debates about some kinds of regulation can be seen as contested incomplete commodification. There the contest is over whether to allow full commodification (a laissez-faire market regime) or something less. If we see the debates this way, residential rent control, minimum-wage requirements, and other forms of price regulation, as well as residential habitability requirements, safety regulation, and other forms of product-quality regulation all become contests over the issue of commodification. As background for exploring these contests, I turn to the relationship between commodification and economic views of inalienability.

Inalienability in Market Rhetoric: The Transaction Costs Model

The archetype of economics talk, universal commodification, leads to a characteristic way of understanding inalienability in general and market-inalienability in particular. When seen through the conceptual lens of universal commodification, market-inalienability is not seen as just one among many kinds of inalienability. In a conceptual scheme that supposes, for purposes of explanation and justification, that every human interaction is a sale, all inalienabilities collapse into nonsalability. Economic analysis is blind to all inalienabilities other than market-inalienability because it is blind (conceptually speaking) to all human interactions other than sales.

Two premises follow from this conceptual blindness. First, no inalienability or restraint on alienation should exist unless market methodology—cost-benefit analysis—itself requires it. It follows that market failure is the only reason to allow inalienability. Second, when market failure requires it, inalienability is accounted for in market terms and described in market rhetoric. It is said that the presence of free-riders or holdouts can make inalienability an efficient solution to the problem of resource allocation. These two premises combine to produce a transaction costs model of inalienability. In this model, inalienability is a means of controlling externalities that prevent the market from achieving an efficient result.

The transaction costs model is developed by Guido Calabresi and A. Douglas Melamed in their treatment of "inalienability rules."[7] Calabresi, formerly a law professor and dean, and now a circuit judge, is one of the pioneers of economic analysis of law. Even though its discussion of inalienability is limited, the Calabresi and Melamed article has been seminal for those who conceive of inalienability in the market mode.

Calabresi and Melamed divide protection of entitlements into property rules, liability rules, and inalienability. Property rules signify a scheme of free transfers between willing sellers and buyers, with no coerced transfers. Liability rules signify a scheme of allowable coerced transfers at market prices set by official entities, such as courts. Inalienability signifies that sales are not permitted.

Calabresi and Melamed argue that property rules are prima facie efficient and therefore desirable. Liability rules are an exception to the property-rule regime, justifiable only when transaction costs of various kinds cause market failures to undermine the prima facie efficiency of property rules.[8] Both the property-rule regime and the exception to it are generated by market methodology and the pursuit of efficiency.

Calabresi and Melamed conceive of inalienability as similarly generated by the pursuit of efficiency. In their approach, alienability is prima facie correct or justified, and inalienability must be the exception that proves the rule. Their definition of inalienability fails to distinguish between prohibiting all loss or transfer and prohibiting sale: "An entitlement is inalienable to the extent that its transfer is not permitted between a willing buyer and a willing seller."[9] Thus, Calabresi and Melamed exemplify the characteristic collapse, in economic analysis, of all inalienabilities into market-inalienability.

Calabresi and Melamed argue that external costs can explain or justify inalienability. One category of external cost that might be prevented by inalienability is large-scale social cost that sellers can inflict on the public. Calabresi and Melamed use pollution as an example, but their reasoning could just as well apply to assault weapons, heroin, or cigarettes:

> For instance, if Taney were allowed to sell his land to Chase, a polluter, he would injure his neighbor Marshall by lowering the value of Marshall's land. Conceivably, Marshall could pay Taney not to sell his land; but, because there are many injured Marshalls, freeloader and information costs make such transactions practically impossible. . . .
> . . . where there are so many injured Marshalls that the price required under [a] liability rule is likely to be high enough so that no one would be willing to pay it . . . [b]arring the sale to polluters will be the most efficient result because it is clear that avoiding pollution is cheaper than paying its costs—including its costs to the Marshalls.[10]

The argument evokes the archetype of universal commodification in two respects. First, its logic applies to gift transfers as well as to sales, but only sales are mentioned, perhaps because all interactions between humans qualify as sales. Second, Calabresi and Melamed describe injury to third parties in market rhetoric. In this rhetoric, pollution harms people "by lowering the value of [their] land" in dollars rather than by degrading their health and quality of life, which in turn could lower their land value—among other things not measurable in dollars.

The other category of external cost that might be prevented by inalienability involves what Calabresi and Melamed, along with many other economic analysts, call "moralisms." The term "moralism" assimilates moral and political right to the market by conceiving of people's moral tenets as goods and assigning them a dollar value. This assimilation represents the ultimate reach of market rhetoric. For example:

> If Taney is allowed to sell himself into slavery, or to take undue risks of becoming penniless, or to sell a kidney, Marshall may be harmed, simply because Marshall is a sensitive man who is made unhappy by

seeing slaves, paupers, or persons who die because they have sold a kidney. Again Marshall could pay Taney not to sell his freedom to Chase the slaveowner; but again, because Marshall is not one but many individuals, freeloader and information costs make such transactions practically impossible. . . . [And] since the external cost to Marshall does not lend itself to an acceptable objective measurement . . . liability rules are [also] not appropriate.[11]

The authors refer to slavery, spendthrift trusts, and organ-selling, but they could just as well have chosen child labor, gambling, or prostitution. This argument, too, evokes the archetype of universal commodification. Because the argument logically prohibits gifts as well as sales, it may not capture the moral rejection of organ-selling. "Taney" could die just as well from giving away a kidney as from selling it. If the authors mean that "Marshall" is made unhappy by "Taney's" death, and that this is a reason to make kidneys inalienable, they fail to recognize our moral approval of kidney-giving. If they mean that "Marshall" is made unhappy only by death after kidney-selling, on the other hand, and that this is a reason to make kidneys inalienable, they are postulating a "moralism" that distinguishes between gifts and sales in a way that market rhetoric cannot. Because they define inalienability as nonsalability, their theoretical apparatus cannot distinguish market-inalienability from other kinds, and hence ignores the moral distinction between gift and sale.

On a deeper level, the argument disturbingly suggests that the inalienability rule against slavery would not be justified if the rule were inefficient. If enough of the "Marshalls" liked slavery, so that the prohibition would be a cost rather than a benefit to them, slavery would be efficient and therefore, at least according to this argument, acceptable. Anyone who has no qualms about this argument bears witness to a (literally) demoralizing triumph of market methodology.

In addition to the two categories of external costs, the reasons Calabresi and Melamed adduce for the existence of inalienability in an otherwise free market system include two categories of paternalism, and "distributional goals."[12] Their paternalistic reasons for inalienability are characterized (surprisingly) as efficiency reasons. In "self-paternalism," the individual furthers her own long-run welfare maximization by forbidding herself certain contrary transactions in the short run. The classic illustration is Ulysses tying himself to the mast to avoid succumbing to the Sirens.[13] In "true paternalism," "the most efficient pie is no longer that which costless bargains would achieve, because a person may be better off if he is prohibited from bargaining."[14] The examples the authors have in mind are prohibitions of certain activities by minors. True paternalism, they say, unlike the situations involving "moralisms," involves "the notion that at least in some situations the Marshalls know better than Taney what will make Taney better off."[15]

It is hard to understand how one can make sense of the notion that the person under a prohibition would be "better off" in some view other than her own, given the moral subjectivism revealed in the discussion of "moralisms" as external costs. That is, if society is better off without slavery only because those who like it are imposing too much cost on those who don't, how can anyone know that another's preferences are wrong? Thus, Calabresi and Melamed's paternalism-efficiency argument may collapse into their moralism-externality argument. By imposing paternalistic restraints, the argument then would go, we are benefiting people whose subjective moral beliefs include the "knowledge" that others would be better off if restrained, and who attach subjective value to seeing them better off. (Perhaps the argument can be saved from this collapse by supposing that in appropriate situations, such as restraining minors, we can confidently predict that the person herself will eventually come to realize she is better off.)

In showing how "distributional goals" bear on inalienability, Calabresi and Melamed suggest that we should be on guard against the "danger ... that what is justified on, for example, paternalism grounds is really a hidden way of accruing distributional benefits for a group whom we would not otherwise wish to benefit."[16] Thus, they say, "prohibiting the sale of babies makes poorer those who can cheaply produce babies and richer those who through some nonmarket device get free an 'unwanted' baby."[17] Although this argument is directed toward distribution rather than toward efficiency, it is expressed in the market rhetoric of universal commodification: one is "poorer" if she cannot sell a baby she can "cheaply produce." The commitment to market rhetoric in fact seems to have made it difficult for Calabresi and Melamed to talk about "other justice reasons" relevant to entitlements:

[W]e may as well admit that it is hard to know what content can be poured into ["other justice reasons"], at least given the very broad definitions of economic efficiency and distributional goals that we have used. . . . We defined distribution as covering *all* the reasons, other than efficiency, on the basis of which we might prefer to make Taney *wealthier* than Marshall. So defined, there obviously was no room for any other reasons.[18]

Although Judge Calabresi himself probably no longer espouses such a thoroughgoing commodified view of inalienability,[19] many subsequent economic writers have adopted the Calabresi-Melamed analysis. According to Richard Epstein, the only sound justification for inalienability is "the practical control of externalities."[20] According to Epstein, "Rules restraining alienation are best accounted for, both positively and normatively, by the need to control problems of external harm and the common pool."[21] Epstein's common-pool argument is about costs that arise when a resource must be shared. It is in fact a variant of the tragedy of the commons.[22] Like the argument for the tragedy of the commons, Epstein's argument assumes that, absent restraint, people will maximize individual short-run gain to the ultimate degradation of a resource.[23]

For Epstein as for Calabresi and Melamed, inalienability is the exception that proves the market rule. It comes into being only to achieve what the market "would" achieve but cannot, because of various kinds of transaction costs. Epstein's argument about external harm is akin to the Calabresi and Melamed arguments about external costs and efficiency-based paternalism. The external harms he mentions fall into three categories: aggression against third parties, over-exploitation of the common pool, and exploitation of infants and insane persons. The primary examples of inalienability Epstein has in mind are prohibitions: guns, liquor, and drugs. He speaks of them as restrictions or bans on sales, but the logic of the argument extends to gifts and to possession and use as well. The distinctions between market-inalienabilities and other kinds are not noticeable when everything is thought of as part of the market.

In Epstein's view, restraints voluntarily imposed by individual bargaining are presumptively efficient. Restraints imposed by law are to be regarded much more warily, but his common-pool argument can justify a few of them. As examples of common-pool types of restraints imposed by law rather than by individual bargaining, Epstein mentions water rights and voting rights in corporate and political elections.[24] In universal commodification, of course, these are not qualitatively different kinds of "goods." Epstein sees the English common law of riparian rights, which tied water rights to land rights and limited water rights to uses that did not disturb the natural flow, as steering between two extremes: inefficiencies caused by free alienability (the tragedy of the commons), and inefficiencies caused by permanent entitlement of users who do not value the resource highly (which might be called inefficiencies of status).[25] In effect he proposes that a properly tailored status-inalienability is a cure (or a palliative) for the tragedy of the commons.

Epstein's analysis of vote-selling as an externality problem reveals the scope of his market methodology and market rhetoric.[26] If an entrepreneur could buy the votes to put herself into public office, Epstein argues, she could then pay off the sellers with public money, thus depleting the common pool of assets for her own gain.[27] This argument relies on the commodified version of interest-group pluralism, conceiving of politics as rent seeking by those who put their friends and sympathizers in office in order to line their own pockets.

Although Epstein's theory purportedly rests on libertarian rights as well as on economic efficiency,[28] it differs little from the Calabresi and Melamed view. Epstein does not recognize distinctions between market-inalienability and other forms of inalienability, because for him the only real issue is whether a market is under the circumstances self-defeating so that market results must be achieved by other means. For him, the harms caused by treating rights of persons or citizens (such as voting) as alienable commodities are market types of harm—external costs.

Susan Rose-Ackerman, another legal economist who carries forward the view of Calabresi and Melamed, takes a slightly more eclectic view. She finds three normative rationales for inalienabilities: economic efficiency, "certain specialized distributive goals," and incompatibility of unfettered market processes with "the responsible functioning of a democratic state."[29] Rose-Ackerman's concern with democratic functioning implicates what I called community-inalienability; and the fact that she does not fold it into her efficiency analysis may indicate that she does not conceive of politics in market rhetoric quite so single-mindedly as many economists do.

Nevertheless, efficiency is the focus of Rose-Ackerman's analysis, and unless one of her other two concerns is implicated, unfettered market trading is presumptively desirable.[30] The efficiency rationale is a broadened transaction-costs analysis along the lines of Calabresi and Melamed's, adding information and coordination problems to the more familiar externalities. According to Rose-Ackerman too, market failure is what justifies inalienabilities; they are "second-best responses."[31] In order to understand market-inalienability as something other and more than a second-best response, we must escape from the discourse of commodification and its reliance on market failure as the explanation for any and all deviations from laissez-faire.

Rose-Ackerman recognizes that the Calabresi-Melamed definition of inalienability refers only to nonsalability (in my terms, market-inalienability). She recognizes that the reason for this narrowness is that their "treatment of inalienability is colored by [the] emphasis on quid pro quo transfers"—that is, sales—that forms the basis of their treatment of property rules and liability rules.[32] To avoid this narrowness, Rose-Ackerman posits a many-celled matrix of inalienabilities, representing all possible combinations of three variables: limits on who may hold an entitlement; limits on uses of it (uses that are permitted, required, or forbidden); and limits on transfers (what kinds of transfers are permitted or forbidden). Even though she distinguishes ninety-six varieties of inalienability, her matrix does not distinguish among the various types of losses, such as abandonment, forfeiture, and cancellation, that inalienability might prevent. She appears to concentrate on *transfers* just as Calabresi and Melamed concentrate on quid pro quo transfers. Indeed, she gives the name "pure inalienability" to nontransferability.[33]

Rose-Ackerman does not present a normative framework for evaluating inalienabilities according to distributive justice. The rationale for inalienability based on distribution is "narrowly focused," referring to situations in which an inalienability can be used to single out recipients of a benefit. For example, Rose-Ackerman suggests that the Homesteading Acts can be justified as a means of transferring land to formerly landless people willing to live on the land and farm it.[34]

More generally, Rose-Ackerman argues, along the lines of Calabresi and Melamed, that using inalienability to achieve distributive goals is unjustified "except to prevent monopoly gains,"[35] and that "distributive costs" that arise when efficiency-based restrictions burden a particular group might render the restrictions unjustified.[36] Although her treatment of the distributive rationale thus seems undeveloped relative to her commitment to efficiency,[37] Rose-Ackerman's is a hybrid analysis. By raising the issue of distributive justice and by considering the incompatibility of market processes with democratic functioning, she means to combine economic analysis "with a sensitivity to noneconomic ideas."[38] Her analysis shows us how far you can (and cannot) go with market rhetoric. Just as Calabresi and Melamed did, she has trouble talking about issues of distributive justice in terms other than as market failures.

Rose-Ackerman pushes the envelope a bit further, perhaps, in connecting certain inalienabilities (such as voting) with ideals of citizenship. This connection espouses a kind of compartmentalization, a separation of politics and markets. Compartmentalization has been traditional in liberal thought, and it will be the topic of Chapter 3.

3

Problems for the Idea of a Market Domain

According to a traditional liberal view, the market appropriately encompasses most desired transactions between people, with a few special exceptions. Those few exceptions—for example, the way we acquire a spouse or a child—are morally and legally protected from the market. Eventually I want to claim that the traditional view wrongly implies the existence of a large domain of pure free-market transactions to which special kinds of personal interactions form a special exception. It also wrongly suggests that a laissez-faire market regime is prima facie just. The traditional liberal view prevents us from appreciating the nonmarket aspects of many of our market relations; it prevents us from seeing fragments of a nonmarket social order embedded or latent in the market society.

That there should be a domain of inalienable "political" rights and a domain of alienable "property" rights seems fundamental to those who hold a traditional worldview that divides up the social world into politics and markets. In the domain of politics there are familiar inalienable individual rights such as life, liberty, and the pursuit of happiness; there are also autonomy, liberty, and equal respect for persons. In the domain of the market there are alienable property rights and free trade. I will sometimes refer to this regime as liberal compartmentalization. I suggest in this chapter that liberal compartmentalization has borne within it the seeds of universal commodification.

Three prominent theoretical features of liberal compartmentalization are an understanding of freedom as negative liberty, an understanding of the person as abstract subject, and a conceptual notion of property. These three features fit the free market and its institutions, private property and free contract. Subjectivity of personhood and negative liberty are expressed in convictions that inalienable things are metaphysically internal to the person, and that inalienabilities are paternalistic, merely overriding a person's own free choices on the ground that society knows better what's good for her. Conceptualism is reflected in arguments that alienability is inherent in the concept of property. These convictions make the case for liberal compartmentalization uneasy, always threatening to assimilate to universal commodification, that is, to a globalization of private property and free contract.

Inalienability and the Market Infrastructure

The legal infrastructure required for a functioning laissez-faire market system includes not merely private property, but private property plus free contract. In order for the exchange system to allocate resources, there must be both private entitlement to resources and permission to transfer entitlements at will to other private owners. The market infrastructure is reflected, for example, in the two parts of Robert Nozick's libertarian ideal theory of justice—justice in acquisition represents private property, and justice in transfer represents free contract.[1]

Liberal theorists have expressed or reflected the market infrastructure in a variety of ways. One recurring kind of argument is conceptual. Both of the necessary market attributes can be incorporated either into a property theory, by claiming that free alienability is inherent in the concept of property, or into a contract theory, by claiming that private entitlement is inherent in the concept of freedom of contract. In other kinds of arguments, property and contract split the market infrastructure between them. As an example, the common law of restraints on alienation seems to reflect both a conceptualist and a more pragmatic approach. To strike down restraining conditions because they are said, without more, to be "repugnant to a fee" is merely to say that free alienability is implicit in the concept of the fee simple absolute.[2] On the other hand, when restraining conditions

have been weighed to determine their "reasonableness," alienability
is potentially a social variable separate from private ownership.[3]

How have these strategies functioned in liberal theory? Some writers, notably Kant and Hegel, used separate arguments to justify private property and free contract. In such discussions the justifications
for entitlement and alienability, though separate, are interlocking
parts of the same picture. Other writers, notably John Stuart Mill,
asserted that (market) alienability is inherent in the concept of private
property. This argument structure submerges the issue of alienability
and makes justification of it seem less necessary: once property is
justified, the task of justifying the market is done.

Benthamite positivist functionalism takes the final step: entitlement
and free alienation are justified by more direct reference to the requirements of the free market.[4] The market is made the explicit goal in light
of which private property and free contract are to be constructed.
Benthamite reasoning leads directly to universal commodification because of its commitment to value commensurability and its conception
of all things valuable in terms of wealth. I confine my investigation
here to other liberal market theories whose links to commodification
are less straightforward.

The Conceptualist Strategy

Many of those who find the archetype of universal commodification
intellectually attractive are conceptualists. Richard Epstein, for example, argues that property has a timeless and uncontested meaning from
which legal results can be deduced.[5] But the conceptualist strategy
cannot consistently admit any inalienabilities without denying that the
objects of them are property. Conceptualists who are firmly committed to property get pushed toward making everything that can be
called property into a "pure" (laissez-faire) market commodity.

John Stuart Mill's treatment of property in his *Principles of Political
Economy* illustrates the problem that pushes conceptualists toward
complete commodification, although he himself stopped short of that
position. Mill declared that "included in the idea of private property"
is a right of each person "to the exclusive disposal of what he or she
have produced by their own exertions, or received either by gift or by
fair agreement without force or fraud, from those who produced it."
The right of property "includes . . . the freedom of acquiring by

contract," because to prevent those who produce things from giving or exchanging them as they wish violates the producers' property rights. Also "implied in property" is the right to whatever a producer can get for her products "in a fair market."[6] Taken together, these declarations establish that Mill's idea of property inherently requires contracts and markets. It would be a logical contradiction for him to postulate the inalienability of property.

In other passages, Mill countenanced inalienabilities and restraints on alienation: the laws of property "have made property of things which never ought to be property, and absolute property where only a qualified property ought to exist." He rejected the notion that public offices, monopoly privileges, professional brevets—and human beings—could be considered property.[7] In refusing to countenance certain things as property at all, Mill was able to avoid the contradiction that inalienable property poses for his conceptualism. Saying that some things simply are not property is one way for a liberal to be a compartmentalizer. Then the social world is divided into a "pure" property realm, in which the laissez-faire market is inherent in the concept of property, and a nonproperty realm, in which things people value must belong to another category or categories.

Yet Mill also thought that people could justifiably hold only "qualified," and not "absolute," property rights in land and presumably in other natural resources:

> The essential principle of property being to assure to all persons what they have produced by their labour and accumulated by their abstinence, this principle cannot apply to what is not the produce of labour, the raw material of the earth. . . . Whenever, in any country, the proprietor . . . ceases to be the improver, political economy has nothing to say in defense of landed property, as there established.[8]

Here Mill could not avoid the contradiction. What he said about property in land implies some inalienability (and some curtailment of the right to exclude others), thus contradicting his general conceptual vision of property. For example, from the passage quoted, we might infer that land, although it is property, should not be owned by nonimprovers.

The tension between the property rights Mill actually thought could be justified and what he said was required for something even to be property is also evident in his views on bequest. Although he considered bequest "one of the attributes of property," he was opposed to unlimited bequest.[9] Mill's opposition to unlimited transmission of property at death seems to contradict both the unlimited right to dispose (for the testator) and the unlimited right to receive (for the devisee or legatee) that he asserted are inherent in the concept of property.

One who thinks that some things can be "property," but not fully alienable, is a different kind of compartmentalizer from one who holds that some things are not property at all. A conceptualist can be a compartmentalizer by holding that some things are not property at all, but she cannot consistently be one by holding that some things that are property are not fully alienable. The logical contradiction invites a move from the latter kind of compartmentalization toward complete commodification: everything that is property must be fully alienable, because property is necessarily suitable for trade in a laissez-faire market. When this move is made, there is no room for Mill's "qualified" property rights—or rather, property rights could be qualified only if necessary to avoid externalities that would otherwise create market failure, and we would have arrived at the typical economic view of inalienability.[10]

The Subject/Object Dichotomy: The Kantian Person versus the Thing-in-Itself

Theorists who do not argue conceptually in this way avoid the problem of having to view all restraints on the laissez-faire market as incompatible with property. The kind of argument made by Kant and Hegel, who justified property and alienability (free contract) on the basis of their connection with freedom and actualization of the person, does not lead so readily to the worldview of commodification. The central thesis that Kant and Hegel have in common, however they differ in other respects, is that only objects separate from the self are suitable for alienation. Although this kind of theory avoids the difficulty that everything called property must conceptually be a "pure" free-market commodity, it has a serious difficulty of its own. It must distinguish things internal from things external to the person—the subject/object problem.

The subject/object dichotomy metaphysically divides the universe into opposed subjective and objective realms. Kantian personhood is the subject side of the dichotomy. Kantian persons are essentially abstract, fungible units with identical capacity for moral reason and no concrete individuating characteristics.[11] They are units of pure subjectivity acting in and upon the world of objects.

Compartmentalization—separation of a market realm from a non-market realm—must be clear on what things belong on which side of the subject/object divide. Only the object side is suitable for commodification. Yet it seems the subject side, at least as traditionally conceived, might readily collapse. The Kantian conception of personhood makes us all interchangeable and thus engenders liberal political equality: equal treatment of persons as ends, not means; equality before the law; one person, one vote; and the rule of law. By postulating such a world of fungible, subjective, autonomous units, however, Kantian personhood also facilitates conceiving of concrete personal attributes as commodified objects.[12] This is one of the problems that modern Kantians who adopt his thin theory of moral personhood need to confront.

The difficulties caused by Kantian personhood become clear from a brief examination of Hegel's views on property and contract. For both Kant and Hegel, private property is necessary to realize or actualize the will of a person in order to achieve freedom.[13] Contract is also necessary in order to be free and well-developed selves; we must be able to alienate external things, and we must not be able to alienate internal things.

For Hegel, alienability of property (both transfer and relinquishment) followed from the premise that the presence of a person's will makes something property: "The reason I can alienate my property is that it is mine only in so far as I put my will into it. Hence I may abandon . . . anything that I have or yield it to the will of another . . . provided always that the thing in question is a thing external by nature."[14] It follows that whatever is mine but is not "a thing external by nature" will be inalienable (nonrelinquishable and nontransferable). Substantive characteristics of personality are not things external by nature and are hence inalienable.

What Hegel had in mind here are "personality as such," "universal freedom of will," "ethical life" *(Sittlichkeit),* and "religion." These "goods, or rather substantive characteristics," constituting personality itself and the essence of self-consciousness, are inalienable. Under alienation of the personality itself, Hegel included slavery, serfdom, disqualification from holding property, encumbrances on property, "and so forth." Superstition, and ceding to someone else full power to direct one's actions or to prescribe duties of conscience or religious truth, "etc.," for Hegel counted as forbidden alienation of intelligence and rationality, of morality and religion.[15]

In order to apply the Hegelian form of argument to delineate inalienabilities, we need to draw clearly the distinction between things external by nature and substantive constitutive elements of personality, even though (if we are true Hegelians) that distinction must eventually be transcended. If something is external by nature, it must be propertizable and alienable so that persons can achieve freedom and proper self-development. If something is a substantive characteristic of personality, it must be inalienable for the same reasons.

In these respects (propertization and inalienability), Kant and Hegel had similar views. With respect to propertization, Kant argued: "It is possible for me to have any external object of my choice as mine, that is, a maxim by which, if it were to become a law, an object of choice would *in itself* (objectively) have to *belong to no one (res nullius),* is contrary to rights."[16] Hegel argued that persons have the right to put their will "into any and every thing [*Sache*]" and make it property.[17]

Kant and Hegel also had similar views on the inalienability of substantive characteristics of personality. Kant had put the subject/object problem in starker form:

Man cannot dispose over himself because he is not a thing; he is not his own property; to say that he is would be self-contradictory; for in so far as he is a person he is a Subject in whom the ownership of things can be vested, and if he were his own property, he would be a thing over which he could have ownership. But a person cannot be a property and so cannot be a thing which can be owned, for it is impossible to be a person and a thing, the proprietor and the property.[18]

Thus, inalienability is either required or proscribed, and which it is turns on the distinction between external things and substantive characteristics. Whatever is inside the person is required to be inalienable, and cannot be property; whatever is outside the person is required to be available for alienable property.

By "things external by nature," Hegel apparently meant objects in the environment that have (or can be thought to have) an existence independent of our will, at least in the earlier stages of development.[19] Hegel posited an "initial gulf" between the abstract will of the person and the world of unowned objects, which expresses the dichotomy between subject and object. It is only an "initial" gulf because as *Geist* (mind or spirit) becomes actualized, the wills of persons will become actualized in objects, and objects will be enlivened by the wills of persons.[20] Mind and nature do not remain dichotomized as the world develops. For Kant, and perhaps for many neo-Kantians, it is a permanent gulf; although persons (subjects) must control all things (objects) as property in order to be free, their character as subjects and objects is not thereby metamorphosed.[21]

The gulf between subject and object creates practical problems in deciding which items belong on which side of the divide. There are cases in which it does not seem intuitively obvious even to one who thinks the subject/object dichotomy itself is intuitively obvious. Wage labor and intellectual property are two examples.

Faced with explaining why wage labor is justified while slavery is not, Hegel, for example, seems merely to have stated his desired conclusion that wage labor is "external" to personality:

Single products of my particular physical and mental skill and of my power to act I can alienate to someone else and I can give him the use of my abilities for a restricted period, because, on the strength of this restriction, my abilities acquire an external relation to the totality and universality of my being. By alienating the whole of my time, as crystallized in my work, and everything I produced, I would be making into another's property the substance of my being, my universal activity and actuality, my personality.[22]

The argument that wage labor can become external because it is only part of one's creative capabilities and not the whole of them seems to be a non sequitur. Hegel did not claim that for something to be an internal, substantive characteristic of personality it had to be the whole of one's personal capacities. But even if we assume that the argument is valid, it does not show that these capabilities are external by nature. Rather the external relation is "acquire[d]" by virtue of the fact that something less than one's whole being is alienated. Thus, Hegel's argument seems to contradict his own premise for alienability.

If alienable property must be an object, intellectual property is also difficult to theorize. Here again, Hegel provides an example. Hegel thought that the method or medium of expression could externalize mental products and hence render them propertizable.[23] But this is not the same as saying they are a thing external by nature. The picture of intellectual property as an external object becomes more problematic every day, as intellectual property comes to exist in a digital world and is not embodied in any objects we can point to.[24]

The general point is that it is hard to see our work, either physical or intellectual, as belonging intrinsically (even if only "initially") to the object realm. Perhaps Hegel's discussion is a troubled apology for the market. The market agenda, however, is not apparent on the face of his property theory. In fact, his theory might seem to be compatible with a noncommodified view of society, because it is based upon embodiment of the will in objects and not upon trade. For Hegel, the essence of property is just that it is necessary to embody the will and actualize personality:

As *immediate* individuality, a person in making decisions is related to a world of nature directly confronting him, and thus the personality of the will stands over against this world as something subjective. For personality, however, as inherently infinite and universal, the restriction of being only subjective is a contradiction and a nullity. Personality is that which struggles to lift itself above this restriction and to give itself reality, or in other words to claim that external world as its own.[25]

For Hegel, objects may start out external, but they do not remain so: they become constitutive of personality. Indeed, the right to hold property is an inalienable attribute of personality.[26] Because personality is inalienable, one could argue that property might also become inalienable once personality is invested in it and constituted through it. One could argue that property ceases to be completely commodified. Instead, Hegel's argument is that any inalienability of property is itself a violation of inalienable personality rights. Hegel argued that encumbrances on property (probably meaning what we would call restraints upon alienation, like conditions or entails) are themselves a disallowed alienation of substantive personality rights.[27]

An underlying market agenda may appear more clearly in Hegel's contract theory. Hegel said that "the concept" compels alienation of external objects *qua* property "in order that thereby my will may become objective to me as determinately existent."[28] This may parallel

Kant's thought that no object could be permanently *res nullius* without impermissibly curtailing the scope of the human will; similarly, perhaps, objects must be movable by the will in order that its scope not be curtailed. Hegel was at least uncritical of the notion that exchange and trade are necessary to self-actualization. It remains unclear why "reason" or "the concept" compels "gift, exchange, trade, etc.,"[29] just as it is unclear why wage labor is external to the person and why any inalienability of property rights would violate personality.

Contract is the situation in which this compulsion of the concept is realized. Contract is the unity of different wills, and hence "the means whereby one identical will can persist within the absolute difference between independent property owners."[30] If Hegel's property theory is a picture of the person's relationship with external objects, his contract theory is a picture of the person's relationship with other persons. Since it is a picture of two wills relating to each other in will-containing objects, it is no wonder that Marx regarded this kind of contract theory as fetishism.[31]

But although Hegel argued that market exchange of property is required for proper self-development, he did not advocate universal commodification. Not only did he argue that certain things (namely, those belonging to substantive personality) were in principle not conceivable as property, but he also argued that family relationships and political relationships (the state) were not in principle conceivable as contract.[32] In the progress of the ethical Idea from abstract to actual, the family and the state are higher spheres than the sphere of abstract right in which private property and free contract belong.[33] The sphere of private right is the sphere of civil society (that is, the free market); the fully developed state is not merely an association of individual traders, but also (or rather) an organic entity, the embodiment of *Sittlichkeit,* "the actuality of the ethical Idea" and "the actuality of concrete freedom."[34] In these higher spheres, alienability and contract would be transcended by the advancing actualization of *Geist.* It is still open to dispute whether transcendence would mean that property and contract disappear, or that they continue to exist but with new significance. Nevertheless, Hegel's intellectual descendants can find in his work the basis of an evolutionary argument against commodification.

Hegel also cast the argument against alienation of personhood as a "contradiction." To alienate personhood is itself contrary to personhood, in that if I can relinquish my personhood, then no "I" remains to have done the relinquishing. If I treat "the infinite embodiment of self-consciousness" as something external and try to alienate it, Hegel argued, one of two things results: if I really possess these substantive attributes, they are not external and hence not alienated; if they are alienated, I did not possess them in the first place.[35]

Here Hegel might have been trying to say that substantive personhood is simply not capable of objectification. The "contradiction" consists in supposing that one could give up that which, "so soon as I possess it, exists in essence as mine alone and not as something external."[36] If this interpretation is correct, then the contradiction poses the same subject/object problems as Hegel's general view of property and alienation: Why is it that personhood cannot be objectified while at the same time personhood requires objectification (in things)? Exactly what items are permanently "inside" the subject and incapable of objectification?

If the person/thing distinction is to be treated as a bright line that divides the commodifiable from the inalienable, we must know exactly which items are part of the person and which not. The person/thing distinction and its consequences seemed obvious to Kant and Hegel (at least "initially"), but such is not the case for many modern philosophers, among them many neo-Hegelians.[37] One who accepts the arguments of writers like Thomas Kuhn and Richard Rorty rejects the metaphysical bright line between what is inside us, in our minds, and some realm of things-in-themselves, a mind-independent reality outside of us.[38]

Without the bright line, arguments delineating the market realm on the basis of the subject/object distinction lose their force. If the person/thing distinction is not a sharp divide, neither is inalienability/alienability. There will be a gray area between the two, and hence the outer contours of both personhood and inalienabilities based on personhood will remain contested. That there is a gray area need not be fatal for market compartmentalization, but it means that compartmentalization cannot be accomplished in the straightforward way many of its proponents hope. If we lose our grasp of the supposed bright line but remain committed to commodification of objects, then we can lose our grasp of subjectivity. Then the subject/object problem pulls compartmentalization toward universal commodification because there is no obvious stopping place short of that.

Compartmentalization and Paternalism

Two theories about freedom are central to the primary ideological framework in which we have viewed inalienability: the notion that freedom means negative liberty, and the notion that (negative) liberty is identical with, or necessarily connected to, free alienability of everything in markets. "Negative liberty" means roughly the freedom of the individual to be let alone to do whatever she chooses as long as others are not harmed.[39] The distinction between positive and negative liberty was used by Kant, who referred to the kind of arbitrary freedom of the will that we perceive in the phenomenal realm as negative. Positive freedom, in the noumenal realm, was for Kant identical with action necessitated by universal reason in conformity with moral law.[40] In general, the commitment to negative liberty, like the commitment to the Kantian structure of persons versus objects, has caused confusion in liberal compartmentalization and has exerted a pull toward universal commodification.

Inalienabilities are often said to be paternalistic. The discussion of inalienability rules by Guido Calabresi and A. Douglas Melamed, considered in Chapter 2, illustrates a typical use of the notion of paternalism. Paternalism usually means substituting the judgment of a third party or the government for that of a person on the ground that to do so is in that person's best interests. As Duncan Kennedy points out, paternalism involves false consciousness.[41] The paternalist asserts that the actor has made a mistake about what is best for her and that a third party or the government is in a state of true consciousness and can therefore override her choice. Although Kennedy seeks to rescue it for his own purposes, the term "paternalism" has largely been used pejoratively by advocates of negative liberty.

For advocates of negative liberty, to substitute someone else's choice for my own is a naked infringement of my liberty.[42] Paternalism is particularly anathema to libertarians who are also moral subjectivists. They hold that a person's subjective preferences define her interests, and therefore that it is nonsensical to claim that anyone else knows better than she does what is good for her. For these libertarians, among whose number are many practitioners of law and economics, the notion of false consciousness is simply incoherent.

To think of inalienability as paternalism assumes that freedom is negative liberty—that people would choose to alienate certain things if they could but are restrained from doing so by moral or legal rules saying, in effect, that they are mistaken about what is good for them. To say that inalienabilities involve a loss of freedom also assumes that alienation itself is an act of freedom or is freedom-enhancing. As we have seen, this is a traditional liberal view. Someone who holds this view and conceives of alienation as sale through free contract is deeply committed to commodification as expressive of—perhaps necessary for—human freedom. Insofar as theories of negative freedom are allied to universal commodification, so are traditional discussions of inalienability in terms of paternalism.

Joel Feinberg's discussion of the inalienable right to life illustrates the traditional link between inalienability and paternalism, as well as the tension caused by the clash between negative liberty and substantive requirements of personhood. Feinberg distinguishes three conceptions of the inalienable right to life, which he calls "the paternalist," "the founding fathers," and "the extreme antipaternalist."[43] In the view he calls paternalist, to say that the right to life is inalienable means that it is a nonrelinquishable mandatory right, one that ought to be exercised, such as the right to education.[44] In contrast, the view that Feinberg attributes to the founding fathers holds that the inalienable right to life is a nonrelinquishable discretionary right. It is discretionary because the individual may choose whether to exercise it.[45] For example, the right to own property is a discretionary right because I may choose to own nothing; it is a nonrelinquishable discretionary right because I cannot morally or legally renounce the right to own property even if I choose not to own any.[46]

Feinberg concludes that the nonrelinquishable right to life is discretionary, not mandatory:

> [W]e have a right, within the boundaries of our own autonomy, to live or die, as we choose. . . . [T]he basic right underlying each is the right to be one's own master, to dispose of one's own lot as one chooses, subject of course to the limits imposed by the like rights of others. . . . In exercising my own choice in these matters, I am not renouncing, abjuring, forswearing, resigning, or relinquishing my right to life; quite the contrary, I am acting on that right by exercising it one way or the other.[47]

This passage suggests that the right to life is discretionary because it is parasitic on negative liberty, the right to be one's own master. But

Feinberg does not say whether the underlying right to be one's own master is mandatory or discretionary.

The omission points to an apparent contradiction in the argument, a contradiction that stems from a commitment to negative liberty.[48] If the discretionary right to life is nonrelinquishable, as Feinberg claims is the founding fathers' view, then we can infer that the "basic right" to have discretion—liberty—must be mandatory: one cannot choose not to be one's own master, not to dispose of one's lot as one chooses. But to attribute this mandatory conception of liberty to the founding fathers would apparently be to attribute to them a conception of positive liberty, a view that people can be required to be free. Hence, Feinberg attributes to the founding fathers a discretionary, not mandatory, view of the right to liberty. But if the right to liberty is indeed discretionary, then it seems I could choose not to be my own master, not to dispose of my lot as I choose, just as I could choose not to own property. And if I could choose that, I could choose not to have any of the other parasitic nonrelinquishable rights, such as the right to life. The right to life would then be relinquishable.

This contradiction shows why a commitment to negative liberty pulls liberal compartmentalizers toward universal commodification. The commitment to negative liberty usually attributed to the founding fathers forces those who hold it to choose between submerging a contradiction and moving toward conceiving of everything as relinquishable. If the intellectual descendants of the founding fathers want to maintain a nonrelinquishable discretionary right to life, they must adopt a mandatory right to liberty: we are not free not to be free. But adopting a mandatory right moves toward positive liberty, undermining the negative view that generates the nonrelinquishable, but discretionary, right to life. Holding firm to the view that liberty means negative liberty leads to a view that everything, including one's life, is relinquishable.

In this latter view, that of Feinberg's "extreme antipaternalist," the fully informed autonomous individual could sell herself into slavery or sell her right to life. Thus, the antipaternalist is a universal commodifier. This appears to be a more cogent view, once we grant that rights to life and property are parasitic upon a nonrelinquishable, but nonmandatory, right to negative liberty.

Might one hold fast to negative liberty and still claim we are not free not to be free? This difficulty is the root of the tension between compartmentalization and negative liberty, and of the consequent pressure to give up compartmentalization. Mill's well-known attempt to argue against freedom to sell oneself into slavery directly poses this difficulty: "[B]y selling himself for a slave, [a person] abdicates his liberty; he forgoes any future use of it beyond that single act. He therefore defeats, in his own case, the very purpose which is the justification of allowing him to dispose of himself. . . . The principle of freedom cannot require that he should be free not to be free. It is not freedom, to be allowed to alienate his freedom."[49]

The argument is obscure. It is hard to see why Mill thought it obvious that the principle of negative freedom could not require the "freedom not to be free"; only positive freedom clearly holds that a person must be free. In general, what in Mill's view is the connection between free alienation and freedom? (Why is alienation of freedom "not freedom"?) Some commentators have viewed Mill's argument against selling off one's freedom as a lapse into paternalism.[50]

Neither in his conception of freedom nor in his conception of alienability does Mill appear to explain why human beings are non-commodifiable. Given that Mill insisted so strongly on the inherent alienability of property, it is interesting that he elsewhere declared that "the principle of individual liberty is not involved in the doctrine of Free Trade."[51] Hence, for Mill (unlike modern proponents of negative liberty), individual liberty is not involved in most government regulation of trade in commodities. Most trade restrictions, including restrictions on production, are wrong for Mill not because they violate the producers' liberty but because "they do not really produce the results which it is desired to produce by them."[52] They are wrong for utilitarian, not libertarian, reasons. On the other hand, prohibitions, "where the object of the interference is to make it impossible or difficult to obtain a particular commodity," do violate individual liberty, but that of the buyer, not the seller.[53]

This argument seems to make the existence of a liberty interest depend on the motive with which the restraints are enacted. It also seems to imply that freedom is implicated in acquisition of goods but not in disposition of them. Recall that Mill stressed both the right to dispose and the right to acquire as inherent in the idea of property. If freedom is implicated in acquisition rather than in disposition of goods, the idea that alienability and negative freedom are identical or necessarily linked is undermined. If freedom is implicated primarily in acquisition, then perhaps we should ask, as Mill did not, whether a prohibition on slavery violates the would-be slave-owner's freedom instead of (or as well as) the would-be slave's.

One could understand Mill to imply that there is an unstated divide between the domain of the market (free trade) and the domain of politics (liberty). People must be free in order for a free political order to exist; they cannot be free without such a political order; hence, in the nonmarket realm they cannot, without contradiction, be free not to be free. This reconstruction makes Mill a compartmentalizer, as indeed he apparently wished to be; but the reading is not very true to Mill in the way it relinquishes negative liberty.

Again, one way to avoid Mill's problem is to espouse universal commodification. The universal commodifier can hold on to negative liberty and avoid Mill's problem—espousing negative liberty while eschewing voluntary enslavement—because in universal commodification freedom itself is seen as monetizable and alienable. Those who tend toward universal commodification may indeed endorse voluntary enslavement.[54] Those who declare human beings noncommodifiable must do so on the ground of postulated market failure (for example, transaction costs.)[55]

4

Compartmentalization: Attempting to Delineate a Market Domain

Walzer and the Sphere of Free Exchange

Compartmentalization—theorizing the social world in terms of a pure market domain and a pure nonmarket domain—is still attractive to many liberals. Michael Walzer's theory of separation is the most distinguished example of the spatial metaphor I claim we should reject.[1] In Walzer's work, the metaphor is of spheres rather than walls or domains. Nevertheless, I believe we can see in his work the concessions of a modern liberal toward universal commodification.

Walzer posits eleven separate "spheres of justice," with the market as only one of them. Walzer's separation thesis is that justice consists in complex equality. By this he means that the hierarchization that occurs in each sphere—as a result of differences in biological endowments, energy, and luck—is not wrong so long as preeminence in one realm does not spill over, giving the top dogs in one realm automatic dominance in others. In other words, justice consists in keeping the spheres separate. Thus, Walzer assumes that complete commodification in a large sphere is prima facie just.[2]

In light of this separation thesis, one of Walzer's primary tasks, perhaps his most crucial one, is to show how money and power in the free-market sphere can indeed be self-contained in the market realm. Otherwise money and power in the market sphere spill over and give those who dominate the market unjust dominance in the realms of education, free time, security, recognition, public office, and political power. (Thus, Walzer believes there is a slippery slope, which I will call a domino theory: the market, if unchecked, will tend to overstep its bounds.) In order to show how the market may be contained, Walzer must first tell us where the market sphere (normatively) ends and other realms begin. That is, he must map the limits of the sphere. This he does not satisfactorily accomplish; nor, for reasons I hope to make clear, could anyone.

Walzer's term for the transforming of every social good into a commodity (which I have called universal commodification) is "market imperialism." Here is how he poses the problem of market imperialism and proposes a principle for containing it:

> What is at issue now is the dominance of money outside its sphere, the ability of wealthy men and women to trade in indulgences, purchase state offices, corrupt the courts, exercise political power. Commonly enough, the market has its occupied territories, and we can think of redistribution as a kind of moral irredentism, a process of boundary revision. Different principles guide the process at different points in time and space. For my immediate purposes the most important principle has this (rough) form: the exercise of power belongs to the sphere of politics, while what goes on in the market should at least approximate an exchange between equals (a free exchange).[3]

As an attempt to delimit a market sphere, the distinction between "exercise of power" and "free exchange" is not very useful. That only free exchanges should be allowed is no more than the negative liberty that "market imperialists" themselves claim. A contract made under duress is not a valid contract.

Apparently Walzer wants us to understand "free" expansively, so that poverty by itself can count as "coercion" and negate free exchange. Perhaps Walzer just means to argue that without welfare rights or a minimum income or standard of living we cannot count any exchange as free. Does he mean, then, that selling to poor people is an act of political power while selling to middle-class people is an appropriate act in the market realm? Because the concept of economic coercion seems to straddle the supposed boundary between politics (power) and the market (free exchange), it is hard to see how Walzer can use that concept to help draw it.[4]

Walzer lists fourteen types of things that are "blocked exchanges" (off-limits to the market). One of them is "desperate exchanges," by which he means exchanges in the labor market that are motivated by poverty.[5] This "blocked" category of "desperate exchanges" raises theoretical problems that are relevant to the issues surrounding use of the spatial metaphor. Walzer uses this rubric to justify the eight-hour day, minimum-wage regulation, and health and safety regulation. About this Walzer comments: "This is a restraint of market liberty for the sake of some communal conception of personal liberty, a reassertion, at lower levels of loss, of the ban on slavery."[6]

It is unclear whether, for Walzer, market liberty and the communal conception of personal liberty are synonymous with negative and positive liberty, respectively. In general, it is not clear whether Walzer means to reject the idea of negative liberty at all, and, if so, to what extent. As I argued in Chapter 3, the ideological force of negative liberty tends to pull liberal separationist views like Walzer's toward universal commodification. It would be helpful to know, then, how Walzer would treat the libertarian hard question that the idea of "desperate exchanges" doesn't get to: are we justified in prohibiting someone from working long hours under dangerous conditions, if she really freely chooses for reasons of her own to do so? Would Walzer say that this free choice would be an exercise of "market liberty," but one we reject in the name of "personal liberty"?

Perhaps Walzer means to argue that the choice is not "liberty" at all, but coercion. Perhaps he would want to say that the argument about free choice raised by the notion of "market liberty" is a red herring. We should not preoccupy ourselves with the case of some middle-class, well-off, sane, well-educated person suddenly taking it into her head, fully cognizant of what she is doing, to subject herself to hazardous work for long hours at subsistence wages, because this person and these conditions just do not in life confront each other. Those who choose to sell their labor—or their kidneys—under these conditions are poor and oppressed. But even if we think of the exchange as coerced, and not usefully characterized as an exercise of liberty, we are still left with the problem that to the desperate person the desperate exchange must have appeared better than her previous straits, and in banning the exchange we haven't done anything about the straits. It seems to add insult to injury to ban desperate exchanges by deeming them coerced by terrible circumstances, without changing the circumstances.

Walzer's argument seems unsatisfactory because the distinction between market liberty and personal liberty assumes the divide Walzer wants to use the distinction to delineate. Market liberty for Walzer characterizes the permissible domain of commodification, and personal liberty characterizes a domain that is off-limits to the market. If we assume that it is intuitively obvious or a matter of definition which kind of liberty an asserted transaction belongs to, then we have solved the normative issue of the limits of the market. Otherwise, as I think is the case, the categories "personal liberty" and "market liberty" must be the conclusions of a moral argument rather than the basis of one. In my view, that moral argument will turn on our substantive commitments to a theory of proper human flourishing. Those substantive commitments will lead not to a wall, a sphere, or a domain, but rather to a more generalized modification of the market (commodity) scheme.

An Argument Based on Free Choice

The most characteristic form of liberal compartmentalization rests upon an attempt to preserve free choice. Walzer's argument is one example of this kind of theory, though one that countenances the welfare state more than most. If some people wish to sell something that is identifiably self-constitutive, why not let them? In a market society, whatever some people wish to buy and others wish to sell is presumptively alienable. Under these circumstances, liberals who want to limit the scope of the market must formulate an affirmative case for market-inalienability, so that no one may choose to com-modify a particular attribute, right, or thing. The kind of affirmative case that correlates most readily with traditional liberal ideology is a prophylactic argument based on free choice.

For the proponent of free choice it makes sense to countenance both selling and sharing of things, even those close to the self, as the holder freely chooses. If something is close to the self, however, sometimes the circumstances under which the holder places it on the market might arouse suspicion that her act is coerced. Given that we cannot know whether anyone really intends to cut herself off from something "inside" herself by commodifying it, our suspicions might sometimes justify banning sales. The risk of harm to the seller's personhood in cases in which coerced transactions are permitted (especially if the thing sought to be commodified is normally very important to personhood), and the great difficulties involved in trying to scrutinize every transaction closely, may sometimes outweigh the harm that a ban would impose on would-be sellers who are in fact uncoerced. A prophylactic rule aims to ensure free choice—negative liberty—by the best possible coercion-avoidance mechanism under conditions of uncertainty.

This prophylactic argument is one way to justify, for example, the ban on selling oneself into slavery. We normally view such commodification as so destructive of personhood that we would readily presume all instances of it to be coerced. We would not wish, therefore, to have a rule creating a rebuttable presumption that such transactions are uncoerced (as with ordinary contracts), nor even a rule that would scrutinize such transactions case by case for voluntariness, because the risk of harm to personhood in the coerced transactions we might mistakenly see as voluntary is so great that we would rather risk constraining the exercise of choice by those (if any) who really wish to enslave themselves.

In assuming that self-commodification might be acceptable but for uncertainties of knowledge and adjudication, this form of argument countenances commodification of the person, should the person so choose. The argument just doubts that such a choice will in fact take place. As a justification for a rule against self-enslavement, for example, Joel Feinberg mentions the risk of mistaken judgments of voluntariness,[7] and Richard Posner argues that the unenforceability of a self enslavement contract is economically explainable by the high likelihood of making a disastrous mistake.[8]

A liberal compartmentalizer might use a prophylactic justification of this kind to prevent poor people from selling their children, sexual services, or body parts. She would say that these things should be off-limits to the market because attempted sales are best presumed to be outside the realm of free choice. As with Walzer's proposed ban on "desperate exchanges," the compartmentalizer would argue that an appropriate conception of coercion should, with respect to selling these things, include the desperation of poverty. Poor people should not be "forced"—should not be allowed—to give up body parts, because the relinquishment diminishes them as persons, contrary to the liberal regime of respect for persons. We should presume (according to this prophylactic argument) that such transactions are not the result of free choice.

When thus applied to "coercion" by poverty, the prophylactic argument is deeply troubling. If poverty can make some things non-salable because we must prophylactically presume that such sales are coerced, we would add insult to injury if we then do not provide the would-be seller with the goods she needs or the money she would have received. If we think respect for persons warrants prohibiting a mother from selling something that is in some sense "inside" herself to obtain food for her starving children, we do not respect her person-hood more by forcing her to let them starve instead. To the extent that it equates poverty with coercion, the prophylactic argument requires a corollary in welfare rights. Otherwise we would be forcing the mother to endure a devastating loss in her relationship with her children rather than in the one she is willing to sacrifice to protect it. It is as if, when someone "chooses" to hand over her money at gunpoint, we were to direct our moral opprobrium at the victim rather than the gun-wielder, and our enforcement efforts at preventing the victim from handing over her money rather than at preventing the gun-wielder from placing her in the situation where she must.

Thus, this aspect of liberal prophylactic compartmentalization is troubling without a large-scale redistribution of wealth and power that seems highly improbable. And if such a redistribution were to come about, poverty would no longer be presumed a coercive factor, and the prophylactic justification would be less compelling. When someone is coerced at gunpoint, the preferred remedy seems clear: force the gun-wielder to give back whatever was obtained under duress and try to prevent such threats from occurring in the first place. If someone is "coerced" by poverty into selling something she would not otherwise sell, such as a kidney, unwinding the transaction is more problematic. Kidneys cannot readily be reimplanted. The buyer is not the sole cause of the seller's duress, and thus it seems unfair to take back the "goods" and let the seller keep the money. If unwinding the transaction includes restitution of the price paid, then the duress is not removed. To prevent such threats from occurring in the first place entails preventing poverty. A rule saying that those who give up anything at gunpoint will be punished would not be appropriate; thus, it seems clear that a rule saying that those who give up things under the "coercion" of poverty will be punished is not appropriate either. This argument can be understood as one reason why we should not necessarily consider economic need as negating free choice.

The puzzle about whether poverty can constitute coercion is a philosophical red herring that conceals a deeper problem. Insofar as preventing sales seems harmful or disempowering to poor people who otherwise would sell things important to personhood, it is so even if we think of the choice to sell as coerced. Yet allowing sales, even if we think of them as freely chosen, also seems harmful or disempowering. This dilemma is a double bind, a situation in which either commodification or noncommodification might be harmful. (See Chapter 9.)

Although we may nevertheless decide to ban sales of certain things normally understood as "inside" persons, the prophylactic argument, insofar as it rests on equating poverty with coercion, should not be the reason. The prophylactic argument does retain some force with respect to coercion in general. People can be coerced by many nonmonetary factors of power others may have over them. The issue would be whether any nonmonetary factors of power that we wish to characterize as negating free choice could plausibly be presumed to result in people's attempting to sell things.[9] The prophylactic argument may properly recommend that trades of some things—such as the sale of family heirlooms or a homestead—be at least more closely scrutinized for voluntariness than trades of others more clearly understood as "outside" the person. Invalidating "contracts" produced under duress is no more than free-market hygiene. Although we do not scrutinize all contracts for duress, case-by-case analysis of trades of things that are usually "inside" persons could be mandated by the conviction that respect for personhood requires individualized attention.

Notwithstanding the problems with the prophylaxis argument as it stands, it seems clearly to harbor a compelling thought. There is something going on that troubles us with respect to the integrity of the person when we observe someone in poverty who is trying to sell off parts of the body. That we are troubled suggests that we must think through more clearly in general how we can structure society to respect persons, not that we try to wall off a few troublesome transactions that seem less bad than their alternatives to those who are desperate. The next chapter takes up the general issue of how we might structure society to respect persons, in particular whether some realm(s) of noncommodification is (are) constitutive of personhood or human flourishing; or, to put it another way, whether the conception of personhood we are committed to can be consistent with universal commodification.

5

Personhood and the Dialectic of Contextuality

I am looking for a better way to think about market-inalienability, one that does not reproduce the subject/object dichotomy by telling us simply that things "internal" to the person are inalienable and things "external" are freely alienable. At the same time, if the ideological heritage of negative liberty loosens its hold on our imagination, we need not think of all inalienabilities as paternalistic. Reimagining these ideological artifacts will mean reimagining personhood as well. A view of personhood that does not conceive of the self as pure subjectivity standing wholly separate from an environment of pure objectivity should enable us to discard both the notion that inalienabilities relate only to things wholly subjective or internal and the notion that inalienabilities are paternalistic. An attempt to supersede liberal compartmentalization must develop a conception of human flourishing that does not reinscribe the traditional ways of conceiving of self and the world. In this chapter I sketch possible contours of a pragmatic approach to reimagining personhood and human flourishing.

Perspectives on Personhood

There are many different ways to think about personhood. Moral philosophers think about personhood when they construct and deploy their views of human choice and moral agency. For Kantian liberals, personhood is about free will and reason. From the point of view of Kantian moral personality, all of us are identical as persons. Philosophers of mind think about personhood when they try to figure out what constitutes personal identity. For many of these philosophers, personal identity means having a continuous life story that incorporates a past and a future for oneself. From the point of view of personal identity, all of us are different—unique—as persons. Psychoanalysts think about personhood when they relate the constants of human life and development to broad personality structures. From the psychoanalytic point of view, each of us manifests the same dynamic personality structures, yet no two of us do so in exactly the same way; we are all the same and also all different. Welfare rights activists and human rights activists think about personhood: what is the minimum of necessary resources for a fully human life? Medical ethicists think about personhood: at what point does life cease to be a human life worth living? Political theorists think about personhood: what are the basics of individuality that the state should recognize or underwrite? Parents think about personhood: what part do I play in making possible the best kind of life for my children?

In general, the context that provokes thought about personhood has a lot to do with what those thoughts turn out to be. The context of my exploration here is the role of the person in buying and selling in the context of markets, and hence the liberal connection of personhood with notions of property and contract. What can be said about property and contract as tropes for features of personhood?

Freedom and Identity

Traditional ideal theory about personhood stressed freedom and identity. However much the traditional conceptions may now stand in need of transformation, those are not commitments we can give up, so that is a place to begin. The freedom aspect of personhood focuses on will, or the power to choose for oneself. In order to be autonomous individuals, we must at least be able to act for ourselves through free will in relation to the environment of things and other people. The identity aspect of personhood focuses on the integrity and continuity of the self required for individuation. In order to have a unique individual identity, we must have selves that are integrated and continuous over time.

In the conceptual scheme of universal commodification, freedom is negative liberty, indeed is negative liberty in a narrow sense. Freedom is the ability to trade everything in free markets, the ability to use the will to manipulate objects in order to yield the greatest monetizable value. As we have seen, negative liberty has had difficulty with the hypothetical problem of free choice to enslave oneself. Yet even negative liberty can generate an argument against the general notion of commodification of persons. It is plausible to argue that the person cannot be an entity exercising free will (from the person's own point of view) if the person is simultaneously a manipulable object of monetizable value (from the point of view of others).

In universal commodification, personal attributes, relationships, and philosophical and moral commitments are monetizable and alienable from the self. It seems intuitively clear that this conceptualization of the self undermines personal identity, although the matter needs further working out. (See Chapter 6.) I believe that a better view of personhood should understand many kinds of particulars—one's politics, work, religion, family, love, sexuality, friendships, altruism, experiences, wisdom, moral commitments, character, and personal attributes—as integral to the self. To understand any of these as monetizable or completely detachable from the person—to think, for example, that the value of one person's moral commitments is commensurable or fungible with those of another, or that the "same" person remains when her moral commitments are subtracted—is to do violence to our deepest understanding of what it is to be human.

Contextuality and Personhood

A more positive meaning of freedom starts to emerge when one recognizes, in addition to freedom and identity, a contextual aspect of personhood. Contextuality means that physical and social contexts are integral to personal individuation, to self-development. Even the narrowest conception of negative liberty implies a context. To realize this conception of liberty, we would have to bring about a social environment that makes trade possible in order to become the persons whose freedom consists in unfettered trades of commodified objects. A broader conception of negative liberty understands freedom as the ability to make oneself what one will. A context is also implied in order for the conception to be realizable. Self-development in accordance with one's own will requires one to will certain interactions with the physical and social context, because context can be integral to self-development.

The general point is that any (recognizably plausible) conception of freedom of persons comes attached to a particular enabling context. The relationship between freedom of persons and its enabling context requires, if freedom is to be realized, a positive commitment to act so as to create and maintain particular contexts of environment and community. Recognition of the need for such a commitment turns toward a positive view of freedom, in which the self-development of the individual is linked to pursuit of proper social development. This is not a radical point. I believe it goes back to Kant, who argued that property and contract must come into being as juridical (that is, socially mediated) relationships, just because they are necessary for human freedom and cannot exist without a social structure.[1] I think the arena of argument now must be, not whether context is integral to human flourishing, but in what ways it is, and what specific contexts are requisite.

Contextuality and Personal Property

In human life as we know it, self-constitution includes connectedness with other human beings and also with things in the world, with a home, for example. Not everything we might be thus connected with in the world can be property, but in a property-owning culture, some such things can be property. When an item of property is involved with self-constitution in this way, it is no longer wholly "outside" the self, in the world separate from the person; but neither is it wholly "inside" the self, indistinguishable from the attributes of the person. Thus certain categories of property can bridge the gap or blur the boundary between the self and the world, between what is inside and what is outside, between what is subject and what is object.

Lots of things that people own have little to do with self-constitution, however. In the conceptual scheme of commodification, people hold money not for its special relationship to who they are but for what it can buy in the way of other things. In reality, people's relationship with money is more complicated.[2] Nevertheless, most people's holding of money does not implicate self-constitution with particular coins or bills. Many things that people own, such as items of property held only for investment, are just like money in this respect. Property items of this kind are understood as outside the self and do not serve to blur the boundaries of the self or subject.

I have used the term "personal property" to refer to categories of property that we understand to be bound up with the self in a way that we understand as morally justifiable.[3] I have used the term "fungible property" to refer to categories of property that we do not understand to be justifiably bound up with the self, but rather understand to be separate from the self in the sense that they are not implicated in self-constitution. My terms "fungible" and "personal" do not mark out a rigid binary dichotomy but rather mark the end points of a continuum. Nevertheless, the terms are useful. We do understand certain categories as corresponding to the continuum's end points or close to them: we understand certain categories of property items as being completely interchangeable with others of their kind without loss of value to the person (fungible), and certain categories as being bound up with the person so as to be of unique and nonmonetizable value to the person (personal).

These categories of understanding are not transcendent but rather relate to cultural commitments. Not all cultures understand the home as the locus of personal grounding the way we do. A nomadic culture wouldn't, for example. (And who is "we" here? Maybe just "our" dominant culture.) Indeed, it may be peculiar to postindustrial Western culture to enmesh the understanding of personal grounding with the conception of capitalist private property the way our dominant culture does.

These categories of understanding—of social construction—are connected to a number of other categories that we have already explored. All relate to our culture of ownership and exchange: alienability versus inalienability, commensurability versus incommensurability, commodification versus noncommodification.

Fungible Property and Commensurability

Fungible property connects with alienability, which means separability from the holder. Since fungible property is not connected with the self in a constitutive way but is held only instrumentally, nothing is problematic in disconnecting it from the person (from the self). Nothing is problematic in trading it off for some other item that the person would rather have. Moreover, when alienability is understood expansively, so as to include some of the person's endowments and attributes (reproductive capacity, for example), then it presupposes a thin theory of the self. That is, if endowments and attributes are considered readily detachable, and suitable for trade like fungible property, then the self is not defined thickly, in terms of these endowments and attributes, but instead thinly, in terms of whatever remains after they are detached.[4]

Fungible property is related to commensurability. Commensurability is a contested concept, but as I am using it commensurability refers to an understanding of value that is unitary (as opposed to pluralist). Those who understand value in this unitary way believe that all things people value can be reduced to some common metric such as money (a form of simple reductionism), or at least that all things people value can be arrayed in order on one continuous curve from less valuable to more valuable. In the first understanding of commensurability, simple reductionism, values can be unproblematically traded off against each other; six of one really is just as good as half a dozen of the other. In the second understanding, values are at least commensurable in the sense that we can always unproblematically tell whether one thing is more or less valuable than another.

When items are fungible, they are interchangeable with like items and with money. That is, they can be replaced with other items of their kind or with money (which can be used to acquire other items of their kind) without any significance for self-constitution. This may not be exactly the same thing as simple reductionism, but if not, it is close. Fungible items are valued in the same way as money, even if their value for the holder is not identical with money value.

Given our market culture and social structure, these characteristics of fungibility—interchangeability and money value—mean that fungible items are socially constructed as commodities. They are understood instrumentally, as means to satisfy the owner's needs and desires. They are valued in market terms, in terms of exchange.

Personal Property and Incommensurability

Personal property expresses the alternatives to alienability, commensurability, and commodification. Personal property connects with inalienability, which means inseparability from the holder. Since personal property is connected with the self, morally justifiably, in a constitutive way, to disconnect it from the person (from the self) harms or destroys the self. The more something takes on the indicia of an attribute or characteristic of the self, or at least the self as the person herself would wish,[5] the more problematic it seems to alienate it, and the stronger the inclination toward some form of inalienability. Moreover, when the self is understood expansively, so as to include not merely undifferentiated Kantian moral agency but also the person's particular endowments and attributes, and not merely those particular endowments and attributes, either, but also the specific things needed for the contextual aspect of personhood, then this understanding is a thick theory of the self. A thick theory of the self correlates with an expansive role for inalienability because things that are understood as inside the self, or as bridging the boundary between inside and outside, cannot simultaneously be understood as readily detachable from the self they constitute.

Personal property is related to incommensurability. Incommensurability, as I am using the term, refers to an understanding of value that is pluralist; that is, there are different kinds of value that cannot be reduced to one kind (expressed in terms of one common metric) nor arrayed linearly on one scale. When items are personal, they are not interchangeable with like items or with money. They cannot be replaced with a like item or with money without affecting self-constitution. Personal items are not understood instrumentally, as means to satisfy the owner's needs and desires, or at least their significance is not wholly captured by this kind of understanding. They are not valued—or not valued only—in market terms, in terms of exchange. Because they are not, they are noncommodified, or incompletely commodified.

The Dialectic of Contextuality

One aspect of personal contextuality, the one that connects with personal property, relates to a certain stability of one's environment. When things are too chaotic around the person, the person cannot develop adequately; self-constitution is hindered. That is why parents are advised to establish unvarying routines for their children. Moreover, if things are too chaotic around a well-developed person, maintenance of her personhood will be threatened. At the extreme, if *everything* around me were in flux all the time, so that *nothing* I could think or do would have predictable results in the world, it would be hard to say there was a "me" at all. Continuity of context is important both for self-development and for self-maintenance.

At the same time, flexibility of context is just as important for personhood as stability of context. The ability to change oneself, to grow, to make choices that affect oneself, is a mark of personhood as we understand it. That is why parents are advised to enable their children to make choices and experience the consequences. We would find it hard to consider a being with no potential for change in its character to be a person. If I cannot change my environment, it is more difficult to change myself. At the extreme, if *everything* around me is rigid and *nothing* can be changed in response to my thoughts and actions, then it is hard to say that I have the potential for change that is requisite for personhood.

There is a paradox here; or a dialectic. Let us call it the dialectic of contextuality. For appropriate self-constitution, both strong attachment to context and strong possibilities for detachment from context are needed. Because these requirements seem to oppose each other, they exist in tension. This tension causes problems for theory and contradictory tendencies in practice.

For example, for certain inalienability rules in property doctrine I can muster a complex of arguments having to do with the need for stability of context in self-constitution. My libertarian opponent can muster a complex of arguments having to do with the need for flexibility of context in self-constitution.[6] These arguments are undecidable in the abstract. They have to be weighed in practice, with respect to specifics. We have to think whether legal recognition (versus foreclosure) of flexibility or stability is more important under the circumstances. I have argued, for example, that residential rent control can be justified in some contexts because without it a certain kind of stability of context is foreclosed.[7]

Does our society on the whole provide too many opportunities for stability of context (through legal doctrines, among other things) and not enough opportunities for flexibility and change? Some people on the right (such as Robert Ellickson) and some people on the left (such as Roberto Unger) think the answer is yes.[8] Addressing this question is not my project (at least for the moment). I believe, though, that any useful answer to this question of social vision should be developed out of examining and evaluating the many ways both the need for context-embeddedness and the need for context-transcendence are treated in practice.

I believe it is important for theory not to be constructed in such a way as to hamper this kind of pragmatic inquiry. So it is important for a theory of personhood—of human flourishing—somehow to make primary both the need for context-embeddedness and the need for context-transcendence, despite their contradictoriness. Otherwise, its picture of the self becomes distorted. As theory it will not be useful for understanding and evaluating the contradictory strands of our practice; and if we attempt to implement such a distorted theory in practice, it may be harmful to personhood.

In other words, a theory that errs on the side of context-embeddedness may be harmful to personhood; and so, as well, may a theory that errs on the side of context-transcendence. The dialectic of contextuality is an unavoidable complexity about self-constitution. If a theory tries to reduce this complexity by making the need for context-transcendence primary, it leads to what I called a thin theory of the person. In the thinnest theory, where nothing is intrinsic to personhood but bare undifferentiated free will, everything else—such as capacities, relationships, attributes of character—is conceived of as alienable objects, outside the self, part of the severable context. This thin theory of the person is the self in much of traditional liberal theory, as we have seen. It appears to facilitate assimilating aspects of personhood to the realm of commodities, which in turn threatens to make personhood as we know it disappear.

On the other hand, a theory that makes the need for context-embeddedness primary leads to what I called a thick theory of the person. In the thickest theory, much of the person's material and social context is postulated as inside the self, inseparable from the person. This thick theory appears to facilitate social construction of fixed status hierarchies, severely undermining freedom of choice and association, and also threatens to make personhood as we know it disappear.

The task for a theory of human flourishing is to come to grips with the dialectic of contextuality without reinscribing the doctrines of traditional liberalism. The aspect of context-transcendence has hitherto been expressed in terms of freedom of contract (the laissez-faire market), but we need to find a way to express it in terms other than those of commensurability and commodification. Likewise we need to find a way to express the aspect of context-embeddedness in terms other than those of fixed status hierarchies, the "feudal" property that contract ideology is supposed to supplant. In order to find a way to do this, I believe nonideal theory is necessary.

Nonideal Theory

Because of the depth of our commitment to them, it is still worth thinking about past ideal theories about personhood. Our notions of freedom and identity will metamorphose as we recognize the significance of contextuality, but they will not disappear. Yet, as a pragmatist, I believe nonideal theory is also necessary, because our visions about the nature of human beings and of the good life for human beings cannot be too far divorced from the circumstances that give rise to those visions—from what gives them their bite, their urgency. These circumstances include an understanding that our life at present falls short of the good life for human beings, as well as what we understand to be the specifics of its deficiencies.

Theories of personhood, then, should not be too far divorced from the realities of needs, capacities, and circumstances that shape personal development in practice, in the world. Therefore, to be useful to us, personhood theory should pay attention to resources, distributional principles, institutional structures, and the facts of personality development that make a good human life possible. Thus it is important for those of us who think about personhood to draw together insights from various disciplines—moral philosophy, philosophy of mind and identity, psychoanalytic theory, political theory, public health, and others. And in doing this we should pay attention to nonideal theory, relating personhood to cultures, institutions, and other circumstances in the real world.

Amartya K. Sen and Martha Nussbaum have provided a good starting point for this inquiry. Integrating development economics with moral philosophy, Sen has developed an account of justice that rests upon human functionings constitutive of a person's being and the capabilities that support those functionings, with their necessary material and social basis.[9] The philosophical basis for Sen's treatment of human constitutive functionings and capabilities is, according to Sen, Aristotle, as interpreted by Martha Nussbaum.[10] Nussbaum has implicitly brought together facets of many contexts of thought about personhood to make a theory of human nature and the good life, a theory that she calls Aristotelian essentialism. Whether or not her theory is the correct way to understand Aristotle, and whether or not it is usefully denominated "essentialism," it provides a useful starting point for a pragmatic account of personhood, and is therefore worth considering in some detail.

Contextuality and the Role of the Polity

Nussbaum begins by saying that a species of context construction is primary to politics and to justice. The aim of political planning is to provide to people the conditions in which a good human life can be chosen and lived.[11] Her approach, unlike some other liberal approaches, follows Sen in "aim[ing] not simply at the allotment of commodities, but at making people able to function in certain human ways."[12] This approach starts from the premise that people have certain characteristics and capabilities that make it possible for them to develop into fully functioning human beings. This is an ethical premise about what we value in human life. It is thus the task of the polity to provide the conditions under which this fully human functioning is possible.

The Need for Details of Humanity in Context

In order to theorize about political justice, given this basis of polity, we must work on personhood on two levels. We must delineate in detail both human characteristics and capabilities in their undeveloped state, and human functioning in its developed state. In other words, we need an account of human flourishing, Aristotelian *eudaimonia*. As Nussbaum says, the task of the polity "cannot be understood apart from a rather substantial account of the human good and what it is to function humanly."[13] A two-level analysis is needed because practical reason can carry us toward our ideal only if we know the details of where we start and where we want to end up. A pragmatic understanding of the relationship between theory and practice means that the details will change as the journey proceeds, yet the journey cannot start unless we know—however provisionally—some details.

Nussbaum sets about providing the needed two-level analysis: first the list of human characteristics and capabilities that can generate the needed list of developed human functionings; then the list of developed functionings (or rather, the list of developed capabilities for functionings, for it is up to each human being, not the polity, to complete his or her own development once the background enabling conditions are in place).

Nussbaum calls her theory Aristotelian "essentialism" because she means her list to delineate human nature and the good human life in a way that is nonrelative, in the sense of being acceptable cross-culturally. Yet this is not old-fashioned a priori transcendent essentialism, but rather "internal" essentialism.[14] Nussbaum allies herself to Hilary Putnam's "internal realism"—which Putnam also called "pragmatic realism"[15]—and thus it is not surprising that there are substantial affinities between Aristotelian "essentialism" and Deweyan pragmatism. I shall return to these affinities below.

Nussbaum aims for a list of functions that is both "non-detached" and "objective." The list must be nondetached:

> [I]t should not be discovered by looking at human lives and actions from a totally alien point of view, outside of the conditions and experience of those lives—as if we were discovering some sort of value-neutral scientific fact about ourselves. . . . Getting the list of functionings that are constitutive of good living is a matter of asking ourselves what is most important, what is an essential part of any life that is going to be rich enough to count as truly human. A being totally detached from human experience and choice could not, I think, make such a judgement.[16]

The list must also be objective, again not in a transcendent or foundationalist sense, but rather so as to support the possibility of criticizing cultures that are oppressive, while still leaving room for "a certain sort of sensitivity to cultural relativity." We (philosophizers about social justice) do not want "simply to take each culture's or group's word for it," when they tell us what human flourishing is for them: people can be socialized to accept their own oppression.[17] We don't want necessarily to accept female infanticide or enforced female illiteracy merely because these are practices accepted (if they are) by the culture in which they are practiced. At the same time, we do not want to be cultural imperialists. We don't want to be in the position of outsiders telling other cultures what is good for them. That is unjust, and also not useful; it prevents us from becoming involved in cross-cultural dialogue about improving the conditions of human life worldwide.

Thus, the needed list must occupy a middle ground: it must be nonrelative yet also nondetached; it must grow out of human experience yet not be too tied to any particular form of human experience. It must occupy a middle ground in another sense too, for it must attenuate the dichotomy of fact and value. Finding out about the essentials of ourselves and what is a good life for us is simultaneously an empirical and a normative inquiry. We make ethical judgments about what it is to be one of us, a human being, and about what it is to lead a truly human life, as opposed to a life that is alien or merely animal. Certain empirical circumstances are necessary to support such a life; among other things, we cannot have life at all without food. But how much food? Are we prevented from leading a truly human life if we must spend all our time trying to fend off starvation? The answer to this kind of question blends into ethical judgment.

A Pragmatic Theory of the Good

Nussbaum calls her two-level, mixed empirical and ethical, nondetached yet essentialist, theory of human nature the "thick vague theory of the good."[18] It is, I think, a pragmatic theory of the good, which need not be called "essentialist" if that word conjures up foundationalist baggage. It is "thick" because it is nondetached; it grows out of our experience of being human and thinking about what it is to be human, rather than out of a transcendent or a priori starting point. It is "vague" because it is nonrelative; it leaves room for different cultures and communities to have specific (perhaps conflicting) embodiments of its requirements. It is quite promising for thinking about human flourishing in light of the dialectic of contextuality.

In the stylized version necessary for exposition, Nussbaum's formulation has two levels, although actually they blend into a continuum. Level 1, the characteristics and innate capabilities that mark us as human beings, with the potential to develop into human beings capable of leading the good life, is "the shape of the human form of life."[19] Level 2, the developed capabilities for functioning that humans need in order to be capable of the good life, and hence the starting point for the obligations of a socially just polity, is a list of "basic human functional capabilities."[20]

The Level 1 list includes both limits and capabilities that define our humanness. Nussbaum lists ten items:[21]

Mortality: the fact of death "shapes more or less every other element of human life."

The human body: at minimum, we all need food, drink, and shelter; we all experience sexual desire and the need to move about.

Pleasure and pain: aversion to bodily pain is "surely primitive and universal, rather than learned and optional."

Cognitive capability: sense perception, imagination, reasoning and thinking.

Practical reason: "all human beings participate (or try to) in the planning and managing of their own lives."

Early infant development: "all humans begin as hungry babies, perceiving their own helplessness, their alternating closeness to and distance from those on whom they depend, and so forth."

Affiliation: we are social animals and feel some sense of affiliation and concern for other human beings.

Relatedness to other species and to nature: "human beings recognize . . . that they are animals living alongside other animals and also alongside plants in a universe that, as a complex interlocking order, both supports and limits them."

Humor and play: no aspect of human life is more culturally varied, yet laughter seems common to all cultures.

Separateness: however absent individualism is in some societies, "[w]hen we count the number of human beings in a room, we have no difficulty figuring out where one begins and the other ends."

The Level 2 list sets forth, with respect to each of the items in Level 1, the circumstances necessary to be able to live a good human life.[22] The circumstances are both external (things that must pertain in the social and physical environment) and internal (things that must pertain with respect to one's own development).

[Mortality:] "Being able to live to the end of a complete human life, as far as is possible; not dying prematurely, or before one's life is so reduced as to be not worth living."

[The body:] "Being able to have good health; to be adequately nourished; to have adequate shelter; having opportunities for sexual satisfaction; being able to move from place to place."

[Pleasure and pain:] "Being able to avoid unnecessary and non-beneficial pain and to have pleasurable experiences."

[Cognitive capability:] "Being able to use the five senses; being able to imagine, to think, and to reason."

[Practical reason:] "Being able to form a conception of the good and to engage in critical reflection about the planning of one's own life."

[Early infant development:] "Being able to have attachments to things and persons outside ourselves; to love those who love and care for us, to grieve at their absence, in general, to love, grieve, to feel longing and gratitude."

[Affiliation:] "Being able to live for and with others, to recognize and show concern for other human beings, to engage in various forms of familial and social interaction."

[Relatedness to other species and to nature:] "Being able to live with concern for and in relation to animals, plants, and the world of nature."

[Humor and play:] "Being able to laugh, to play, to enjoy recreational activities."

[Separateness:] "Being able to live one's own life and nobody else's; being able to live one's own life in one's very own surroundings and context."

Open-Endedness and Contestability

The thick vague theory of the good as Nussbaum has formulated it is intended as provisional (revisable) in a number of ways. In this her methodology is like the open-endedness of pragmatism. What conception or cultural working-out of any item on the list is the "right" one—the best alternative in its context, the best alternative available now—is properly the subject of cross-cultural debate. The list is merely intended to command enough consensus to get the dialogue started.[23]

Many of the items on it can be debated. Mortality is an important fact about humans, but not all cultures value "being able to live to the end of a complete human life," and some would understand "completeness" in a spiritual rather than biological sense. Practical reason is an important capability that marks humanity in general, but it seems to go too far to say that "all human beings participate (or try to) in the planning and managing of their own lives," although perhaps the point is that we are committed to the idea that they ought to. The notion of affiliation surely needs further work, and I will return to it later in this chapter. At minimum, we must recognize that as things stand, some people are concerned for others, and some aren't, although, again, perhaps the point is that we are committed to the idea that human beings ought to be conceived of in this way. It is also problematic to claim that "human beings recognize . . . that they are animals living alongside other animals and also alongside plants." This goes against important religious commitments of many people and seems needlessly divisive. Again, separateness of physical bodies need not be related to separateness of selves, and where it is not, it may be disputed that separateness belongs on this list at all. Finally, what is said about context on these lists needs explication, and as I shall discuss later, the lists do not adequately capture human dynamism. Nevertheless, they are a starting point.

Because the two levels are a way of marking out a continuum, dialogue should proceed along the lines of what or how much is needed, given the particular conceptions of human functionings prevalent in a culture, to bring people from the bedrock of basic humanness to the minimal threshold of the capabilities they need for the good life.

Although she intends it as nonrelative, Nussbaum recognizes that this particular list is itself culturally situated, as indeed any theory must be. When we truly engage in dialogue with other cultures, we may want to add or subtract items from the list. Perhaps (for example) we will learn from other societies that our relations with animals and plants are more important than we thought, or that our commitment to private property is less important than we thought. In claiming that the list is useful—in fact urgently needed—for evaluating development around the world, Nussbaum claims simply that "in life as it is lived, we do find a family of experiences, clustering around certain focuses, which can provide reasonable starting points for cross-cultural reflection."[24]

The Role of Political Affiliation

Even those of us who haven't studied Aristotle know he said that man is a political animal. He meant by that "an animal whose nature it is to live in a polis." The kind of polis Aristotle had in mind no longer exists. If Nussbaum's theory of human nature is "Aristotelian" essentialism, what is the role of political affiliation in humanness? Affiliation is listed in the thick vague theory, but politics is not mentioned. About the requirement of affiliation, Nussbaum comments that "we define ourselves in terms of at least two sorts of affiliation: intimate family and/or personal relations and social or civic relations."[25] The need for "social or civic relations" apparently includes, at least, "relationships of a political kind, the function that is constituted by playing one's role as a citizen alongside other citizens." So Nussbaum comments that the Aristotelian conception is one in which all citizens share in ruling. Since "planning the conception of the good that shapes a citizen's life" takes place, in part, in the political sphere, "good functioning in accordance with practical reason requires that every citizen should have the opportunity to make choices concerning this plan."[26] It seems puzzling that Nussbaum's formulation of the thick vague theory of the good does not directly include political affiliation as part of our human nature. Level 2 might well include something like "being able to engage in meaningful political participation with one's fellows." And if one reads Aristotle as foreclosing meaningful political activity except within the kind of polis that no longer exists, then here is where it ceases to be useful to think of this theory as Aristotelian.

True to her roots in Aristotelian thought, Nussbaum does ask us to understand both practical reason and affiliation (sociability) as special to human nature: "these two play an architectonic role in human life, suffusing and also organizing all the other functions—which will count as truly human functions only in so far as they are done with some degree of guidance from both of these."[27] It is unclear whether Nussbaum intends sociability in this formulation to be coextensive with political affiliation; in other words, whether she intends a very broad understanding of the political. At least we can say the whole enterprise of ethical debate that generates her list is political, since its aim is to discover the minimal obligations of the polity; and anyone who participates in these debates affirms the importance of both political affiliation and practical reason.[28]

Nussbaum so far has not set about elaborating how the other functions cannot be truly human unless arranged, organized, and suffused by practical reason and sociability. Someone might say that practical reason and sociability come in only at Level 2, that is that they are necessary for leading the good life, a well-developed human life, but not for the bare minimum of being human at all. Nussbaum, however, does not say this. For her, practical reason and sociability are architectonic at Level 1 and not just at Level 2: the form of life described by her list cannot be characteristically human at all unless "organize[d] and arrange[d]" by these two capabilities.[29]

Here some questions remain to be explored. In general, as a pragmatist I suspect that the attempt to reduce the experientially and ethically generated lists to two "architectonic capabilities" will turn out to be too wholesale to be useful in working out an understanding of personhood.

Exactly how do the cross-cultural psychoanalytic insights related to early infant development, for example, depend for their humanness on practical reason and social or political affiliation? Perhaps Nussbaum would want to say here just that without proper nurturing as infants we cannot *become* sociable beings, or beings with practical reason, so that we could never reach Level 2, "being able to have attachments to . . . persons outside ourselves," "being able to engage in critical reflection about the planning of one's own life."

But this seems to make practical reason and sociability derivative rather than architectonic. So perhaps Nussbaum would want to say instead that adult humans organize their infant caretaking by means of their practical reason and in conjunction with other humans, and that that makes practical reason and sociability architectonic for humanness in the sense she means, which is to say that which distinguishes human infant development from infant development in other animals. Yet this reading doesn't make one's own practical reason and sociability the organizing principles in one's own development, but rather the organizing principles in how one's caretaker(s) relate to one; whereas it seems to be one's own development (one's having been a helpless, hungry baby, and the way that fact shapes personality) that is relevant for the list.

What Nussbaum may be groping for, I suspect, is that the very concept of practical reason must belong to a social group (consisting of babies and caretakers) and cannot even be conceptualized as belonging only to one individual. The irreducibly social nature of practical reason does not by itself provide a basis for declaring practical reason to be architectonic, though, because all concepts are social in this sense.

Nurturing and Feminism

Whatever the relationship between early infant development and the capabilities of practical reason and sociability, it is salient that Nussbaum places the constants of early infant development on the list of those things basic to the human form of life. Other theories of human nature that are put forth as underwriting a view of the function and obligations of the polity do not do this; they start from the full-grown human being. The Kantian considers moral agency without considering how our personalities come to embody it. The Benthamite doesn't ask how we developed the instrumental self-interested rationality of economic man. It is possible that as a student of Aristotle Nussbaum is better situated to pay attention to what we might think of as a modern version of human teleology. Yet I am inclined to think something else is at work here as well.

That something is a feminist receptiveness to connectedness, to the recognition that human life is impossible without nurturing from those who care for us when we are helpless and dependent. Nussbaum builds human connectedness into her theory at a more basic level than the need of independent grown-ups to affiliate socially or politically. Early connectedness to another—nurturing—is what makes the social and political possible for us. It is not just that we can be happier, or better adjusted, or lead a better life if we experience the development from helpless dependence on our caretakers to independence from them; it is that without this experience we would not be human at all. Thus, theorizing about human nature in political theory cannot omit this salient human experience. In using abstract models of human nature that do not take this into account, both Kantians and Benthamites are missing something crucial.

Beyond Traditional Liberalism

In stressing the role for political theory of our personal developmental trajectory, pragmatic theory of the kind I have been discussing differs from traditional forms of liberalism that take off either from Kant or from Bentham. There are other important respects as well in which this theory differs from traditional liberalism.

First, in this theory the role of the polity is to structure social life and use of resources so that everyone can cross the threshold into capability to choose well.[30] It certainly doesn't resemble utilitarian liberalism, in which the goal is to maximize social wealth no matter how many are left out in the cold. Nor need it track Rawls's difference principle, in which more is always better even if it goes to those already wealthy, just so long as the worst off are made even a little better off. Depending on the height of the threshold and on material and social circumstances, it seems that in some possible Rawlsian worlds those who are worst off may remain below the threshold.

Thus, if we want to evaluate how well a nation or culture is doing with respect to providing opportunities for the good life for its people, we will not ask merely about gross national product, nor even about per capita income or assets.[31] Since policy analysts do predominantly evaluate societies this way, the Sen-Nussbaum approach has urgent results for what we should do in the real world of international development and international human rights.

Second, this theory is primarily about structuring of institutions and not primarily about mere distributions of goods. The amount of money a polity has, and the quantity of commodities its citizens consume, will not tell us all we need to know about whether good human functioning is taking place.[32]

Third, this is nonideal theory. It asks us not to imagine the just polity in the abstract, but to consider what would make each particular polity more just, given its particular situation with respect to cultural heritage and material resources. It is not like liberal ideal theories that assume away almost all the oppressive and unjust circumstances that need ameliorating.

Fourth, this theory undermines liberal neutrality (which I will discuss further in Chapter 14). It does not suppose that it is possible for the polity to be neutral among alternative conceptions of the good life. Quite the contrary, unless the polity structures institutions and resource use so as to bring as many people as possible across the threshold into capability for good human functioning (that is, unless it embraces a conception of the good for human beings), its citizens will not be enabled to choose their own conceptions of the good, and the good life for human beings cannot get off the ground.

Fifth, this theory, like some early writings of Marx, clearly implies that "some forms of labor are incompatible with good human functioning."[33] The kind of labor that contradicts our humanity is impermissible no matter how lucrative it might be for a society. It is not enough for the polity to make sure people have enough money and commodities to provide food and shelter—although many workers do not have even that kind of minimal assurance. Some forms of labor simply are mindless and exhausting enough to make it impossible for the worker to lead a fully human life, and the worker himself becomes a commodity. Nussbaum calls for "a searching examination of the forms of labor and the relations of production, and for the construction of fully human and sociable forms of labor for all citizens, with an eye to all the forms of human functioning."[34] This call for meaningful work for all people goes well beyond what is required by most forms of welfare rights liberalism.

Sixth, unlike many kinds of traditional liberalism, education has a central role in this theory. As in John Dewey's theory of democracy and human nature, a particular kind of education is a primary requirement if the polity is to support human flourishing. What is required of the polity is not just commitment of resources to education, either, but commitment to educational institutions concretely worked out so as to bring people to fully human functioning.[35]

As Dewey elaborated it, the ideal of democracy, which he sometimes called "the liberal faith," is a regulative ideal of self-actualization in all aspects of social life.[36] In ideal democracy people will use the method of intelligent inquiry, and the ever-increasing accumulation of cooperatively acquired knowledge its use will gain them, to solve social problems by their own actions. This is a rich and contextualized understanding of the abstract commitment of liberalism that the polity must treat people as—must consist of—free and equal citizens.[37] This kind of political participation and intelligent cooperative choice cannot come into being without a detailed commitment to education for democratic citizenship—a commitment that, despite Dewey's lifelong efforts, our own polity is farther than ever from making.

Incommensurability

The pragmatic open-ended theory of the good I have been discussing implies a commitment to incommensurability, or pluralism in the nature of value, similar to the commitment I symbolized with the notion of personal property. The items on the list cannot be traded off against each other. For example, having more food than you need does not make up for having less nurturing than you need. Otherwise, an eating disorder would not be a "disorder."

Nussbaum finds "especially repellant" the reductionist notion of universal commodification, that "all this can be modeled by attaching a monetary value to the relevant human functionings."[38] To treat the elements of self-constitution as fungible does violence to the self—to *ourselves*. As Nussbaum puts this, drawing on the arguments I have made,

> To treat the functions themselves as commodities that have a cash value is to treat them as fungible, as alienable from the self for a price; this implicitly denies what the Aristotelian asserts: that we define ourselves in terms of them and that there is no self without them. To treat deep parts of our identity as alienable commodities is to do violence to the conception of the self that we actually have and to the texture of the world of human practice and interaction revealed through this conception.[39]

The Role of Private Property

What results does this sort of theory of the good have for the role of private property? In nonideal theory we start with the property culture we have. But we can also be slightly more ideal, and slightly more visionary, and abstract away from the property culture in which we find ourselves. Without taking a culture of property for granted, how does an open-ended, pragmatic theory of the good approach the question, Is private property required for human flourishing?

It may be shown that certain functionings *can* be served by a form of private property; individual separateness, in particular, and the need to live one's life in one's very own context. When property actually serves this function in a justifiable way, I have called it personal. As Nussbaum says, however, this form of justification of private property is "contingent and controversial," since it will collapse as a justification if someone shows, to the contrary, that the context of noninterference required for human functioning does not include private property.[40] Moreover, it is certainly open to other cultures to see to this particular human functioning in other ways—or even to convince us that living under a property system has distorted its importance for us. (Marx said, "Private property has made us so stupid and one-sided that we think a thing is only *ours* when we have it.")[41]

Pragmatic Theory and Dynamism

The conception of human flourishing we have been considering generates a basic requirement of "being able to live one's own life in one's very own surroundings and context." This requirement follows from the basic understanding that human beings are separate individuals; the idea is that separation from other human beings, individuation, is accomplished in part by particularized connection with things.

In other words, in this conception of human flourishing separation does not connote the idea of alienability of all of the self's attributes and possessions, but rather something like its opposite: it refers not to separation of the person from her environment, but rather to separation of one person from another person, with the premise being that for that kind of separation to be instantiated in the world, a certain kind of specific connection to one's environment may be needed.

The pragmatic conception of the good as Nussbaum has formulated it, and as I have recounted it, has not yet fully recognized the dialectical nature of contextuality. As it must, Nussbaum's list does include in certain ways both the need for stability (which I called context-embeddedness) and the need for change (which I called flexibility of context or context-transcendence) as part of our conception of humanness. The need for stability is expressed in the idea of "being able to have attachments to things and persons outside ourselves," "being able to engage in various forms of familial and social interaction," "being able to live . . . in relation to animals, plants, and the world of nature," and "being able to live one's own life in one's very own surroundings and context." These requirements relate to the need for human situatedness in a minimally stable context of relationships to other human beings and to the nonhuman environment. The need for change is expressed in "being able to move from place to place" and perhaps in the very notion of practical reason, "being able . . . to engage in critical reflection about the planning of one's own life." Having the capability for practical reason seems to imply having the capability to act to change things for oneself.

Elements of the dialectic of contextuality can thus be gleaned from Nussbaum's theory. Yet, as she has formulated it so far, it submerges the role in human flourishing of the potential for self-alteration. Her recognition of the indispensable role of early infant development in the human form of life shows that she sees human life as a developing story. Yet I think that (what seems to me to be) the human need to construct a narrative for ourselves should be highlighted.

I think we should recognize that we seem to understand ourselves as *dynamic* beings, as beings whose life is a journey, and that this self-conception is no less central to our understanding of ourselves as human than is our understanding of the need for stable contexts.[42] Humanness is not just a static set of capabilities or even the results, considered on their own, of what we make of them. It seems to me that the list that for Nussbaum expresses the thick vague theory of the good does not really capture the salience of our experience of dynamism, the ever-present potential for change.

The idea of potential for change has been overstressed in traditional liberalism, partly through the primacy of contract ideology and the notion that everything people value is nevertheless freely alienable. Overstressing context-transcendence in trying to build a cross-cultural theory of human nature could be a form of modern Western cultural imperialism. Perhaps indeed I am still overstressing it here. Ideologies other than Western liberalism might stress it less. Yet I think context-transcendence, no less than context-embeddedness, has a place on the list of human characteristics.

A changeless being, or rather a being without the potential for change, even if possessed of all the capabilities on Nussbaum's list, would not be considered fully human. We seem to be committed to the idea that the potential to change ourselves—our character, our context, our emotional and philosophical commitments—is part of our essential humanity. At the same time, we are committed to the necessity of stability of context. A being that changed itself all the time, by changing all its relationships all the time, would not be considered fully human either.

Traditional liberal political theory expressed the potential for change in the principle of free contract: wherever we are, we can buy our way to somewhere else. But this is an alienated expression of the context-transcendence necessary for personhood, and it is chimerical. Acquiring different commodities is acquiring more of same; that is the meaning of commensurability. Commodification imagines a thin self that does *not* change; the static thin self just changes the set of commodities in its purview. The human capacity for self-mutability, for context-transcendence, is much more mysterious than the reductionism of commodification would portray it. Human dynamism awaits more capacious terms in which to characterize itself.

6

Human Flourishing and Market Rhetoric

Humanist Marxists, taking off from Marx's early writings, have persistently maintained that commodification is inimical to the flourishing of human beings. Attempts to create Marxist economic regimes are currently in disarray all over the world, and states that formerly called themselves Marxist are now trying to create market institutions as fast as they can. It would be foolish to deny that markets are experienced as liberating under some circumstances. Nevertheless, even if the ideal of universal noncommodification (abolition of the market) seems to be a chimera, Marx's polemics against the commodification of human beings still have some bite. And critical theorists' cognizance of the role of discourse in commodification—their attention to social construction and market rhetoric—reflects an issue that is philosophically very much alive.

The ideology of noncommodification generates a counterarchetype to universal commodification. Universal noncommodification holds that the hegemony of profit-maximizing buying and selling stifles the individual and social potential of human beings. This hegemony is dehumanizing, contrary to human flourishing. Capitalist buying and selling stunts humanity through its organization of production, distribution, and consumption because it creates and maintains persons as objects of trade (workers) and self-aggrandizing profit- and preference-maximizers (owners).

Universal noncommodification, as a counterarchetype, assumes that we are living under a regime of universal commodification, with its attendant full-blown market methodology and market rhetoric. It assumes that universal commodification is a necessary concomitant of commodification in the narrower sense—the existence of market transactions under capitalism. It links rhetoric and reality: our material relationships of production and exchange are interwoven with our discourse and our understanding of ourselves and the world. The social world is partly constituted by our concepts and categories of belief. This link between words and the world can be taken seriously even outside the context of the worldview of complete noncommodification.

Alienability and Alienation: Fetishism

For critics of the market society, commodification simultaneously expresses and creates alienation. The word "alienation" thus harbors an ironic double meaning.[1] Freedom of alienation is the paramount characteristic of liberal property rights, yet Marx saw a necessary connection between this market alienability and human alienation.

In his early writings, Marx analyzed the connection between alienation and commodity production in terms of estranged labor. Marx portrayed workers' alienation from their own human self-activity as the result of laboring to produce objects that become market commodities. By objectifying the labor of the worker, commodities create object-bondage. Commodities alienate workers from the natural world in and with which they should constitute themselves by creative interaction. Ultimately, laboring to produce commodities turns the worker from a human being into a commodity, "indeed the most wretched of commodities." Marx continued: "The worker becomes an ever cheaper commodity the more commodities he creates. With the *increasing value* of the world of things proceeds in direct proportion the *devaluation* of the world of men. Labour produces not only commodities; it produces itself and the worker as a *commodity*—and does so in the proportion in which it produces commodities generally."[2]

In this view, commodification brings about an inferior form of human life. As a result of this debasement, Marx concluded that people themselves, not just their institutions, must change in order to live without the market. To reach the postcapitalist stage, "the alteration of men on a mass scale is necessary." Revolution was necessary "not only because the *ruling* class cannot be overthrown in any other way, but also because the class *overthrowing* it can only in a revolution succeed in ridding itself of all the muck of ages and become fitted to found society anew."[3]

Later, in *Capital,* Marx introduced the notion of commodity fetishism. The fetishism of commodities represents a different kind of human subjection to commodities (or a different way of looking at human subjection to commodities).[4] By fetishism Marx meant a kind of projection of power and action onto commodities. This projection reflects—but disguises—human social interactions. Relationships between people are disguised as relationships between commodities, which appear to be governed by abstract market forces.[5]

One interpretation of this fetishistic displacement is to consider the experience of responding to market forces. I do not decide what objects to produce; rather, "the market" does. Unless there is a demand for paperweights, they will have no market value, and I cannot produce them for sale. Moreover, I do not decide what price to sell them for; "the market" does. At market equilibrium, I cannot charge more or less than my opportunity costs of production without going out of business. In disequilibrium, my price and profit are still set by "the market"; my price depends upon how many of us are supplying paperweights in relation to how many people want to buy them and what they are willing to pay for them. Thus, the market value of my commodity dictates my actions, or so it seems.[6] As Marx put it, producers' "own social action takes the form of the action of objects, which rule the producers instead of being ruled by them."[7]

In an analysis that has profoundly influenced many contemporary critics of the market, Georg Lukács, developing Marx's concept of commodity fetishism, found commodification to be "the central, structural problem of capitalist society in all its aspects."[8] That is, he found capitalism to express universal commodification. Lukács thought it might justifiably be claimed that Marx's "chapter dealing with the fetish character of the commodity contains within itself the whole of historical materialism," and that we can "gain an understanding of the whole of bourgeois society from its commodity structure."[9]

Lukács linked the trend to commodify the worker with Weberian "rationalization" of the capitalist structure.[10] The more efficient production becomes, the more fungible are the laborers. Moreover, commensurability becomes pervasive:

> [T]he principle of rational mechanisation and calculability [embraces] every aspect of life. Consumer articles no longer appear as the products of an organic process within a community (as for example in a village community). They now appear, on the one hand, as abstract members of a species identical by definition with its other members and, on the other hand, as isolated objects the possession or nonpossession of which depends on rational calculations.[11]

These falsely objectified commodities are said to be reified. According to Lukács, reification penetrates every level of intellectual and social life. As Lukács argued, commodification extends to the attributes and characteristics of the self:

> The transformation of the commodity relation into a thing of "ghostly objectivity" cannot therefore content itself with the reduction of all objects for the gratification of human needs to commodities. It stamps its imprint upon the whole consciousness of man; his qualities and abilities are no longer an organic part of his personality, they are things which he can "own" or "dispose of" like the various objects of the external world. And there is no natural form in which human relations can be cast, no way in which man can bring his physical and psychic "qualities" into play without their being subjected increasingly to this reifying process.[12]

False objectification—false separateness from us—in the way we conceive of our human attributes, our social activities, and our environment reflects and creates dehumanization and powerlessness. The rhetoric, the discourse in which we conceive of our world, affects what we are and what our world is. For example, Lukács thought that the universal commodification of fully developed capitalism underlies physicalist reductionism in science and the tendency to conceive of matter as external and real. He thought commodification entails epistemological foundationalism and metaphysical realism. In reified bourgeois thought, "facts" are the highest form of fetishism:

> [I]n the "facts" we find the crystallisation of the essence of capitalist development into an ossified, impenetrable thing alienated from man. And the form assumed by this ossification and this alienation converts it into a foundation of reality and of philosophy that is

perfectly self-evident and immune from every doubt. . . . Thus only when the theoretical primacy of the "facts" has been broken, only when *every phenomenon is recognised to be a process,* will it be understood that . . . the facts are nothing but the parts, the aspects of the total process that have been broken off, artificially isolated and ossified.[13]

Lukács thought that universal commodification also underlies both our rigid division of the world into subjects versus objects ("the metaphysical dilemma of the relation between 'mind' and 'matter' "), and the "Kantian dilemma" that places objective reason, purportedly the foundation of metaphysics and ethics, in the noumenal realm forever beyond our reach.[14] For Lukács, thought and reality are inextricably linked. Discourse matters for what is. That is why every phenomenon is a process. Our ability to see it as a particular phenomenon depends upon the categories we use to organize the world, and those categories depend upon both our thought and our material circumstances.[15]

Lukács warned against conceiving of the link between thought and reality in a way that reintroduces foundationalism:

It is true that reality is the criterion for the correctness of thought. But reality is not, it becomes—and to become the participation of thought is needed. . . . Thus thought and existence are not identical in the sense that they "correspond" to each other, or "reflect" each other, that they "run parallel" to each other or "coincide" with each other (all expressions that conceal a rigid duality). Their identity is that they are aspects of one and the same real historical and dialectical process.[16]

For Lukács and his many intellectual descendants, commodification in discourse and practice are inseparable and all-pervasive. They underwrite not only an economy of industrial capitalism but also a philosophy of atomistic individualism and a culture of consumerism.[17]

Market Rhetoric: Does it Matter?

Do these humanist Marxist critiques of universal commodification have any relevance for us? I believe they do, because they expose the link between our conceptual schemes and our world. This link has been perceived by writers as diverse as Clifford Geertz and Frank

Michelman.[18] Discourse matters for what is. The search for a conception of human flourishing must confront the problem of market rhetoric. It must confront the discourse of commodification—commodification as a worldview.

Once we start thinking about social construction through discourse, there arises an argument that the worldview of commodification cannot support the traditional Kantian ideal of personhood, even if we accept the appropriateness (or entrenchment, at any rate) of that ideal. The argument is that conceiving of persons or of essential attributes of personhood as fungible commodities tends to make us think of ourselves and others as means, not ends. Conceiving of the person as a commodity is harmful, in other words, because it undermines the conception of personhood involving the Kantian agent as end-in-itself: the Kantian person cannot be conceived of as a fungible exchangeable object.

This conception of personhood is a cultural artifact. Maintaining this conception—this construction of ourselves and of others—means maintaining a firm cultural commitment to it. Thus, if we do not want to lose hold of Kantian personhood, we might think that market rhetoric should be culturally discouraged in cases in which market conceptualization harms personhood. Moreover, law is culture-shaping. Thus, we might also think that market rhetoric should be legally discouraged in those cases, or in some of them. (But wouldn't legally discouraging market rhetoric, or any rhetoric, transgress freedom of expression? I will explore this issue in Chapter 12.)

Perhaps, though, we are moving too fast. Why should discourse matter? "The word is not the thing," we were taught, when I was growing up.[19] Rhetoric is not reality; discourse is not the world. Why should it matter if someone conceptualizes the entire human universe as one giant bundle of scarce goods subject to free alienation by contract, especially if reasoning in market rhetoric can reach the same result that some other kind of normative reasoning reaches on other grounds? Three answers suggest themselves: it matters because the rhetoric might lead less-than-perfect practitioners to wrong answers in sensitive cases; it matters because the rhetoric itself is insulting or injures personhood regardless of the result; or it matters because there is no such thing as two radically different normative discourses reaching the "same" result. The third answer involves the kind of social construction, the link between words and the world, that I have been discussing. And the other two can usefully lead up to it.

Risk of Error

The rhetoric of commodification might lead imperfect practitioners to wrong answers, even if the sophisticated practitioner would not be misled.

To see this, it may be helpful to compare a normative heuristic like cost-benefit analysis to a flat map of the world. Such a map is easy to use at the point of projection, but difficult and misleading at the edges. The difficulty of certain philosophical problems may signify we are at the edges of a chosen map. An example might be found in the justification of punishment. For utilitarian deterrence theorists, deciding whether to punish strict liability or *malum prohibitum* offenses (involving activities not inherently harmful) does not cause problems, but deciding whether to punish innocent people or undeterrable offenses requires fancy footwork. For deontological retributivist theorists, the situation is reversed.

The situation with the cost-benefit map may be analogous. Cost-benefit analysis is in principle not difficult when two firms deal with each other, at least if we define firms as profit-maximizing black boxes and no difficult externalities exist. By contrast, cost-benefit analysis involving people's subjective well-being is difficult to get right when many different people are involved and we are talking about interests they hold dear.

For example, the economic analysis of residential rent control could take into account not only the monetary costs to landlords and would-be tenants but also the monetized "costs" of the decline in well-being of tenants who are forced to lose their homes, break up their communities, and endure the frustration, disruption, and other "costs" of moving. But in practice the analysis proceeds differently.[20] Reasoning in market rhetoric, with its characterization of everything that people value as monetizable and fungible, tends to make it easy to ignore these other "costs." Money costs and easily monetizable matters are at the center of the map, and personal and community disruption are at the edges. Because it tends to ignore "costs" that are not readily monetizable, commodification-talk tends to err on the side of alienation.

Injury to Personhood

In some cases market discourse itself might be antagonistic to interests of personhood. Richard Posner conceives of rape in terms of a marriage and sex market. Posner concludes that "[r]ape bypasses the market in sexual relations (marital or otherwise) . . . and therefore should be forbidden." In the passage in which this sentence appears, Posner is examining the argument that rape should not be punished criminally if there is "no market substitute" for rape. Presumably, the market substitutes would be marriage, dating, and prostitution; there would be no market substitute if some rapists "derive extra pleasure from the fact that the woman has not consented."[21]

Posner cites two objections to this argument. One is the fact that rapists who derive further pleasure from the nonconsensual nature of their acts are "hard to distinguish empirically from mere thieves of sex." The other is the concern that "free reign" for such rapists would "induce women to invest heavily in self-protection, requiring correspondingly heavy investment by would-be rapists to overcome this protection."[22] Posner does not cite as an objection the idea that the purported pleasures of the rapist should not count at all, because this argument is not cognizable within the framework of market rhetoric. Rape is no different from any other preference satisfaction.

Posner takes up the question of marital rape by noting reasons that "until recently" marriage precluded rape charges. Among them is the argument that the nature of the harm is "a little obscure," because "the fact of [the wife's] having intercourse one more time with a man with whom she has had intercourse many times before seems marginal to the harm inflicted." Posner responds to this reasoning by noting "the increasing control [women] demand over their sexual and reproductive capacity." As women become less economically dependent on men, "the terms of trade between wives and husbands may alter in favor of the wife." Posner concludes that the decline of marriage as a complete defense to rape is a corollary of these altered forms of trade: "In part because she does not need a husband as much as was once the case, a woman (at least a woman with good opportunities in the job market) no longer is forced to give up control over her sexual and reproductive capacity in order to get a husband."[23]

It mustn't go unnoticed here that a venerable critical tradition takes a commodified view of marriage.[24] Many feminists would agree with

Posner in this thoroughly unromantic view of marriage. They would agree that as things have developed under patriarchy, marriage is indeed an economic bargain, and one in which wives have the worst of it.[25] Few feminists, however, would want to conceive of marriage monolithically (uncritically) in market rhetoric as Posner does, for doing so precludes the possibility of envisioning a progressive transformation of its structure and meaning.

Guido Calabresi and A. Douglas Melamed also use market rhetoric to discuss rape. In keeping with their view that "property rules" are prima facie more efficient than "liability rules" for all entitlements, they argue that people should hold a "property rule" entitlement in their own bodily integrity. Further, they explain criminal punishment in terms of the need for an "indefinable kicker," an extra cost to the rapist "which represents society's need to keep all property rules from being changed at will into liability rules."[26] Unlike Posner's view, that of Calabresi and Melamed can be understood as compartmentalized;[27] but like Posner's, their view conceives of rape in market rhetoric. Bodily integrity is an owned object with a price.

Calabresi and Melamed conceive of crimes against property and bodily integrity as exactly parallel but for the concession that we should not "presume collectively and objectively to value the cost of rape to a victim against the benefit to the rapist."[28] Like Posner's, their argument must presume that benefits to rapists do count.

What is wrong with this rhetoric? The risk-of-error argument discussed above is one answer. Unsophisticated practitioners of cost-benefit analysis might tend to undervalue the "costs" of rape to the victims. But this answer does not exhaust the problem. Rather, for all but the deepest enthusiast, market rhetoric seems intuitively out of place here, so inappropriate that it is either silly, or somehow insulting to the value being discussed, or both.

One basis for this intuition is that market rhetoric conceives of bodily integrity as a fungible object. A fungible object can pass in and out of the person's possession without effect on the person as long as its market equivalent is given in exchange; trading commodified objects is just like trading money. To speak of personal attributes as fungible objects—alienable "goods"—seems intuitively wrong to many people, because they do not conceive of bodily integrity as commodified. Thinking of rape in market rhetoric implicitly conceives of as fungible something that we know to be personal, in fact con-

ceives of as fungible property something we know to be too personal
even to be personal property. Bodily integrity is an attribute and not
an object. The effect of "detaching" it from the person is nonmonetizable. We feel discomfort or even insult, and we fear degradation or even loss of the value involved, when bodily integrity is
conceived of as a fungible object.

Systematically conceiving of personal attributes as fungible objects
is threatening to personhood because it detaches from the person that
which is integral to the person. Such a conception makes actual loss
of the attribute easier to countenance. For someone who conceives
bodily integrity as "detached," the same person will remain even if
bodily integrity is lost; but if bodily integrity cannot be detached, the
person cannot remain the same after loss. Moreover, if my bodily
integrity is an integral personal attribute, not a detachable object, then
hypothetically valuing my bodily integrity in terms of money is not far
removed from valuing me in terms of money.

I don't mean to argue that someone who is raped is changed into a
completely different person. To assert either that she is altogether the
"same" or completely "different" afterward would trivialize her experience: we must have a way of conceptualizing our understanding
both that she is different afterward, so that we recognize that she has
been changed by the experience, and simultaneously that she is the
same afterward, or else there would be no "she" that we can recognize
to have had the experience and been changed by it. Just as personal
attributes should not be seen as separate from an abstract self, neither
should our experiences be seen as separate from ourselves.

The "Texture of the Human World"

The difference between conceiving of bodily integrity as a detached,
monetizable object and finding that it is "in fact" detached is not
great, because there is no bright line separating words and facts. The
philosophical turn toward pragmatist or antifoundationalist theories
means that we cannot be sanguine about radically different normative discourses reaching the "same" result. Our conceptualizations of
what is matter for what is. Because words and the world are linked,
the result at which a normative discourse arrives is not detachable
from that discourse without altering the meaning of the result. Even
if everybody agrees that rape should be punished criminally, the

normative discourse that conceives of bodily integrity as detached and monetizable does not reach the "same" result as the normative discourse that conceives of bodily integrity as an integral personal attribute.

This integration of discourse into a state of affairs follows from the pragmatist rejection of foundationalism. Pragmatism denies that rationality or truth consists of linear deductions from an unquestioned foundational reality or truth. Many pragmatists endorse coherence theories stressing holistic interdependence of an entire body of beliefs and commitments; they judge truth or rightness by fit, not by correspondence with an external foundational standard. For example, John Rawls's "reflective equilibrium" is a moral methodology based on coherence,[29] and W. V. O. Quine's "field of force" is a metaphor for the coherence view of metaphysics.[30] The need to reevaluate reality and truth in light of the rejection of foundationalism can readily be understood from the revolution wrought by Ludwig Wittgenstein and Thomas Kuhn (among others).[31] In a famous example, Kuhn suggests that "the scientist who looks at a swinging stone can have no experience that is in principle more elementary than seeing a pendulum. The alternative is not some hypothetical 'fixed' vision, but vision through another paradigm, one which makes the swinging stone something else."[32]

If we accept the gist of the antifoundationalist theories, facts are not "out there" waiting to be described by a discourse. Facts are theory-dependent and value-dependent. Theories are formed in words. Commitments to facts and values are present in the language we use to reason and describe, and they shape our reasoning, our description, and the shape (for us) of reality itself.[33]

Hilary Putnam's striking parable of the super-Benthamites, which I will recount in a moment, gives me the title of this section ("the texture of the human world"). The parable illustrates how a view of values can alter one's view of the facts, alter the discourse in which one conceives and describes both fact and value, and thus alter the human world.[34] The parable also shows how pervasive value-commensurability is inconsistent with life as we know it.

Putnam asks us to suppose that the continent of Australia is inhabited by people whose sole ethical imperative is that one should always act to maximize "hedonic tone."[35] (This term, referring to the aggregate level of satisfaction or pleasure, derives from the use of a hedonic calculus like Bentham's to judge the good.) Because they are single-minded, these people would do what appears to us to be ruthless:

> [W]hile they would not cause someone suffering for the sake of the greatest happiness of the greatest number if there were reasonable doubt that in fact the consequence of their action would be to bring about the greatest happiness of the greatest number . . . in cases where one knows with certainty what the consequences of the actions would be, they would be willing to . . . torture small children or to condemn people for crimes which they did not commit if the result of these actions would be to increase the general satisfaction level in the long run . . . by any positive [increment], however small.[36]

Putnam says that the difference between us and the super-Benthamites is not merely a disagreement about values.[37] Our disagreement about values will entail disagreement about facts and descriptions of facts. For example, super-Benthamites would realize that sometimes the greatest happiness of the greatest number requires telling a lie; it would not count as dishonest in any pejorative sense to tell lies in order to maximize the general pleasure level. Nor would it be wrong to break promises that would not maximize pleasure if kept. The use of the term "honest" among super-Benthamites would be extremely different from our use of that same descriptive term.[38] Terms such as "considerate," "good citizen," or "good person" would likewise be subject to different uses. The vocabulary for describing interpersonal situations would vary greatly between us and the super-Benthamites:

> Not only will they lack, or have altered beyond recognition, many of our descriptive resources, but they will very likely invent new jargon of their own (for example, exact terms for describing hedonic tones) that are unavailable to us. The texture of the human world will begin to change. In the course of time the super-Benthamites and we will end up living in different human worlds.
>
>   In short, it will not be the case that we and the super-Benthamites "agree on the facts and disagree about values." In the case of almost all interpersonal situations, the description we give of the facts will be quite different from the description they give of the facts. Even if none of the statements they make about the situation are false, their description will not be one that we will count as adequate and perspicuous; and the description we give will not be one that they

could count as adequate and perspicuous. In short, even if we put aside our "disagreement about the values," we could not regard their total representation of the human world as fully rationally acceptable.[39]

Putnam concludes that the super-Benthamites' inability rightly to comprehend "the way the human world is" results from their "sick conception of human flourishing"—their inferior theory of the good for human beings. An appropriate theory of the good for human beings, the parable implies, must include an understanding of value incommensurability.

Commensurability and Human Flourishing

In his parable, Putnam was aiming to show us how facts and values are intertwined. He also was aiming to show us the link between words and the world—how "the texture of the human world" depends upon our conceptual schemes. He did not focus on the super-Benthamites' commitment to commensurability, yet it is an important part of their story. Commensurability, in its broadest sense, is the view that all values can be arrayed on a single orderly scale;[40] they differ from one another only in quantity. The super-Benthamites' hedonic calculus treats value this way, and that it does is perhaps the main reason the super-Benthamites seem so different from us, and the reason their conception of human flourishing seems "sick," at least to most of us.

According to Martha Nussbaum, the longing for commensurability—an algorithmic ethical calculus—goes back as far as Plato. She points out what a radical transformation commensurability would entail. She asks questions about its logical/metaphysical coherence, its psychological plausibility, and its ethical desirability. Nussbaum argues that we cannot decide the ethical issue without a detailed imagining of the life of commensurability:

We need not just philosophical examples . . . we also need novels about the whole way of life of people who really think and live the life of commensurability, about how they got there and how they now deal both with others and with themselves. . . . Any social theory that recommends or uses a quantitative measure of value without first exercising imagination along these lines seems to me to be thoroughly irresponsible.[41]

Putnam's parable and Nussbaum's warnings are both relevant to
the conceptualization of rape as theft of a property right. Putnam's
parable suggests that a particular conception of human flourishing is
advanced by the pervasive use of market rhetoric. Those who have
conceived of rape as just a "cost" commensurate with the "benefit"
to the rapist have been irresponsible in the way Nussbaum suggests.
To think in terms of costs to the victim and her sympathizers versus
benefits to the rapist is implicitly to assume that raping "benefits"
rapists.

The assumption must be questioned. Do we want our conception
of human flourishing to regard rape as benefiting the rapist? Or do we
want to regard rapists as pursuing a life that is not aimed at the good
of human beings, so that the more they rape the less it benefits them?
As a reason for criminalizing rape, Posner blandly says, "Supposing
it to be true that some rapists would not get as much pleasure from
consensual sex, it does not follow that there are no other avenues of
satisfaction open to them."[42] For Posner, the "pleasure" and "satisfaction" of maintaining one's bodily integrity are commensurate with
the "pleasure" and "satisfaction" of someone who invades it. Thus,
there could be circumstances in which the satisfactions or "value" to
rapists would outweigh the costs or "disvalue" to victims.[43] In those
situations rape would not be morally wrong and might instead be
morally commendable.

In order to decide what conception of human flourishing is properly
ours, all we can do is reflect on what we now know about human life
and choose the best from among the conceptions available to us.
Whatever turns out to be best, it will not be the life of universal
commodification. It will not be a conception in which rape benefits
rapists.

The question remains whether use of market rhetoric commits the
speaker to the conception of human flourishing implied by it. "After
all," the neoclassical economist might say, "What's wrong with using
reductionist models if they succeed in explaining behavior? Mere use
of the models doesn't commit me to believing that they accurately
reflect human values." I do not believe a speaker can be completely
divorced in this way from the implications of her rhetoric. Rhetoric
does have an influence on the world, and on the speaker herself,
although in what way it does so is complex.[44] And when a proffered
"explanation" of human activity implies a conception of human

flourishing that is foreign to the actors themselves we should question the extent to which it can be considered explanatory.

Noncommodification of Personal Rights, Attributes, and Things

The critique of market rhetoric tells us that the way we conceive of things matters to who we are. To conceive of something personal as fungible assumes that the person and the attribute, right, or thing, are separate. This view imposes the subject/object dichotomy to create two kinds of alienation, depending upon whether or not the bearer of the attribute, right, or thing internalizes the commodified conception.

If the discourse of commodification is partially made one's own, it creates disorientation of the self that experiences the distortion of its own personhood. For example, workers who internalize market rhetoric conceive of their own labor as a commodity separate from themselves as persons; they dissociate their daily life from their own self-conception. On the other hand, when the discourse of commodification is not internalized, it creates alienation between those who use the discourse and those whose personhood they wrong in doing so. For example, workers who do *not* conceive of their labor as a commodity are alienated from others who do, because, in the workers' view, people who conceive of the workers' labor as a commodity fail to see them as whole persons.

To conceive of something personal as fungible also assumes that persons cannot freely give of themselves to others. At best they can bestow commodities. At worst—in universal commodification—the gift is conceived of as a bargain. (The gift would be seen as an exchange by assuming that giving you something that I value yields me monetizable value in return, or by assuming that I am doing it so that you will treat me with favor, and this favorable treatment yields monetizable value to me.) Conceiving of gifts as bargains not only conceives of what is personal as fungible; it also endorses the picture of persons as profit-maximizers.

A better view of personhood should conceive of gifts not as disguised sales, but rather as expressions of the interrelationships between the self and others. A gift takes place within a personal relationship with the recipient, or else it creates one.[45] Commodification

stresses separateness both between ourselves and our things and between ourselves and other people. To postulate personal interrelationship and bonding requires us to postulate people who can yield
personal things to other people and not have them instantly become
fungible. Seen this way, gifts diminish separateness. This is why (to
take an obvious example) people say that sex bought and paid for is
not the "same" thing as sex freely shared.[46] Commodified sex leaves
the parties as separate individuals and perhaps reinforces their separateness; they engage in it only if each individual considers it worth-
while. Noncommodified sex ideally diminishes separateness; it is conceived of as a union because it is ideally a sharing of selves. (I will
return to the issue of commodified sex in Chapter 10.)

Market-Inalienability as Prohibition of Commodification

If a commodified good (like commercial sex) is not the "same" thing
as an analogous noncommodified experience (like noncommercial
sex), what follows? It is sometimes thought that the disparity can
generate a moral requirement that the commodified version not be
permitted to exist. Such a requirement can be expressed with a market-inalienability.

What might be the basis of such a moral requirement? Something
might be prohibited in its market form because it both creates and
exposes wealth- and class-based contingencies for obtaining things
that are critical to life itself—for example, health care—and thus
undermines a commitment to the sanctity of life.[47] Another reason for
prohibition might be that the use of market rhetoric, in conceiving of
the "good" and understanding the interactions of people respecting
it, creates and fosters an inferior conception of human flourishing. For
example, as I have argued, we accept an inferior conception of personhood (one allied to the extreme view of negative freedom) if we
suppose people may freely choose to commodify themselves.

The prohibition argument—that commodification of things is bad
in itself, or because these things are not the "same" things that would
be available to people in nonmarket relationships—leads to the universal noncommodification pursued by many utopian humanist
Marxists. If commodification is bad in itself, it is bad for everything.
Once we have understood the point about social construction, any

social good is arguably "different" if not embedded in a market society.[48]

To restrict the argument in order to permit compartmentalization, we have to accept either that certain things are the "same" whether or not they are bought and sold, and others are "different," or that prohibiting the commodified version on moral grounds matters only for certain things, but not for all of them. At present we—at least the mainstream group of "us"—tend to think that nuts and bolts are pretty much the "same" whether commodified or not, whereas love, friendship, and sexuality are very "different"; we also tend to think that trying to keep society free of commodified love, friendship, and sexuality morally matters more than does trying to keep it free of commodified nuts and bolts.

These arguments would undoubtedly seem unsatisfactory to anyone really committed to the idea that commodification is bad for human beings. Commodified nuts and bolts are produced by commodified labor, and prohibiting commodified labor morally matters as much as prohibiting commodified love, friendship, and sexuality. Moreover, commodification of their labor may force workers to experience only the commodified versions of love, friendship, and sexuality.

Contagious Commodification? A Domino Theory

Once we get the point about social construction it becomes natural to wonder whether commodification is contagious and monolithic. If it is both, then once some commodification enters the arena, there is a slippery slope—a domino effect—leading to market domination. At the extreme, as Lukács apparently thought, universal commodification becomes inevitable once the commodity form exists.

The domino theory assumes that for some things, the noncommodified version is morally preferable; it also assumes that the commodified and noncommodified versions of some interactions cannot coexist. To commodify some things is simply to preclude their noncommodified analogues from existing. Under this theory, the existence of some commodified sexual interactions will contaminate or infiltrate everyone's sexuality so that all sexual relationships will become commodified. If it is morally required that noncommodified sex be possible, market-inalienability of sexuality would be justified. This result can be conceived of as the opposite of a prohibition: there is assumed to exist some moral requirement that a certain "good" be socially available. The domino theory thus supplies an answer (as the prohibition theory does not) to the liberal question why people should not be permitted to choose both market and nonmarket interactions: the noncommodified version is morally preferable when we cannot have both.

We can now see how the prohibition and domino theories are connected. The prohibition theory focuses on the importance of excluding from social life commodified versions of certain "goods"—such as love, friendship, and sexuality—whereas the domino theory focuses on the importance for social life of maintaining the noncommodified versions. The prohibition theory stresses the wrongness of commodification—its alienation and degradation of the person—and the domino theory stresses the rightness of noncommodification in creating the social context for the proper expression and fostering of personhood. If one explicitly adopts both prongs of this commitment to personhood, the prohibition and domino theories merge.[49]

The Domino Theory and Opportunities for Altruism

A well-known argument that market-inalienabilities are necessary to encourage altruism relies upon the domino theory. With regard to human blood, Richard Titmuss argues that a regime permitting only donation fosters altruism.[50] The altruistic experience of the donor in being responsible (perhaps) for saving a stranger's life is said to bring us closer together, cementing our community in a way that buying and selling cannot. The possibility of reciprocity is also a part of this cementing process, because a donor's sense of obligation could be partially founded on the recognition that she could be a recipient someday. From the recipient's perspective, it is said that knowing one is dependent on others' altruism rather than on one's own wealth creates solidarity and interdependence, and that this knowledge of dependence better preserves and expresses the ideal of sanctity of life.

But why do we need to forbid sales to preserve opportunities for altruism for those who wish to give? According to this argument, altruism is foreclosed if both donations and sales are permitted. If sales are not allowed, donations have no market value and remain unmonetized. If sales are allowed, then even gifts have a market equivalent. My giving a pint of blood is like giving fifty dollars of my money. According to this argument, such monetization discourages giving. We are more willing to give health, perhaps life itself, to strangers than we are to give them fifty dollars of our money.

Something like this argument can be made for certain cases of human organ donation, as well. Imagine the case of grief-stricken parents being asked to donate the heart of a brain-dead child to a newborn victim of congenital heart disease in a distant hospital. The parents are being asked to give up the symbolic integrity of their child and face immediately the brute fact of death. The act of donating the heart may be one of those distinctively human moments of terrible glory in which one gives up a significant aspect of oneself so that others may live and flourish.

But now imagine the experience if the grieving parents know that the market price of hearts is $50,000. There seems to be a sense that the heroic moment now cannot be, either for them to experience or for us to observe, in respect and perhaps recognition. If the parents take the money, then the money is the reason for their action; or at best, neither we nor they themselves will ever know that the money was not the reason for the action. But if they don't take the money, then their act can seem like transferring "their" $50,000 to the transplant recipient. It can seem so, that is, if the domino theory is true, and once something is monetized for some it is monetized for all. No matter what choice the parents make, the opportunity for a pure act of caring is foreclosed.

I think many people would intuitively object, however, to the domino idea that whatever is monetized for some people is necessarily monetized for themselves as well. As I shall argue in the next chapter, this objection has a deeper theoretical basis. For the domino theory to hold, we must "naturally" tend to commodify. This "natural" tendency seems to be merely a debatable ideological postulate, and, at that, not one that utopian noncommodifiers can afford to endorse.

A domino-style argument can also be made about adoption. People (sometimes) give up children in pain and in hope that they will have a better life elsewhere. There is at least some human glory in being able to do this. Perhaps it disappears if the child bears a market value. If money is paid, it would contaminate the experience of the adoptive parents as well as that of the birth parents, since they will be aware that they valued the child at $10,000, perhaps, but not at $100,000. The adopted child herself, if she finds out what price was paid for her, may always wonder whether a higher asking price would have left her without parents. Even if the birth parent doesn't accept the money, doesn't take the price that the market will bear, perhaps knowledge of the price could contaminate the experience, making it seem as though the birth parent is giving the adopting parent $10,000 out of her pocket.

In addition, if children have a market value, then even parents who do not put their children up for adoption will know what their children are worth, and how much money they are losing by not doing so. All children will also know how much they are worth and how much their parents are losing by keeping them. We will all know how much we cost our parents. We will all conceive of ourselves as objects bearing monetary value. But this worry too assumes the domino theory is true, which we have yet to investigate.

Although the example of organ donation involved donation of a child's heart, it seems that the argument about opportunities for altruism also fits the case of donating one's own organs, especially donating to strangers. But it may not fit the case of donating to one's friends and relatives. That depends upon whether this situation can properly be described as altruism. Perhaps altruism means giving unselfishly in the context of a presupposition of selfishness; altruism is to go against one's "natural" selfishness.

Perhaps, at any rate, altruism means this in the context of a hard-line individualism. Insofar as it connotes impersonal giving, perhaps altruism is an artifact of alienation. Ties of family and friendship already overcome one's "natural" selfishness. So, perhaps, actions expressing those ties, though unselfish, would not count as altruistic, since there is no selfishness to overcome in doing them.

I do not think we should grant the assumption that permitting any commodification engenders a domino effect. Even if we grant the assumption for the sake of argument, however, there is a problem with the argument about opportunities for altruism, which I think turns out in the end to be a virtue. It is too general to carve out a few exceptional kinds of interactions that must remain unmonetized. Suppose we grant that opportunities for altruism must be kept open because (suppose) we think altruism is required for proper human flourishing and community cohesion. Still, how are we supposed to know which, and how many, opportunities must be kept open? Why focus on blood, for example? Many (perhaps even most) kinds of work—such as social worker, teacher, and police officer—present opportunities for altruism.

Maybe those who make the argument would cabin it by suggesting that, given our pervasive "natural" selfishness, only things that can be given without special training or on a onetime basis are practicable avenues for altruism in the market society. It is not quite clear why this should be so, however. Can we not say that people ought to give their services when they can? But the problem is that we cannot argue that any of these services must remain completely unmonetized. If we must invest our capital in learning skills or developing our talents, then we must expect (in a market society) to be paid for them once they are developed, in order to supply ourselves with those things we need in order to keep on living and working—food, shelter, and so on. If the domino effect that is implicit in the argument about opportunities for altruism really does hold, then all such services given altruistically will in fact feel like transferring money from donors to recipients, because the services bear a market value. Altruism requires nonmonetized vehicles.

Even accepting a need to find gift objects that must remain completely unmonetized, it still seems that the argument about opportunities for altruism is more general than its proponents have thought. Many kinds of gift objects or volunteer services that can be given on a onetime basis and do not require much special training might still fit the argument: gifts of old clothes or books; services such as reading to blind people, being a subject for experimentation, driving voters to the polls, and censustaking. Why do we not think of keeping these things completely unmonetized? Maybe those who make the argument about opportunities for altruism would try to cabin it further by suggesting that, in addition to being things that can be given on a onetime basis, the things that must be kept unmonetized are extremely important, perhaps meaning the difference between life and death, to the recipient. But such an attempt to cabin the argument must fail, because it is unclear why the level of importance should matter in this way. There seems to be no reason why we must make altruism dramatic in order to preserve it.

Sex, Babies, and the Domino Theory

To summarize: The domino theory holds that there is a slippery slope leading from toleration of any sales of something to an exclusive market regime for that thing; and there is a further slippery slope from a market regime for some things to a market regime encompassing everything people value. The domino theory implicitly makes two claims: first, as a background normative premise, that it is important for a nonmarket regime to exist; and second, as an empirical premise, that a nonmarket regime cannot coexist with a market regime.[51] The market drives out the nonmarket version; hence the market regime must be banned.

Although it is a necessary supposition of the argument about opportunities for altruism, the domino theory is more often brought up in connection with prostitution and sale of babies. Here the domino theory covers more than just the territory supposedly conducive to altruism, since those who argue that sexuality must remain nonmonetized do not argue that the reason is so that it may be altruistically given. Indeed, as I suggested earlier, it seems that the concept of altruism already presupposes more distance, remoteness, or impersonality between people than we wish to countenance in our ideals of sexuality. Those who are against monetized sex are probably against altruistic sex also. Giving it to strangers is not deemed praiseworthy.

Preserving opportunities for altruism does not, then, seem to be the main reason for asserting that noncommercial sex must remain possible. Nor does it seem to be the main reason at work in the inclination to ban baby-selling, although it can play a part, as my earlier discussion indicated. Rather, it appears that the uncommodified version must remain possible because commodification somehow destroys or deeply disfigures the possible value of sex or of the baby itself.

In the case of babies this impulse does not seem difficult to understand. Superficially, at least, it seems to fail to treat children as persons to make them all realize that they have a definite commercial value, and that this is all their value amounts to, even if their parents did not choose to sell them or did not obtain them by purchase. The domino theory asserts that this will be the result of permitting sales for those who choose them.

Is it similarly an injury to personhood to commercialize sex? If noncommercial sex becomes impossible, as we are here assuming, the argument that the answer is yes asserts that we shall all be deprived of a significant form of human bonding and interrelation. Under this analysis, noncommercial sex is a component of human flourishing, like the need for opportunities to express altruism. Commercial friendship is a contradiction in terms, as is commercial love. If opportunities for noncommercial friendship and love were not available, we would not be human. The argument we are reviewing asks us to see sexuality analogously.

But let us finally focus on the domino part of the theory. Is it the case that if some people are allowed to sell babies or sexual services, those things will be thereby commercialized for everyone? The argument that the answer is yes assumes that once the fact of market value enters our discourse, it must be present in, and dominate, every transaction. The argument is a simple postulate about the nature of the link between words and the world. It says the fact of pricing necessarily brings with it the conceptual scheme of commodification. We cannot know the price of something and know at the same time that it is priceless. Once something has a price, money must be a part of the interaction, and the reason or explanation for the interaction, when that something changes hands. A sale cannot simultaneously be a gift. If our children know that the going rate of babies is $10,000, they will know that they are worth $10,000. They will know that they are worth as much as an economy car but not as much as a house. Worse, if they know that the market price of "good" babies is $10,000, whereas the price of "medium-grade" babies is only $8,000, they will be anxiously comparing themselves with the "good" grade of child in hopes that they measure up. One can fill in the analogous argument regarding sexuality.

Like Lukács and the humanist Marxists, the domino theory assumes that we cannot both know the price of something and know that it is priceless. We cannot have a sale that is also, and "really," a gift. Is this assumption correct? Or, perhaps, does it grant too much to universal commodification at the outset, by assuming that thinking in money terms is what comes most "naturally" to us? Perhaps it is not true that an interaction cannot be both a sale and a gift at the same time; that we cannot both know the price of something and know that it is unmonetizable, or priceless. This kind of resistance to the domino theory would see a nonmarket aspect to much of the market. In the next chapter I shall elaborate it by considering work and our ideals about work.

7

Incomplete Commodification

What if it is not true that we cannot both know the price of something and know that it is priceless? What if commodified understandings of certain transactions can coexist with noncommodified understandings? There seem to be several different perspectives from which we might explore such a coexistence. I begin with a tentative distinction between two possible states of affairs in our discourse. One, which I will call contested concepts, can be thought of as external to the person. The other, which I will call internally conflicted (or plural) meanings, can be thought of as internal to the person.

When we have a contested concept, conflicting understandings are well crystallized. Some people adhere unambivalently to one and some to the other, as, for example, when some people are certain a fetus is a person and others are certain it isn't. Our understanding of a transaction such as adoption is a contested concept when a commodified understanding (for some people) coexists with a noncommodified understanding (for others). This social state of affairs can be denominated a species of incomplete commodification, because in this case only one segment of society accepts the commodified understanding. (As I will argue in Chapter 13, I believe this describes the situation with respect to compensation for personal injury.)

If, however, conflicting understandings of an interaction are not well crystallized, each can characterize one of its aspects. The same person can understand an interaction in different, and conflicting, ways, as, analogously, she can both feel a painting is priceless and yet have it appraised for insurance purposes. Then neither commodification nor noncommodification can accurately describe the way such a person conceives of an interaction. That second kind of coexistence of market and nonmarket understandings can also can be denominated a species of incomplete commodification.

Social policy reflects our understandings of the meaning(s) of human interactions. I will also use the term "incomplete commodification" to refer to the social state of affairs envisioned by such policies. Contested concepts and internally plural meanings can be reflected in policy decisions. Where different meanings coexist in society as a whole or in persons themselves, it becomes simplistic to think of our social policy choice as binary: either complete commodification or complete noncommodification. Instead, it becomes important to recognize both our social division over commodification and the nonmarket aspect of many transactions that can be conceived of in market terms.

The domino theory we considered in Chapter 6 assumes that anytime we find market and nonmarket understandings coexisting, either as a contested concept or as internally plural meanings, it is inevitable that the market understanding will win out. This theory holds that it is inevitable that a monolithic market understanding will be the end result of any conflicted coexistence of market and nonmarket understandings.

I want to urge, on the contrary, that such a preordained victory of market understandings should not be presumed. If we do presume it, we are implicitly subscribing to the commodified theory of human nature that makes market understandings more powerful than their possible alternatives. Such an implicit and broad-based commitment must be avoided if we wish to achieve a more nuanced understanding of where we stand with respect to commodification.

We do need to investigate why market understandings seem so powerful. Someone fully committed to the archetype of universal commodification (Gary Becker, perhaps) would say they are powerful because they are true: market understandings best explain and order our world. Someone committed to Marxist critique (Lukács, perhaps) might say that market understandings seem powerful because they "naturally" link up with the entrenched power structure of capitalism.

Someone interested in the characteristic ways in which discourse persuades us (Kuhn, perhaps?) might say that market understandings are powerful because the algorithmic structure of commensurability is so simple and elegant. Certainly numbers do seem to command us more than they should. Think, for example, how employers and academics prefer applicants with higher test scores even if those scores have no statistical significance or are based on very loose judgments.[1]

Whatever the reason(s) for the power of the market as a conceptual scheme, for each case of contested commodification I believe we should look and see how powerful the market conceptualization is in context. We should consider whether under some circumstances market understandings and nonmarket understandings can stably coexist, either as contested concepts or as internally conflicted (plural) meanings.

Once we recognize that commodification and noncommodification can pervasively coexist, assuming that we judge that in some circumstances the coexistence can be stable, a broad range of policy alternatives becomes available. Complete noncommodification and complete commodification can be seen as largely hypothetical end points of a continuum of possible meanings and corresponding policy choices. To think of the problem of the market domain as simply drawing a boundary line between a completely nonmarket realm and a laissez-faire market realm ignores the continuum. Under present circumstances, when we draw such a line we understand the market as a presumptive norm in a large realm, as liberal compartmentalization does.

As an alternative to compartmentalization, I think we should recognize a continuum reflecting degrees of commodification that will be appropriate in a given context. An incomplete commodification—a partial market-inalienability—can sometimes reflect the conflicted state of affairs in the way we understand an interaction. And an incomplete commodification can sometimes substitute for a complete noncommodification that might accord with our ideals but cause too much harm in our nonideal world.

Work and Incomplete Commodification

Because this is a market society, most people must be paid for their work if they are to live. Yet the kind of work most of us hope to have—I think—is that which we would do anyway, without money, if somehow by other means our necessities of life were taken care of. Ideals about work—at least for many of us—do not turn on capitalist rationality. What one hopes to get out of working is not all money nor understandable in monetary terms (unless the archetype of universal commodification describes one's conceptual scheme).[2]

Inspired by Hannah Arendt, I think it is helpful here to introduce a distinction between work and labor, although it is not the same one she had in mind.[3] It is possible to think of work as always containing a noncommodified human element; and to think of the fully commodified version as labor. The fully commodified version is what Marx thought to be actual for the nineteenth-century proletariat. The worker who produces commodities becomes himself a commodity.

We can understand the difference between working and laboring in much the way we understand the difference between playing notes and playing music. Laborers play notes, we might say, and workers play the music. Laborers are sellers; fully motivated by money, exhausting the value of their activity in the measure of its exchange value. Laborers experience their labor as separate from their real lives and selves. Workers take money but are also at the same time givers. Money does not fully motivate them to work, nor does it exhaust the value of their activity. Work is understood not as separate from life and self, but rather as a part of the worker, and indeed constitutive of her. Nor is work understood as separate from relations with other people.

Many teachers and scholars identify this way with their work. So, of course, do many performers, artists, and writers; and editors and publishers. So do many doctors, and nurses, and people who care for children, the elderly, the retarded, the handicapped; and people who counsel students, or married couples, or those who have trouble with drugs or alcohol. Firefighters, paramedics, and law enforcement officers can do their work as givers to others while being paid. So can military people and judges. Certainly that is what we hope for from political officials (unless we accept a commodified political theory; see Chapter 14).

The nonmarket aspect of work is not limited to the arts, public servants, teaching, and the helping professions. (Even if it were, it would be significant to recognize that so many activities can be in the market but not wholly of it.) The concept of the personal touch in one's work, of doing a good job for the sake of pride in one's work, for the sake of the user or recipient, and for the sake of one's community as a whole is intelligible for much of the market economy. Plumbers, housecleaners, carpenters, financial advisers, and clerks can all work with personal care for those who need their services. Those who sell products can genuinely care about the needs of people to whom they are selling. It is possible to fix a vacuum cleaner and care whether it works; it is possible to sell shoes and care whether they fit; it is possible to design software and care whether people can actually use it. However mechanized and technological and rational is the market society, it is still true that the worker we consider the good worker is working and not just laboring.

These are prevalent ideals about work; they are sometimes seen played out in practice. It is true, of course, that the market also contains grinding assembly-line jobs that hardly anyone could treat as humane work. With few exceptions those who labor at these jobs do not feel that they are living while working, but only do the labor so that they may have some time to live during the hours they are not on the job. But I think these jobs run counter to deep-seated ideals about work. Even in these jobs many people can express their humanity in their relationships with coworkers; humanity is hard to suppress completely. Yet I think that basically we agree with Marx that these jobs involve inhumane commodification of people.

Many people have the sense that humane ideals about work are declining. As market rationality takes over, they feel, there is less and less room for working with care. They feel that many kinds of work are becoming impersonal. (Health care is a primary example.)[4] What does it mean to say they are becoming impersonal? That seems to be simply to say that market rhetoric fully characterizes the process of interaction between seller and buyer. This is to say that to the participants in the interaction the services or things are completely commodified. It is to say that the relation between health-care provider and patient, for example, is no different from that between the proverbial seller and buyer of widgets.

Putting it this way suggests that complete noncommodification—complete removal from the market—is not the only alternative to complete commodification. Once we give up the search for a theory that will accomplish clean compartmentalization, we can begin thinking in terms of pervasive incomplete commodification. Incomplete commodification can describe a situation in which things are sold but the interaction between the participants in the transaction cannot be fully or perspicuously described as the sale of things. If many kinds of sales retain a personal aspect even though money changes hands, those interactions are not fully described as sales of commodities. They exhibit internally plural meanings. There is an irreducibly non-market or nonmonetized aspect of human interaction going on between seller and recipient, even though a sale is taking place at the same time. That there should be the opportunity for work to be personal in this sense does seem to be part of our conception of human flourishing—which is why those who see increasing depersonalization deplore it. Complete commodification of work—pure labor—does violence to our notion of what it is to be a well-developed person.

Now it may be clear why I think it concedes too much to commodification to argue that certain specific items (for example, blood) must remain completely noncommodified so as to keep open opportunities for altruism, especially if those who argue this way hope that these sporadic opportunities may lead to a less commodified society. The way to a less commodified society is to see and foster the non-market aspect of much of what we buy and sell, to honor our internally plural understandings, rather than to erect a wall to keep a certain few things completely off the market and abandon everything else to market rationality.

Regulation as the Social Aspect of Incomplete Commodification

Recall that the term "incomplete commodification" can refer either to people's understandings of an interaction or to the social policy choices that reflect those understandings. It will now be useful to denominate these senses as the participant and social aspects of incomplete commodification. The discussion so far has focused on the participant aspect, which can reveal either a contested concept or internally plural meanings. Now I want to turn to the social aspect.

The participant aspect of incomplete commodification draws attention to the meaning of an interaction for those who engage in it. The social aspect draws attention instead to the way in which society as a whole recognizes that things have nonmonetizable participant significance. In legal culture this social recognition may be reflected in regulating (curtailing) the free market.

Work and housing are possible examples of incomplete commodification. We have so far considered the participant aspect with
respect to work. For many of us, work is not only the way we make
our living but also a part of ourselves. What we hope to derive from
our work, and the personal importance we attach to it, are not
understandable entirely in money terms, even though we demand and
accept money. These ideals about work seem to be part of our
conception of human flourishing, and thus the loss of this personal
aspect of work would be considered inhumane.[5] Consider also our
attachment of meaning to housing. Although a house has market
value and we can express our investment in terms of dollars, there is
a nonmonetizable, personal aspect to many people's relationships
with their homes. (Many other things can become, for the person who
buys them and comes to depend upon them or care about them,
meaningful in a nonmonetizable way).

Now consider the social aspect of incomplete commodification with
respect to work and housing. Although work has not been fully
decommodified, it is incompletely commodified. Reforms such as
collective bargaining, minimum-wage requirements, maximum-hour
limitations, health and safety requirements, unemployment insurance,
retirement benefits, prohibition of child labor, and antidiscrimination
requirements reflect an incompletely commodified understanding of
work. The regulation of residential tenancies also reflects an incompletely commodified understanding. Rent control, habitability requirements, restrictions upon termination of tenancies, and antidiscrimination requirements can all be seen as indicia of incomplete
commodification. In general, where many people tend to become
attached to a certain kind of thing in a way that makes, to them,
simple market rhetoric inappropriate to describe their relationship
with it, we are likely to see a social order in which the distribution of
that thing deviates from laissez-faire.

I don't mean to deny the utility of the well-entrenched market-ori-
ented ways of looking at regulation. From the point of view of
universal commodification, regulations would be unjustified unless
they promoted efficiency. The kinds of regulations I have been discussing have not been readily seen as efficiency enhancing, however, so
they are recurring targets of Chicago-style economists.[6]

The kinds of regulations I have been discussing may also be seen as
examples of wealth redistribution under liberal welfare rights. I also

don't mean to deny the utility of this approach. Yet it seems to me that an understanding in terms of welfare rights may evoke commodification in a way that is somewhat at odds with the participant meanings of the interactions involved in work and housing. Understanding the regulations as redistribution of wealth seems to assimilate work and personal property to fungible wealth of the holders.

When we see certain regulations, such as those affecting work and housing, as reflecting incomplete commodification, we conceive of work and housing (at least partially) in other than market rhetoric. Insofar as we do see regulation as the social aspect of incomplete commodification, moral reasoning and not market failure will be the focus of debates over its proper extent. If we think that because of their desperate poverty and the pricing policies of landlords and employers, tenants and workers would not wish to have the regulations, that is, would choose complete commodification, then the fact that complete commodification seems best on balance to those we think it harms places us in a double bind caused by nonideal circumstances. (I address this issue in Chapter 9.) The regulations are not necessarily rendered unjustified, however, if they are now our best available alternative.

In this view, work and housing are not conceived of as completely monetizable and fungible objects of exchange that are separated from persons. Instead, regulation of work and housing is seen as an effort to take into account workers' and tenants' personhood, to recognize and foster the nonmarket significance of their work and housing.

Regulation of residential tenancies can be seen as attempting to ensure that tenants are not forced to move from their homes for ideological, discriminatory, or arbitrary reasons or by a sudden rise in market prices, and to ensure that rental housing is decent to live in and a decent place for family life. Thus, regulation can be seen as connected to identity and contextuality: attempting to make possible and protect the constituting of one's personhood in one's home, and one's continuity of residence there, because the home is a justifiable kind of personal property. This shows how the category of personal property may be seen as related to incomplete commodification. For those things that we accept as being appropriately identified with the person, a range of protections exists to shield them from market forces and wrongful treatment as fungible. The ability to establish oneself in relationship with things is promoted by the social aspect of incomplete commodification; once the relationship is established, the thing is personal.

Regulation of work can be seen as attempting to make more possible the realization of personal ideals about work, which are related to human flourishing: a self-conception inseparable from one's work (contextuality), continuity of work (identity), and control over one's own work (freedom). Regulation can be seen as attempting to ensure that employees are not forced to leave their jobs for ideological, discriminatory, or arbitrary reasons; to ensure that the workplace is safe, and free from sexual or racial harassment; and to ensure that employees have some say in workplace decisions, and the opportunity to understand how their work is helpful or significant to other people. Although complete decommodification of work or housing is not now possible, these social incomplete commodifications can be seen as responses in our nonideal world to the harm to personhood caused by complete commodification of work and housing.

Some regulation, then, can be seen as socially structured incomplete commodification. This, where morally justified, forms a nonefficiency justification for regulation—that is, socially mandated deviations from the laissez-faire market regime for many things that are bought and sold. If everything is appropriately fully commodified unless efficiency dictates otherwise, then exceptions from the laissez-faire regime are justified only where the market for some reason cannot achieve efficient outcomes. This in fact is the position of many economists on regulation. It makes many types of regulation (for example, residential rent control) difficult to justify; when these types of regulation are frequently imposed anyway by the political order, they are seen as obvious examples of selfish rent-seeking by powerful interest groups. But there is another way to view regulation of many things that are important to human personhood and community, and that is as incomplete commodification. To the extent that we are stubbornly committed to the idea that these things that are very important to human life, health, and self- and community development ought not to be completely monetized, regulation that does not (theoretically) meet an efficiency test can in principle be justified. Then the response of the political order in imposing the constraints on commodification may be seen as a good-faith working out of cultural values.

Social Justice

Incomplete commodification can also be related to the way we think about social justice. In one kind of theorizing, we concentrate on justice for the community as a whole. In this kind of theory, justice is often conceptualized in terms of distribution of goods or wealth. A theory of justice in this form can (though it need not) cohere with a universal commodifying view of the social order. For example, Robert Nozick's unpatterned entitlement theory replicates the market in its global reliance on entitlement (private property) and just transfer (free contract).[7] Neo-Hobbesian theories likewise conceive distributive justice to be the outcomes of unfettered market trades, with adjustments for market failures that mimic what a free market would have achieved.[8]

In another kind of theorizing, we concentrate on social justice as just deserts for individuals, or respect for personhood. This kind of theory too can be captured by the conceptual scheme of commodification; for example, when the person's deserts are conceived of as negative freedom to buy and sell all things in markets. Even John Rawls's theory seems to be tinged with market methodology and rhetoric. As set forth in *A Theory of Justice*, Rawls's ideal scheme "makes considerable use of market arrangements." Rawls says, "It is only in this way, I believe, that the problem of distribution can be handled as a case of pure procedural justice. Further, we also gain the advantages of efficiency and protect the important liberty of free choice of occupation."[9] Although Rawls has since reinterpreted his theory of justice in significant ways, he has not sought to abjure market rhetoric. The bases of self-respect necessary to respect persons are still conceived of as primary "goods," which may perpetuate the rhetoric of fungible possessions and objectification.[10]

Whether we are theorizing about justice for the community or for individuals, the still-prevalent liberal metaphor of social contract seems itself to perpetuate market rhetoric. Modern contractualists do not always mean the language of contract to imply monetary exchange or implicit monetizability of all individual and social value.[11] Yet contract is a linchpin of the commodified conceptual scheme, and in the liberal tradition the contract metaphor must draw its power from the normative power of promises to exchange commodities. Hence it is possible to see theories of justice that are couched in contract rhetoric as evoking universal commodification. Contract rhetoric reduces to market terms the broader normative ideas of social commitment, agreement, and consensus.

Positing the possibility and appropriateness of pervasive coexistence of market and nonmarket aspects to human interactions is an alternative both to theories that imply or can be understood to countenance universal commodification and to compartmentalized theories of social justice like Michael Walzer's. Incomplete commodification would be reflected both in a theory of overall distributive fairness and in a theory of proper treatment of individuals. Key principles for both these aspects of justice in such an alternative theory are that who should get what things of value depends upon the appropriate relation between persons and things, and between persons and other people.

For example, if we accept as appropriate a close connection between persons and their housing, then housing should be socially provided in such a way not only that everyone may have the shelter necessary for physical survival, but also that everyone may have the continuity of residence that in our culture is supposed to provide for the stability of context essential to proper self-development. Housing, both rented and owned, is appropriately incompletely commodified: it has special nonmarket significance to participants in market interactions regarding it, and it is appropriately socially regulated in recognition of the propriety of this self-investment. I don't think this is best described as a species of compartmentalization. The appropriateness of regulation does not rest, as Walzer might have it, on the fact that housing belongs to the "sphere" of security and welfare, where distribution should be based on the principle of need, and not to the "sphere" of money and commodities, where distribution is based on the principle of free exchange.[12] Rather, regulation is appropriate because, although we value the efficiency of the market, at the same time housing must be incompletely commodified in recognition of its connection with personhood.

Who gets what depends upon appropriate relations between persons and other people, and not just upon relations between persons and things. People engaged in market interactions often do not understand themselves as just acquiring things; they are relating to each other as well. A theory of social justice should recognize that these interactions often are (and ought to be able to be) valued for themselves, and specifically, not merely instrumentally and fungibly. As critics of Rawls (for example) have often argued, many kinds of solidarity and interrelations between people are central to our conception of human flourishing in such a way that they must not be excluded from a theory of social justice. If we understand the fact of our having been a helpless infant dependent upon caretakers to be important to a conception of human flourishing, and if we understand the facts of our human development as dependent upon the character of parenting, then family structures and childrearing practices become components of social justice.[13]

Liberal conceptions of personhood and community (individuality and sociality) have been criticized for expressing and creating an alienated, crassly commercial form of life.[14] A central strand of liberalism has conceptualized personhood as an abstract, isolated subject radically separate from a world of objects (and other subjects). A central strand of liberalism likewise has conceptualized society as a whole that is nothing other than the sum of its parts. In this conception of sociality, community is an aggregate of self-interested individuals each striving for her own autonomous ends, and cooperation is normatively conceived of as imposed by a sovereign whose power stems from strategic recognition of otherwise intractable coordination problems.[15]

If we accept to some extent the criticisms leveled against these conceptions of personhood and community, we conceive of the person as more integrally connected to the world of things and other people. And we conceive of community as crucially founded on human interdependence, as a network of processes and relations that expresses and creates value and significance not normatively reducible to an aggregate of self-contained individuals.

Incomplete commodification as an expression of a nonmarket order coexistent with a market order can be related to this shift in conception of the ideals of personhood and community. The kinds of things that deviate most from laissez-faire are those related to human beings' homes, work, food, environment, education, communication, health, bodily integrity, sexuality, family life, and political life. For these things it is easiest to see that preserving and fostering the nonmarket aspect of their provision and use are related to human flourishing and social justice—to personhood and community as reconceived to meet the critique of earlier liberalism.

Once we accept that pervasive incomplete commodification is related to appropriate ideals of personhood and community, it becomes clear why the arguments for piecemeal noncommodification of specific items are unsatisfactory. It seems that the values of personhood and community require not that certain specific exceptional things be insulated by a wall while everything else is governed by market forces and conceived of in market rhetoric. Rather, it seems that the values of personhood and community pervasively interact with the market and alter many things from their pure free-market form.

8

Conceptual Recapitulation

As I said Chapter in 1, one can think of commodification as having two senses, a narrow one (literal markets) and a broad one (market rhetoric). Commodification can be less than universal in literal markets if trade is regulated or foreclosed in various ways, and commodification can be less than universal in rhetoric if other conceptual schemes play a role in various ways. Moreover, actions and discourse (the thought structures giving meaning to action) are not completely disjunct, so that literal market exchanges and market rhetoric are interdependent in whatever way(s) action in general and discourse in general are interdependent.

Senses of Incomplete Commodification

A more accurate way to see our situation with respect to commodification, therefore, is to modify the hypothetical of universal commodification and instead to think of commodification as a matter of degree. We can refer to the hypothetical archetype, universal commodification, as complete commodification, and refer to the more ambiguous and variegated situation in our own world as incomplete commodification, as I have so far done. But this is a complex endeavor because there are many aspects of incompleteness on which we could focus. So far I have not fully untangled the complexities, although I have distinguished between participant and social aspects and have broken down the participant aspect into contested concepts and internal plural meanings. I think we are now in a position to distinguish seven ways in which we might consider commodification to be a matter of degree.

1. There might be a commodification continuum in literal markets: laissez-faire markets represent complete commodification, and regulated markets represent incomplete commodification. Regulated markets represent incomplete commodification in only a weak sense if it is thought that the only explanation for regulation is some kind of market failure. (As I explained in Chapter 2, when the issue of regulation is conceived of in market rhetoric, market failure is the only available explanation or justification.) In practice this indeed may sometimes seem the best explanation (or justification) for regulation. For example, laws prohibiting sale of securities without certain specific disclosures of information may be best understood as making it possible for buyers to know what price they are willing to pay. This is an explanation in terms of market failure.

2. Regulated markets represent incomplete commodification in a stronger sense in situations where they reflect internally plural meaning, that is, where regulation expresses and fosters an important nonmarket aspect of the interactions between persons who buy and sell things. For example, as I argued in Chapter 7, much regulation involving working conditions probably rests more on the respect owed to workers as persons than on market failure. Much regulation involving residential housing probably rests primarily on the minimum decent standards needed to shelter people, especially children, in safety and dignity.

3. Commodification can also be a matter of degree in literal laissez-faire markets in another sense, relating to what portion of the world of things people value is traded in markets. If only automobiles, toys, and clothing are commodified, we have a lesser degree of commodification of the world of desired goods than if housing, health care, and environmental quality are commodified as well. If everything that is scarce that people value is literally bought and sold, then we would have universal commodification in the narrow sense.

4. Another way to think of commodification as a matter of degree involves the difference between literal and metaphorical markets. Then literal laissez-faire markets would correspond to complete com-

modification, and metaphorical laissez-faire markets, in the absence of corresponding literal markets, would correspond to incomplete commodification. In this way of looking at the matter, commodification becomes complete when things people value are actually exchanged for money, in a social context of like exchanges. Commodification remains incomplete when all we do is talk about it. Of course, if there were no literal markets anywhere, then commodification in rhetoric could not be understood as such.

5. Commodification in rhetoric can itself be a matter of degree in a sense analogous to the one involving how much of the world is traded in literal markets. A neoclassical economist could conceive of children as commodities but perhaps not think of morality in general in market rhetoric. But some philosophers do think of morality in market rhetoric.[1] If law, morality, politics, and all aspects of social life are conceived of in market rhetoric, to the exclusion of rival conceptual schemes, then we would have universal commodification in rhetoric.

6. Commodification in rhetoric can be a matter of degree in another way too, relating to how much the discourse of commodification is the actual discourse of ordinary language. If only a few academics conceive of children as commodities, we have a lesser degree of commodification in rhetoric than if that is the only way available to conceive of children in our language as a whole. In that limiting case, not only would there be no way for the economist's rhetoric to trouble us; there would also be no way for it to stand out as market rhetoric. In the real world, there is greater or lesser prevalence of market rhetoric depending upon what is being discussed and who is discussing it, but market rhetoric is always less than monolithic as long as we are able to distinguish it for concern. When certain people conceive of children as a commodity, and other people conceive of children as noncommodified, then two crystallized competing conceptions of children coexist in society. Then the meaning of "having" children is a contested concept.

7. Finally, commodification in rhetoric can range from complete to less complete forms in yet another way, which is the one that mainly interests me in this chapter. This continuum involves the range from core instances of commodification in rhetoric to instances that bear some indicia of commodification but are more attenuated.[2] On this continuum, Gary Becker's conceptualization of the family's desire for children is an example of complete commodification (of children) in

rhetoric, because nothing is lacking from the indicia of the laissez-faire market except literal exchanges of money for children.

Indicia of Commodification

I can now explain commodification more precisely by setting out an analytic structure that has been only implicit in what has gone before. My view is that literal complete commodification is characterized by (1) exchanges of things in the world (2) for money, (3) in the social context of markets, and (4) in conjunction with four indicia of commodification in conceptualization. Those four conceptual indicia characterize complete commodification in rhetoric. They are (i) objectification, (ii) fungibility, (iii) commensurability, and (iv) money equivalence. Literal commodification and commodification in conceptualization need not be coextensive in practice, but they are loosely interdependent. Unless the market conceptual scheme (market rhetoric) were prevalent in the world, literal market exchanges could not have the meaning they do. And unless literal market exchanges were prevalent in world, we would not be able to operate inside the conceptual scheme the way we do.

The indicia of commodification in conceptualization are related to one another, but each of them plays a slightly different role in our understanding of commodification. Objectification relates to ontological commitment. By objectification, I mean ascription of status as a thing in the Kantian sense of something that is manipulable at the will of persons. Fungibility relates to exchange. By fungibility, I mean at least that the things are fully interchangeable with no effect on value to the holder. Fungibility may also mean that the things can be equated with a sum of money. If fungibility has this meaning, it collapses into commensurability. Commensurability relates to the nature of value. By commensurability, I mean that values of things can be arrayed as a function of one continuous variable, or can be linearly ranked. By money equivalence, I mean that the continuous variable in terms of which things can be ranked is dollar value.

As my definitions indicate, the indicia of commodification in rhetoric seem to be at least roughly cumulative. If we have money equivalence, we will also have the other three. Money equivalence implies commensurability, with money as the metric to which value can be reduced. Money equivalence also implies fungibility; things with the same monetary value are interchangeable with one another as well as with a certain sum of money. Likewise, money equivalence seems to imply objectification, because something whose value is perspicuously described as precisely equivalent to a sum of money has no more honorific ontological status than the sum of money itself.

It is possible to have commensurability without money equivalence. This happens if values are deemed commensurable in terms of a utility function but the utility function is not reducible to dollars, or if values can be definitively ranked in terms of one another but cannot be translated into dollars. If we have commensurability, however, it seems we will also have fungibility and objectification. Commensurability as I understand it may imply fungibility: given something of value, it is at least theoretically possible that something else will be equal to it in value. If two things are equal to each other in value, can be valued in terms of each other, then it seems they are interchangeable. Commensurability as I understand it may also imply objectification, but that depends upon whether we think that being able to say that someone's attributes are equal in value to someone else's, in the sense implied by commensurability, implies that we are conceiving of those attributes in a way that is contrary to personhood.

Similarly, it may be possible to have fungibility without money equivalence or commensurability. Perhaps things can be conceived of as interchangeable with each other but with values that cannot be reduced to some third common value; perhaps they need not be conceived of as equal to each other in the sense required for commensurability. If we have fungibility, we will, I think, probably have objectification as well: things that are interchangeable are conceived of as manipulable objects and not as subjects or agents.

Finally, it seems possible to have objectification without fungibility, commensurability, or money equivalence. Treating something as interchangeable with others of its kind is not the only way to treat it as an object. For example, improper subordination of persons could be a form of objectification without the other indicia of commodification.

It may be useful to consider a discourse as involving commodification even if the rhetoric is incomplete in the sense that the discourse does not exhibit all four indicia. No doubt at some point the link to core instances of commodification becomes too attenuated and it becomes inapposite to think of commodification. Maybe, for example, where objectification is the only aspect of the discourse that suggests commodification, we are dealing with a problem of subordination, and it would be more appropriate to confront subordination directly.

Commodification in rhetoric at least remains a useful concept for cases in which we have commensurability (and thus, it seems, fungibility and objectification) even if money equivalence is not part of the discourse. Examples of this may be found in some utilitarian views that do not reduce utility to wealth. Such views treat incommensurabilities that we have been formerly committed to as instead commensurable. This is a form of reductionism that can engender the kind of erosion of the concept of personhood that I have said is the basis for thinking of commodification as potentially harmful.[3] Incomplete commodification in rhetoric is not beyond the purview of concern about commodification, at least prima facie. Conceiving of children's value in terms of "utils" that are ranked on a continuous function with the "utils" produced by other goods seems troublesome in the same way that conceiving of their value in dollars seems troublesome.

Commodification in rhetoric sometimes also remains a useful concept for thinking about cases in which we have fungibility, even if commensurability is not explicitly part of the discourse. Some of the objections to commensurability may really be objections to fungibility. They may be objections simply to treating things or values as interchangeable with each other, and may not depend upon the further idea that the things or values can all be decisively ranked or can be reduced to some third value in a scalar way. Perhaps the interchangeability of children and dollars would be troublesome even if various dollar sums couldn't be linearly ranked. The idea of fungibility, even without commensurability, still undermines the notion of individual uniqueness.

Cognitive Instabilities and the Issue of Translation

The archetype that I have been calling universal commodification is conceptually unstable. It lends itself to easy deconstruction. The literal laissez-faire market privileges competition but presupposes cooperation in order to set up a functioning market. Without (unpoliced) cooperation in setting up and policing a system of enforceable property rights and a system of enforceable agreements to exchange them, there could be no laissez-faire market.[4] Commodified views of politics, such as rational choice contractarianism, eschew commitment to any values prior to choice of those values as, for example, appropriate public goods by individuals conceived of solely as profit-maximizers. Yet these theories nevertheless seem precommitted to particular conceptions of justice and the good for human beings. In particular, they seem committed to some conception of persons as free and equal moral agents.[5]

There also may be a conceptual instability in the notion that all things people value can be understood as commensurable—the notion that the stuff of value is fungible. A metaphorical market, such as the "marketplace of ideas," might be understood as making it possible for all conceptualizations of value to compete freely with one another. (See Chapter 12.) But it appears that the commodified conception of values and social practices, which gives rise to the notion of a metaphorical market in the first place, cannot do that. By assuming that all values can be expressed commensurably in market rhetoric, the commodified conception appears to presuppose suppression of other views in which incommensurability is salient. For example, a neoclassical economist such as Gary Becker "translates" the joys of having children into services that we as parents consume. His precommitment to the assumption that such "translation" is possible automatically silences what is salient about a noncommodified view. Yet if the possibility of such "translation" is not presupposed, the commodified conception of value disintegrates. "Translation"—reduction of everything to one metric—is its essence.

Many neoclassical economists argue that every value that is understood in a noneconomic discourse can be translated into their discourse. Moral commitments can be understood as monetizable "moralisms." (Recall the discussion in Chapter 2 of the wrong of slavery in terms of externalities.) There is no way to prove to such economists that the translation is impossible. What language, what conceptual scheme could I use to prove this to someone who reasons in universal market rhetoric? Can I use market rhetoric to show its own incompleteness? Perhaps a partial way of doing that is to point out conceptual instabilities such as those mentioned above. The notion that I could use market rhetoric to show its own incompleteness in a more complete (more algorithmic?) way seems to involve the contradiction of admitting that market rhetoric is the master paradigm while trying to use it to deny that very thing. On the other hand, any other

discourse I use (incommensurability of value, for example) will immediately be "translated" by the economist into market rhetoric. She will
say my stubborn commitment to incommensurability means I value it
very highly so that it would "cost" me a lot to give it up, and therefore
I'm willing to "trade off" certain other things against it, and so forth.

Commensurability and incommensurability belong to clashing conceptual schemes—conflicting paradigms, if you will. Neither can be
made to subsume the other in some logical sense. At least, as a
pragmatist, I deeply doubt it. Rather than trying to prove that the
economist's "translations" have something logically or analytically
wrong with them, then, I believe it is better to argue for incommensurability—the incommensurability of the wrong of slavery and
"costs" in dollars, for example—by showing how hard it would be in
practice to do without our commitments to it. In practice, the "texture
of the human world" would be unrecognizable, and personhood as
we know it would disappear.

In the main, mine is an argument for discourse pluralism. I don't
mean to deny that the rhetoric of economics is frequently useful as
one among the many ways we can think about relationships and
behavior. I am arguing that something important to humanity is lost
if market rhetoric becomes (or is considered to be) the sole rhetoric of
human affairs, excluding other kinds of understanding. Rather than
saying that market rhetoric must inevitably be "imperialistic" in this
way, I believe we should look and see under what circumstances this
market takeover might happen. I will devote Chapters 10 and 13 to
this sort of investigation.

9

The Double Bind

Nonideal Justice and Never-Ending Transition

There is always a gap between the ideals we can formulate and the progress we can realize. Hence there is always an ambiguity about theorizing about justice, and there is always an ambiguity about seeking justice. Does justice refer to the best general ideals we can formulate? We can call this ideal justice. Or does justice refer to a theoretical working out of what changes would now count as social improvements? We can call this nonideal justice. When we seek justice, should we pursue ideal or nonideal justice?

To avoid all significant harms to personhood and community may be an ideal of justice, at least of ideal justice. Yet it may also be the case that justice (at least for here and now) instead means only that we should choose the best alternative from among those available to us. If that is what justice means, then whatever harms to personhood and community are present in the best alternative cannot be thought of as unjust, although they may come to be unjust when a better alternative becomes available. Doing nothing in the meantime while we wait for circumstances in which we can implement ideal justice may ensure that those circumstances will never come into being.

Pursuing nonideal justice is linked with a dilemma of transition from where we are now to a better world. If we compromise our ideals too much because of the difficulties of our circumstances, we may reinforce the status quo instead of making progress. Some would argue that giving welfare entrenches recipients in an underclass rather than helping them to escape from it. On the other hand, if we are too utopian about our ideals given our circumstances, we may also make no progress. Granted that an underclass in need of welfare would not exist in an ideal state, it still may worsen the situation to abolish welfare now. This practical dilemma of nonideal justice is what I call the double bind.

The link between discourse and practice deepens the dilemma. Our ideals, our visions for a better future, are different from our current circumstances, but at the same time our current circumstances create and underwrite those visions. As we change our circumstances, our visions of the ideal will also change. If we compromise our ideals too much because of the difficulties of our circumstances, we may no longer be able to formulate those ideals.

The double bind is omnipresent in the pursuit of justice because the problem of transition that generates it is simply an artifact of the interdependence of theory and practice. Nonideal justice is the process by which we try to make progress (effect a transition) toward our vision of the good world. In the transition all decisions about justice—as opposed to theories about it—are pragmatic decisions. Ideal theory is equally necessary because we need to know what we are trying to achieve; and ideal theory metamorphoses as our decisions take effect. In other words, our visions and nonideal decisions, our theory and practice, paradoxically constitute each other.

With respect to commodification, the double bind has two main consequences. First, if we sometimes cannot respect personhood either by permitting sales or by banning sales, justice requires that we consider changing the circumstances that create the dilemma. We must consider wealth and power redistribution. Second, we still must choose a regime for the meantime, the transition, in nonideal circumstances. To resolve the double bind, we have to investigate particular problems separately. Decisions must be made (and remade) for each thing that some people desire to sell. At the same time, each separate decision must be made in light of a reevaluation of both our ideals and our circumstances.

Social Justice in Context

If we have reason to believe with respect to a particular thing that the domino theory might hold—commodification for some means commodification for all—we would have reason to try to foreclose market trading. But the double bind means that if we choose market-inalienability, we might deprive a class of poor and oppressed people of the opportunity to have more money with which to buy adequate food, shelter, and health care in the market, and hence deprive them of a better chance to lead a humane life. Those who gain from the market-inalienability, on the other hand, might be primarily people whose wealth and power make them comfortable enough to be concerned about the inroads on the general quality of life that commodification would make. Commodification worries may seem like a luxury. Yet, taking a slightly longer view, commodification threatens the personhood of everyone, not just those who can now afford to concern themselves about it. Whether this elitism in market-inalienability should make us risk the dangers of commodification will depend upon the dangers of each case.

The prophylactic personhood argument discussed in Chapter 4—that people should not be allowed to sell, for example, their organs because to do so is degrading to personhood—calls attention to a more pervasive problem of social justice. If people are so desperate for money that they are trying to sell things we think cannot be separated from them without significant injury to personhood, we do not cure the desperation by banning sales. Nor do we avoid the injury to personhood. Perhaps the desperation is the social problem we should be looking at, rather than the market ban. Perhaps worse injury to personhood is suffered from the desperation that caused the attempt to sell a kidney or cornea than would be suffered from actually selling it. The would-be sellers apparently think so. Then justice is not served by a ban on "desperate exchanges."

These considerations change the arena of argument from considerations of appropriateness to the market to explicit considerations of social justice. If neither commodification nor noncommodification can put to rest our disquiet about harm to personhood in conjunction with certain specific kinds of transactions—if neither commodification nor noncommodification can satisfy our aspirations for a society exhibiting equal respect for persons—then we must rethink the larger social context in which this dilemma is embedded. We must think about wealth and power redistribution.

In other words, sale of one's body parts presents a dilemma because it seems we cannot honor our intuitions of what is required for society to respect personhood, either by permitting sales or by banning them. The dilemma throws into relief the results of inequalities of wealth distribution. It should make us consider the justice of the surrounding circumstances that create the dilemma.

One's body is bound up with one's personhood, which is why when organs are donated it is a significant expression of human interrelation. But to preserve organ donation as an opportunity for altruism is also one way of keeping from our view the desperation of poor people. Hence, one who thinks social progress can be brought about by forcing unjust conditions upon our attention might agree with the universal commodifier that sales should be permitted. The progressive thinks, in other words, that fellow feeling is better served by permitting sales so that the spectacle will awaken fellow feeling in the rest of us, to eliminate poverty. The universal commodifier, on the other hand, thinks that even altruism is monetizable, and, in cases where there are willing buyers and willing sellers, it must be worth less than sales. This ironic alliance between the radical and the libertarian is a sure sign that something is incoherent about the middle way.

In certain cases, for example, organ-selling, it appears that we cannot respect personhood either with commodification or with non-commodification, given the surrounding social circumstances. If we agree that this dilemma means we ought to change the surrounding circumstances, we are still faced with the question of whether we should permit commodification while we try to do that. If we opt to permit sales for those who choose, as both the libertarian and the radical might recommend, we may risk complete commodification. Whether complete commodification is a serious risk depends on whether the domino theory correctly predicts the resulting social consciousness, given the level of commodification already present. Complete commodification makes the supposed goal of greater respect for persons in a less commodified future even less imaginable. But perhaps this risk is not as bad as the degradation of personhood and reinforcement of powerlessness brought about by the regime of enforced noncommodification. Obviously, I have no handy algorithm for making this decision. But the double bind must be taken seriously in all cases in which it is claimed that commodification harms or disempowers persons or contributes to social subordination.

"Women's Issues"

In the struggle for social justice for women, the double bind is pervasive. (In the next chapter I will focus in detail on two of the issues for which it is salient, prostitution and baby-selling.) If the social regime permits buying and selling of sexual and reproductive activities, thereby treating them as fungible market commodities given the current understandings of monetary exchange, there is a threat to the personhood of women, who are the "owners" of these "commodities." The threat to personhood from commodification arises because essential attributes are treated as severable fungible objects, and such treatment denies the integrity and uniqueness of the self. But if the social regime prohibits this kind of commodification, it denies women the choice to market their sexual or reproductive services, and given the current feminization of poverty and lack of avenues for free choice for women, this prohibition also poses a threat to the personhood of women.[1] The threat from enforced noncommodification arises because narrowing women's choices is a threat to liberation, and because their choices to market sexual or reproductive services, even if nonideal, may represent the best alternatives available to those who would choose them.

Thus the double bind: both commodification and noncommodification may be harmful. Harmful, that is, under our current social conditions. Neither one need be harmful in an ideal world. The fact that money changes hands need not necessarily contaminate human interactions of sharing. Nor must the fact that a social order makes nonmonetary sharing its norm necessarily deprive or subordinate anyone. That commodification now tends toward fungibility of women, and that noncommodification now tends toward their domination and continued subordination are artifacts of the current social hierarchy. For a group subject to structures of domination, all roads thought to be progressive can lead to a backlash. In other words, the fact of oppression is what gives rise to the double bind.

Thus, it appears that the solution to the double bind is not to solve but to dissolve it: remove the oppressive circumstances. But in the meantime, if we are practically limited to those two choices, which are we to choose? I think that the answer must be pragmatic. We must look carefully at the nonideal circumstances in each case and decide which horn of the dilemma is better (or less bad), and we must keep redeciding as time goes on. At the same time, we must look for ways to escape seeing our choices as limited in this binary way.

Consider the special treatment/equal treatment debate. When we single out pregnancy, for example, for "special treatment," we fear that employers will not hire women. But if we do not accord special treatment to pregnancy, women will lose their jobs. If we grant special treatment, we bring back, at least to some extent, the bad old conception of women as weaker creatures. If we do not, we hinder women from becoming strong in the practical world.[2]

Feminist theory that tends toward the ideal, the visionary side of our thought about justice, has grasped the point that the dilemma must be dissolved. The framework of the dilemma is the conceptual framework of the oppressors, those who define what is "special" and what is "equal." But feminist theory that tends toward the nonideal, practical side of our thought about justice has also realized that if the dominant conceptions are too deeply held at this time, trying to implement an alternative vision could be counterproductive.

In the case of pregnancy, perhaps the time has come to convince everyone that both men and women should have the opportunity to be parents in a fulfilling sense. As Justice Thurgood Marshall said in a 1987 Supreme Court case, "By 'taking pregnancy into account,' California's pregnancy disability-leave statute allows women, as well as men, to have families without losing their jobs."[3] The old conceptions of the workplace now can begin to give way. Nevertheless I think that each women's issue situation, such as pregnancy, workplace regulation to protect fetuses, and height and weight restrictions, will have to be evaluated separately, and continually reevaluated.

Affirmative action also poses the double bind. Where there is a social commitment to affirmative action, in this nonideal time and place, it is likely to be conflicted, so that a woman or person of color who holds a job formerly closed to women and people of color is likely to be presumed to be underqualified.[4] Affirmative action becomes yet another stigma. Some women and people of color will hold jobs formerly closed to them, but few will be allowed to feel good about it. The dominant group may well be able to make women and people of color meet higher standards than those applicable to white males, and yet at the same time convince everyone, including, often, the beneficiaries of affirmative action themselves, that as beneficiaries they are inferior.

But what is our alternative? If there is no affirmative action commitment in place, institutional racism and sexism, and just plain cronyism, will see to it that far fewer women and people of color will hold these jobs. Yet those who do, whatever vicissitudes they endure, will not endure the particular backlash of affirmative action stigma. The pragmatic answer in most cases, I believe, is that backlash is better than complete exclusion,[5] as long as the backlash is temporary. But if backlash can keep alive the bad old conceptions of women and people of color, how will we evolve toward better conceptions of the abilities of those who have been excluded? There is no easy answer to this question.

Our struggle with how to understand rape seems to be yet another instance of the double bind. Catharine MacKinnon's view—or perhaps an oversimplified version of her view—is that under current conditions of gender hierarchy there is no clear dividing line between the sort of heterosexual intercourse that is genuinely desired by women and the sort that is unwelcome.[6] There can be no clear line because our very conception of sexuality is so deeply intertwined with male dominance that our desires as we experience them are problematic. Our own desires are socially constituted to reinforce patterns of male dominance against our own interest.[7] "Just say no" as the standard for determining whether rape has occurred is both under- and overinclusive. It is underinclusive because women who haven't found their voices mean "no" and are unable to say it; and it is overinclusive because, like it or not, as sexuality has been constituted in a culture of male dominance, the male understanding that "no" means "yes" was often, and may still sometimes be, correct.[8] MacKinnon's view is painful. If there is no space for women to experience heterosexuality that is not suspect, what does that do to our self-esteem and personhood in a social setting in which sex is important to selfhood?

The other prong of the double bind—roughly represented by the views of Robin West—is that we should greet all of women's subjective experience with acceptance and respect.[9] That view is less threatening to personhood in one way but more so in another. How can we progress toward a social conception of sexuality that is less male-dominated if we do not regard with critical suspicion some of the male-dominated experiences in which we now take pleasure?[10]

The last example of the double bind I want to mention is the conceptualization of marriage. Is marriage to be considered a contract

in which certain distributions of goods are agreed to between autonomous bargaining agents?[11] Upon divorce, such a conception of marriage makes it difficult for oppressed women who have not bargained
effectively to obtain much. Or is marriage to be considered a noncontractual sharing status in which the partners' contributions are not to
be monetized?[12] Upon divorce, such a conception makes it difficult for
oppressed women who have contributed unmonetized services to their
husbands' advantage to obtain much. The idea of contractual autonomy may be more attractive in our nonideal world if the alternative
is for women to be submerged in a status that gives all power to men.
Yet the autonomy may be illusory because oppression makes equal
bargaining power impossible. At the same time, the reinforcement of
individualist bargaining models of human interaction is contrary to
our vision of a better world and may alter that vision in a way we do
not wish.[13]

Perhaps it is obvious that the reason the double bind recurs
throughout feminist struggles is that it is an artifact of the dominant
social conception of the meaning of gender. The double bind is a series
of dilemmas in which both alternatives are, or can be, losers for the
oppressed. Once we realize this, we may say it is equally obvious that
the way out of the double bind is to dissolve these dilemmas by
changing the framework that creates them. That is, we must dissolve
the prevalent conception of gender.

Calling for dissolution of the prevalent conception of gender is the
visionary half of the problem. Yes, we must create a new vision of the
meaning of male and female in order to change the dominant social
conception of gender and change the double bind. In order to do that,
however, women need the social empowerment that the dominant
social conception of gender keeps us from achieving.

Then how can we make progress? The other half of the problem is
the nonideal problem of transition from the present situation toward
our ideal. The pragmatist solution is to confront each dilemma as it
occurs and choose the alternative that will hinder empowerment the
least and further it the most. Appropriate solutions may all differ,
depending on the current stage of women's empowerment, and how
the proposed solution might move the current social conception of
gender and our vision of how gender should be reconceived for the
future. Indeed, the "same" double bind may demand a different
solution tomorrow from the one we find best today.

10

Prostitution and Baby-Selling: Contested Commodification and Women's Capacities

Payment in exchange for sexual intercourse and payment in exchange for relinquishing a child for adoption are nodal cases of contested commodification. They express the double bind for women especially clearly. They implicate issues of race and class. They show how our culture stubbornly insists on conceiving of the person as a moral agent, as a subject distinct from a world of objects, yet how at the same time our culture persistently commodifies and objectifies.

Social policy decisions about these practices, which have become focal mirrors for the crosscurrents of our culture, cannot help but symbolize how we view ourselves now, and how we envision our future. In pursuit of our vision of the future we might see certain changes as desirable for our culture as a whole. But policy decisions are made piecemeal, and our vision of what the whole is, and should be, keeps changing as those piecemeal decisions are made. It is in this context that we try to make incremental changes for the better, as we see the better. Our vision of the whole is always implicated.

In fact any decision, including the decision to avoid decision (the decision to privilege the status quo), gets made in the context of our entire situation, whether or not we explicitly recognize its larger context. As a pragmatist, I can't claim that explicit recognition of larger cultural context is always useful or important, regardless of the practice to be evaluated. It depends on the practice and the circumstances. But explicit recognition of the symbolic meaning of the practices targeted for discussion here, in light of the surrounding cultural institutions and practices, is indeed useful and important. As we decide what to do about them, for now (for we may well need to decide again, later, in different circumstances), we should try explicitly to make whatever sense we can of the cultural/conceptual crosscurrents pervading commodification and the general issue of objectification.

Prostitution

Start with the traditional ideal of sexual interaction as equal non-monetized sharing. In an ideal theory of justice, we might hold that the "good" commodified sexuality ought not to exist: that sexual activity should be market-inalienable. But considerations of nonideal justice might tell us that prohibiting sale of sexual services in order to preserve sexuality as nonmonetized sharing is not justified under current circumstances. One reason to say this is that sex is already commodified. Legalized prostitution has existed in many places, and there has always been a large black market of which everyone is well aware. Those who purchase prostitutes' services are often not prosecuted, at least in traditional male-female prostitution.[1] This practice tolerates commodification of sexuality, at least by the purchasers.[2]

Moreover, in our nonideal world, market-inalienability—especially if enforced through criminalization of sales—may cause harm to ideals of personhood instead of maintaining and fostering them, primarily because it exacerbates the double bind. Poor women who believe that they must sell their sexual services in order to survive are subject to moral opprobrium, disease, arrest, and violence. The ideal of sexual sharing is related to identity and contextuality, but the identity of those who sell is undermined by criminalization and powerlessness, and their contextuality, their ability to develop and maintain relationships, is stunted in these circumstances.

Despite the double bind and the harms of the black market to prostitutes, fear of a domino effect—the discourse contagion of market rhetoric—might be thought to warrant market-inalienability as an effort to ward off conceiving of all sexuality as commodified. To this suggestion many people would protest that the known availability of commodified sex does not by itself render noncommodified sexual interactions impossible or even more difficult. They would say that the prevalence of ideals of interpersonal sexual sharing despite the widespread association of sex and money,[3] is proof that the domino effect in rhetoric is not to be feared.

But we must evaluate the seriousness of the risk if commodification proceeds. What if sex were fully and openly commodified? Suppose newspapers, radio, TV, and billboards advertised sexual services as imaginatively and vividly as they advertise computer services, health clubs, or soft drinks. Suppose the sexual partner of your choice could be ordered through a catalog, or through a large brokerage firm that has an 800 number, or at a trade show, or in a local showroom. Suppose the business of recruiting suppliers of sexual services was carried on in the same way as corporate headhunting or training of word-processing operators.

If sex were openly commodified in this way, its commodification would be reflected in everyone's discourse about sex, and in particular about women's sexuality. New terms would emerge for particular gradations of sexual market value. New discussions would be heard of particular abilities or qualities in terms of their market value. With this change in discourse, when it became pervasive enough, would come a change in everyone's experience, because experience is discourse dependent. The open market might render an understanding of women (and perhaps everyone) in terms of sexual dollar value impossible to avoid. It might make the ideal of nonmonetized sharing impossible. Thus, the argument for noncommodification of sexuality based on the domino effect, in its strongest form, is that we do not wish to unleash market forces onto the shaping of our discourse regarding sexuality and hence onto our very conception of sexuality and our sexual feelings.

This domino argument assumes that nonmonetized equal-sharing relationships are the norm or are at least attainable. That assumption is now contested. Some feminists, notably Catharine MacKinnon, argue that male-female sexual relationships that actually instantiate the ideal of equal sharing are under current social circumstances rare or even impossible.[4] According to this view, moreover, women are oppressed by this ideal because they try to understand their relationships with men in light of it, and conceal from themselves the truth about their own condition. They try to understand what they are doing as giving, as equal sharing, while their sexuality is actually being taken from them. If we believe that women are deceived (and deceiving themselves) in this way, attempted noncommodification in the name of the ideal may be futile or even counterproductive. Noncommodification under current circumstances is part of the social structure that perpetuates false consciousness about the current role of the ideal.

Some feminists also argue that many male-female sexual relationships are (unequal) economic bargains, not a context in which equal sharing occurs.[5] If that is true, attempted noncommodification of sexuality means that prostitutes are being singled out for punishment for something pervasive in women's condition. They are being singled out because their class or race forecloses more socially accepted forms of sexual bargaining. This situation returns us to the double bind.

Perhaps the best way to characterize the present situation is to say that women's sexuality is incompletely commodified, perhaps both in the sense that it is a contested concept and in the sense that its meaning is internally plural. Many sexual relationships may have both market and nonmarket aspects: relationships may be entered into and sustained partly for economic reasons and partly for the interpersonal sharing that is part of our ideal of human flourishing. Under current circumstances the ideal misleads us into thinking that unequal relationships are really equal. Yet because the ideal of equal sharing is part of a conception of human personhood to which we remain deeply committed, it seems that the way out of such ideological bondage is not to abandon the ideal, but rather to pursue it in ways that are not harmful under these nonideal circumstances. Market-inalienability (attempted noncommodification) seems harmful as it is practiced in our world. Yet complete commodification, if any credence is given to the feared domino effect, may foreclose our conception of sexuality entirely.

So perhaps the best policy solution, for now, is a regime of regulation expressing incomplete commodification. The issue becomes how to structure an incomplete commodification that takes account of our nonideal world yet does not foreclose progress to a better world of more nearly equal power (and less susceptibility to the domino effect of market rhetoric). In my opinion, we should now decriminalize the sale of sexual services. We should not subject poor women to the degradation and danger of the black market nor force them into other methods of earning money that seem to them less desirable than selling their bodies. At the same time, in order to check the domino effect, I believe we should prohibit the free-market entrepreneurship that would otherwise accompany decriminalization and could operate to create an organized market in sexual services. Such regulation would include, for example, such deviations from laissez-faire as banning brokerage (pimping) and worker training (recruitment).

In structuring a regulatory regime expressing incomplete commodification for sexual activity, an important issue is whether contracts to sell sexual services should be enforced. The usual reason given for precluding specific performance of personal service agreements is that forcing performance smacks of slavery. If sexual service contracts were to be specifically performed, persons would be forced to yield their bodily integrity and freedom. This is commodification of the person. Suppose, then, that we decide to preclude specific performance but allow a damage remedy. Enforceable contracts might make the "goods" command higher prices. Prostitutes might welcome such an arrangement; it might be on the procommodification side of the double bind. The other side is that having to pay damages for deciding not to engage in sex with someone seems very harmful to the ideal of sexuality as integral to personhood. Moreover, it seems that determining the amount of damages due is tantamount to complete commodification. Granting a damage remedy requires an official entity to place a dollar value on the "goods"; commodification is thus officially imposed.

In this context both specific performance and damages seem to go all the way to complete commodification. Thus, we should continue to make prostitution contracts unenforceable, denying the most important factor of commodification—enforceable free contract. We could either provide for restitution if the woman reneges or let losses lie. If we let losses lie, we preclude any increased domino effect that official governmental (court) pronouncements about commodified sexuality might cause. But letting losses lie would also allow men to take and not pay when women are ignorant or powerless enough to fail to collect in advance. Similar two-edged results are reached by the doctrine of nonenforcement of illegal contracts, under which contracts to render sexual services are currently unenforceable because of the illegality of prostitution.

An incomplete commodification regime for prostitution might also include banning advertising. Trying to keep commodification of sexuality out of our discourse by banning advertising does have the symbolic effect of failing to legitimate the sales we allow, and hence it may fail to alleviate significantly the social disapproval suffered by those who sell sexual services. It also adds "information costs" to their "product," and thus fails to yield them as great a "return" as would the full-blown market. But these nonideal effects must be borne if we really accept that extensive permeation of our discourse by commodification-talk would alter sexuality in a way that we are unwilling to countenance.

Baby-Selling

Just as some women wish to sell their sexual services, some wish to sell their children. Is a regulatory regime expressing incomplete commodification also now warranted for baby-selling? In my opinion, the answer is no, but the issues are very complex.

Let me start with the general issue of selling babies to would-be parents. If our regime were to allow would-be parents to approach a woman of their choice and commission a pregnancy for a fee, with the woman releasing the baby to them at birth, we would no doubt characterize this regime as one in which babies are being produced for sale. I refer to this scenario as "commissioned adoption." A regime allowing commissioned adoption would provide for a full-blown market in babies. The supply of newborn babies for sale would be related primarily to the demand of the would-be parents who wanted to buy them; that is, the quantity of children supplied would depend on the prices would-be parents would pay and how many would be willing to buy children at a given offering price.

If our regime were to allow would-be parents to approach a woman who is already pregnant, or who has already given birth, and for a fee have her release the baby to them, we would also characterize this regime as one in which babies are sold, though not one in which babies are being produced for sale. I refer to this scenario as "paid adoption of 'unwanted' children." This regime would not be a full-blown market in babies, because the supply of newborn babies for sale would not be related primarily to the demand of the would-be parents who wanted to buy them. Instead, supply would probably be related primarily to access to birth control information and education, and to cultural characteristics having to do with sexuality and permissibility of abortion. Of course, this regime could approach a black-market version of a commissioned adoption regime, because some women might conceive babies without any prearranged purchaser but hoping to put them up for sale.

As far as I know, no jurisdiction permits paid adoption of "un-wanted" children; it is universally prohibited as baby-selling. (Many jurisdictions permit the birth mother to be paid expenses, and this arrangement creates a gray market.) A fortiori, no jurisdiction permits commissioned adoption. Our status quo "official" social regime—and the "official" regime is the one that has the most symbolic cultural significance—bans the exchange of children for money. That cultural significance makes troubling even the market rhetoric I have been using in these paragraphs.

Like relationships of sexual sharing, parent-child relationships are closely connected with personhood, particularly with personal iden-tity and contextuality, and the interest of would-be parents is a strong one. Moreover, poor women caught in the double bind raise the issue of freedom: they may wish to sell a baby on the black market, as they may wish to sell sexual services, perhaps to try to provide adequately for other children or family members.[6] But the double bind is not the only problem of freedom implicated in baby-selling. Under a market regime, prostitutes may be choosing to sell their sexuality, but babies are not choosing for themselves that under current nonideal circum-stances they are better off as commodities. If we permit babies to be sold, we commodify not only the mother's (and father's) babymaking capacities—which might be analogous to commodifying sexual-ity—but also the baby herself.

When the baby becomes a commodity, all of her personal attrib-utes—sex, eye color, predicted I.Q., predicted height, and the like—be-come commodified as well. Hence, as Gary Becker says, there would be "superior" and "inferior" babies, with the market for the latter likened to that for "lemons."[7] As a result, boy babies might be "worth" more than girl babies; white babies might be "worth" more than nonwhite babies.[8] Commodifying babies leads us to conceive of potentially all personal attributes in market rhetoric, not merely those of sexuality.

Moreover, to conceive of infants in market rhetoric is likewise to conceive of the people they will become in market rhetoric, and this might well create in those people a commodified self-conception.

Hence, the domino theory has a deep intuitive appeal when we think about the sale of babies. Yet perhaps we are being too pessimistic about our "nature" as market actors if we succumb to it. Maybe the fact that we do not now value babies in monetary terms suggests that we would not do so even if our official regime allowed babies to be sold. Maybe. Perhaps babies could be incompletely commodified, valued by the participants in the interaction in a nonmarket way, even though money changed hands. Perhaps. Although this outcome is theoretically possible (see Chapters 6 and 7), it seems risky to commit ourselves to this optimistic view in our nonideal world.

If a free-market baby industry were to come into being, with all of its accompanying paraphernalia, how could any of us, even those who did not produce infants for sale, avoid measuring the dollar value of our children? How could our children avoid being preoccupied with measuring their own dollar value? This measurement makes our discourse about ourselves (when we are children) and about our children (when we are parents) like our discourse about cars.[9]

Perhaps we should separately evaluate the risk in the cases of selling "unwanted" babies and selling babies commissioned for adoption or otherwise "produced" for sale. The risk of complete commodification may be greater if we officially sanction bringing babies into the world for purposes of sale than if we sanction accepting money once they are already born. Such a distinction would probably be quite difficult to enforce, however, because nothing prevents a would-be seller from declaring any child to be "unwanted." Permitting the sale of any babies (any kind of paid adoption) is perhaps tantamount to permitting the production of them for sale (commissioned adoption).

I suspect that an intuitive grasp of the injury to personhood involved in commodification of human beings is the reason many people lump baby-selling together with slavery.[10] But this intuition can be misleading. Selling a baby, whose personal development requires caretaking, to people who want to act as the caretakers is not the same thing as selling a baby or an adult to people who want to act only as users of her capacities. Moreover, if the reason for our aversion to baby-selling is that we believe it is like slavery, then it is unclear why we do not prohibit baby-giving (release of a child for adoption) on the ground that enslavement is not permitted even without consideration. Perhaps most important, we might say that respect for persons prohibits slavery but may require adoption. There might be cases in which only adoptive parents will treat the child as a person, or in the manner appropriate to becoming a person.

But this answer is still somewhat unsatisfactory. It does not tell us whether biological parents who are financially and psychologically capable of raising a child in a manner we deem proper nevertheless may give up the child for adoption, for what we would consider less than compelling reasons. If parents are morally entitled to give up a child even if the child could have (in some sense) been raised properly by them,[11] our aversion to slavery does not explain why infants are subject only to market-inalienability. There must be another reason why baby-giving is unobjectionable.

Baby-giving is unobjectionable, I think, because we do not fear relinquishment of children unless it is accompanied by—understood in terms of, structured by—market rhetoric. Relinquishing a child may be seen as admirable altruism. Some people who give up children for adoption do so with pain, but with the belief that the child will have a better life with someone else who needs and wants her, and that they are contributing immeasurably to the adoptive parents' lives as well as to the child's. Baby-selling might undermine this belief because if wealth determined who gets a child, we would know that the adoptive parents valued the child as much as a Volvo but not as much as a Mercedes. If an explicit sum of money entered into the birth parent's decision to give the child up, then she would not as readily place the altruistic interpretation on her own motives. Again, however, if babies could be seen as incompletely commodified, in the sense of coexistent commodified and noncommodified internal rhetorical structures, the altruism might coexist with sales.

The objection to market rhetoric as the discursive construction of the relinquishment of a child may be part of a moral prohibition on market treatment of any babies, regardless of whether nonmonetized treatment of other children would remain possible. To the extent that we condemn baby-selling even in the absence of any domino effect, we are saying that this "good" simply should not exist. Conceiving of any child in market rhetoric wrongs personhood. To the extent the objection to baby-selling is not (or is not only) to the very idea of this "good" (marketed children), it stems from a fear that the nonmarket version of human beings themselves will become impossible because of the power of market discourse (the domino effect).

A Special Case of Commissioned Adoption

Surrogacy is a special case of commissioned adoption. The question is whether the circumstances that make it a special case render it morally distinguishable from commissioned adoption in general, so as to justify creating a legal exception to permit the practice. In what has been the usual use of surrogacy so far, one of the would-be parents, the man, contributes his genetic material to the child to be adopted by supplying sperm. This couple approaches a woman and commissions a pregnancy. The woman promises, in return for a fee, that the child she gives birth to will be turned over to them for adoption. (There can also be the more unusual situation in which both would-be parents contribute their genetic material. Perhaps such cases will become more prevalent in the future.)

Paid surrogacy can be seen as tantamount to permitting the sale of babies. A surrogate is paid for the same reasons that an ordinary adoption is commissioned: to conceive, carry, and deliver a baby. Surrogacy appears even more like a commissioned adoption if what is important to the adopting couple is not primarily the genetic link between father and baby, but rather the opportunity, as some adopting parents have testified, to exercise control over the mother's background and genetic makeup and to monitor her pregnancy.[12]

Even if we do not see surrogacy as commissioned adoption, what difference is there between paid surrogacy and any paid adoption? There seems to be no substantive difference between paying a woman for carrying a child whom she then delivers to the employers, who have found her through a brokerage mechanism, and paying her for an already "produced" child whose buyer is found through a brokerage mechanism (perhaps called an "adoption agency") after she has paid her own costs of "production." Both are adoptions for which consideration is paid.

Others view paid surrogacy as better analogized to prostitution (sale of sexual services) than to baby-selling. They would say that the commodity being sold in the surrogacy interaction is not the baby itself, but rather some form of service provided by the birth mother.[13]

The different conceptions of the good being sold in paid surrogacy can be related to the primary difference between this interaction and (other) baby-selling: the genetic father is more closely involved in the surrogacy interaction than in a standard adoption.

The disagreement about how we might conceive of the "good" reflects a deeper ambiguity about the degree of commodification of mothers and children. Why might someone think that ordinarily a birth mother paid to relinquish a baby for adoption is selling a baby, but that if she is a surrogate, she is merely selling gestational services? Someone who thinks this way seems to be assuming that the baby cannot be considered the surrogate's property, so as to become alienable by her, but that her gestational services can be considered property and therefore become alienable. It seems to be assumed, that is, that the "good" being sold in an ordinary paid adoption is the baby, which sale we condemn, but the "good" being sold in paid surrogacy is not the baby, so we need not condemn the sale.

This way of thinking could reflect a commitment that a baby cannot be property at all—cannot be objectified—cannot even be thought of or spoken of as property. But this interpretation is implausible because of our willingness to refer to the ordinary paid adoption as baby-selling. If we were assuming that babies cannot be property, we would more readily envision an ordinary adoption for a price not as baby-selling, but rather as sale of gestational services, or fetal growth support services, followed by the gift of an unmonetized child. No one argues for commissioned adoption in general this way.

A more plausible interpretation of some people's conception of the "good" in paid surrogacy as gestational services is that this conception reflects a covert understanding that the baby is already someone else's property—the father's. This characterization of the interaction can be understood as both complete commodification in rhetoric and an expression of gender hierarchy. The would-be father is "producing" a baby of his "own," but in order to do so he must purchase these "services" as a necessary input. In a celebrated surrogacy case, *Baby M,* the trial judge was quite open about male ownership: "At birth, the father does not purchase the child. It is his own biological genetically related child. He cannot purchase what is already his."[14]

Indeed, the very label we now give the birth mother reflects the father's ownership: she is a "surrogate" for "his" wife in her role of bearing "his" child. Thus, surrogacy raises the issue of commodification and gender politics in how we understand even the description of the problem. An oppressive understanding of the interaction is the more plausible one: women—their reproductive capacities, attributes, and genes—are fungible in carrying on the male genetic line.[15]

Paid surrogacy involves a potential double bind. The availability of the surrogacy option could create hard choices for poor women. In the worst case, rich women, even those who are not infertile, might employ poor women to bear children for them. It might be degrading for the surrogate to commodify her baby (or her gestational services), but she might find this preferable to her other choices in life. So far surrogates have not tended to be rich women or middle-class career women, but neither have they (so far) seemed to be the poorest women, the ones most caught in the double bind.[16] Perhaps legitimating paid surrogacy but not permitting commissioned adoption would worsen the double bind for poor women, who are less likely to be chosen as surrogates by the kind of couples who seek this arrangement. To underscore the irony of the double bind, consider the testimony of an adopting mother who fears that surrogacy "can exploit the lower classes and the women of the Third World," and thus finds it "unconscionable" to choose as surrogates women who are poverty-stricken and need the money.[17]

Whether surrogacy is paid or unpaid, it may harbor an ironic self-deception for the women who engage in it. Acting in ways that current gender ideology characterizes as empowering might actually be disempowering. Surrogates may feel they are fulfilling their womanhood by producing a baby for someone else. Yet they may actually be reinforcing oppressive gender roles, in particular the role of the mother image in women's subordination. Even if surrogate mothering is subjectively experienced as altruism, the surrogate's self-conception as nurturer, caretaker, and service-giver might be viewed as a kind of gender role-oppression.[18]

It is also possible to view would-be fathers as (perhaps unknowing) oppressors of their own partners. Infertile women, believing it to be their duty to raise their male partners' genetic children, could be caught in the same kind of false consciousness and relative powerlessness as surrogates who feel called upon to produce children for others. Some women might have conflicts with their partners that they cannot acknowledge, either about raising children under these circumstances instead of adopting unrelated children, or about having children at all.

In addition to the concerns about commodification and gender hierarchy, permitting any kind of commissioned adoption (including surrogacy) would, it seems, given our nonideal world, injure the chances of proper personal development for children awaiting adoption. Unlike a mother relinquishing a baby for adoption (the case of paid adoption of an "unwanted" child), surrogacy is commissioned adoption. The surrogate mother bears a baby only in response to the demand of the would-be parents; their demand is the reason for the child's being born. There is a danger that "unwanted" children might remain parentless even if only unpaid surrogacy is allowed, because those seeking children will turn less frequently to adoption. Would-be fathers may strongly prefer adopted children bearing their own genetic codes to adopted children genetically strange to them; perhaps women prefer adopted children bearing their partners' genetic codes.

There is a more visionary reason one might consider for prohibiting all surrogacy. The demand for surrogacy expresses a limited view of parent-child bonding, a view in which bonding is based on genetics rather than relationship. In a better view of personal contextuality, it may be urged, bonding should be reconceived. Some people do defend surrogacy on the basis of (the genetic interpretation of) bonding. People who are sensitive to what men lose by not having the bonds with children traditionally thought characteristic of motherhood might argue that if we hope for "new" men who are more bound up with their children, we should foster progress toward this ideal by assuming a deep and personal bond between men and their genetic offspring.

It is unclear, however, why we should assume that the ideal of bonding depends especially on genetic connection. Many people who adopt children feel no less bonded to their children than do responsible genetic parents;[19] they understand that relational bonds are created in shared life more than in genetic codes. True, there is usually a deep bond between a baby and the woman who carries it, but it seems that this bond too is created by shared life, the physical and emotional interdependence of mother and child, more than by the identity of the genetic material. (It will be difficult to study this question unless—until?—childbearing by embryo transfer, in which a woman can carry a fetus that is not genetically related to her, becomes widespread.) We might make better progress toward ideals of interpersonal sharing—toward a better view of contextual personhood—by breaking down the notion that children are fathers' (or parents') genetic property.[20]

It is true that artificial insemination—and for that matter traditional procreation—pose a similar issue of genetic property. It is just as inappropriate to conceive of parent-child bonding in terms of women's genetic "property" as in terms of men's. But in the context of the present gender structure, the desire to carry on the woman's genetic line is less likely to reinforce cultural stereotyping of men as fungible child-producers. Moreover, the interests of women and men are asymmetrical because the carrying of the child in the woman's body (whether or not it is hers genetically) is a stronger factor in interrelationship with a child than an abstract genetic relationship.

All of these concerns, if taken seriously, suggest a social policy banning surrogacy, even unpaid surrogacy. But such a ban would be hard to enforce because it infringes on people's choices. At present, many people seem to believe that they need genetic offspring in order to fulfill themselves; at present, some surrogates believe their actions to be altruistic.[21] Perhaps an appropriate policy would be to permit only unpaid surrogacy. Concerns about commodification of children (and women) underwrite our society's general ban on commissioned adoption, and the difficulties with finding a justifiable basis on which to exempt paid surrogacy suggest that paid surrogacy should not be legitimated. Maybe, in other words, market-inalienability is warranted, even when a commissioned adoption involves genetic contribution from the would-be parent(s).

Market-Inalienability versus Incomplete Commodification

Market-inalienability might be grounded in a judgment that commodification of women's reproductive capacity is harmful for the identity aspect of their personhood, and in a judgment that the difficulty of distinguishing surrogacy from baby-selling harms our self-conception too deeply. In a social regime permitting any type of commissioned adoption, there is certainly the danger that women's attributes, such as height, eye color, race, intelligence, and athletic ability, will be monetized. Birth mothers with "better" qualities will command higher prices in virtue of those qualities. This monetization commodifies women more broadly than merely with respect to their sexual services or reproductive capacity.

If we wish to avoid the dangers of commodification and, at the same time, recognize that there are some situations in which a surrogate—or indeed any woman willing to become pregnant for the purpose of giving a baby to someone else—can be understood to be proceeding out of love or altruism and not out of economic necessity or desire for monetary gain, we could prohibit sales but allow a surrogate—or indeed any woman—to give her services. We might allow her to accept payment of her reasonable out-of-pocket expenses—a form of market-inalienability similar to that governing ordinary adoption.[22]

Fear of a domino effect might also counsel market-inalienability. At the moment, it does not seem that women's reproductive capabilities are as commodified as their sexuality. Of course, we cannot tell whether this means that reproductive capabilities are more resistant to commodification or whether the trend toward commodification is still at an early stage. Reproductive capacity, however, is not the only thing in danger of commodification. We must also consider the commodification of children. The risk is serious indeed because, as I have argued above, if there is a significant domino effect, commodification of some children means commodification of everyone. We have all been children. Yet, as long as fathers have an unmonetized attachment to their genes (and as long as their partners tend to share it), even though the attachment may be nonideal, we need not see children born in a paid surrogacy arrangement—and they need not see themselves—as fully commodified. Does this mean there may be less reason to fear the domino effect with paid surrogacy than with commissioned adoption in general?

The most credible fear of a domino effect—one that paid surrogacy shares with ordinary commissioned adoption—is that all women's personal attributes will be commodified. The pricing of surrogates' services will not immediately transform the rhetoric in which women conceive of themselves and in which they are conceived, but that is its tendency. This fear, even though remote, seems grave enough to warrant steps to ensure that paid surrogacy does not become the kind of institution that could permeate our discourse.

Thus, for several reasons market-inalienability seems an attractive policy solution. But it also has its drawbacks, having to do with the personal freedom of would-be buyers who yearn for children and would-be sellers caught in the double bind. There might be degrading simulations of altruism by those who would find living on an expense allowance preferable to their current circumstances.[23] Furthermore, the fact that they are not being paid "full" price exacerbates the double bind and is not really helpful in preventing a domino effect. We would also have to recognize that there would probably not be enough altruistic surrogates available to alleviate the frustration and suffering of those who desire children genetically related to fathers, if this desire is widespread. In light of the apparent strength of people's desires for fathers' genetic offspring, the ban on profit would also be difficult to enforce. As with adoption, we would see a black market develop in surrogacy.

Another policy choice to consider, therefore, is a regulatory regime that reflects incomplete commodification, perhaps similar to the one suggested for sale of sexual services. The problem of surrogacy is more difficult, however, primarily because the interaction produces a new person whose interests must be respected. An incomplete commodification regime could permit performance of surrogacy agreements by willing parties, yet stop short of forcing any kind of performance or penalty on women who change their minds.[24]

The issue of whether surrogacy agreements should be specifically performed—whether the mother who changes her mind should nonetheless be forced to hand over the baby—has received the most popular attention. In the *Baby M* case, the New Jersey Supreme Court decided that contract pregnancy was contrary to public policy and that specific performance could not be granted. (The "best interests of the child," however, were found in that case to support granting custody to the adopting couple who paid the surrogate.) If we do decide to permit an exception for surrogacy from the ban on commissioned adoption, we should not think that granting specific performance of such contracts automatically follows. To conceive of surrogacy as a special situation requiring specific performance seems to place undue weight on the supposed genetic interests of would-be fathers in their unique "property," and to undervalue both the personal development of "unwanted" children they might otherwise adopt (and become bonded to) and the personal identity of women torn between economic need and deep attachment to a baby.

A regime expressing incomplete commodification would allow a woman who changes her mind to decide to keep the baby.[25] Yet we would need to decide upon a reasonable time limit during which she must make up her mind, for it would be injurious to the child if her life were in limbo for very long. The limitation could be established analogously with statutory waiting periods for adoption to become final after birth.[26] We might wish to make the birth mother's decision to keep the child not an absolute right but only a very strong presumption, such as would be used in a custody dispute over a newborn baby in a divorce. In my view, however, ordinary adoption is the better analogy: except in very special cases, both surrogates and others who are considering relinquishing children for adoption should be able to decide after birth to keep the child.[27]

In an incomplete commodification regime, those who hire a surrogate and then change their minds should not be forced to keep and raise a child they do not want. But if a baby is brought into the world and nobody wants her, the surrogate who intended to relinquish the child should not be forced to keep and raise her. Instead, those who, out of a desire for genetically related offspring, initiated the interaction should bear the responsibility for providing for the child's future in a manner that can respect the child's personhood and not create the impression that children are commodities that can be abandoned as well as alienated. The special dangers of commodification in the surrogacy situation should serve to distinguish it from the way we treat children generally. Perhaps a regulatory scheme should require bonding, insurance policies, or annuities for the child in case the adoptive parents die or renege.[28] Perhaps a better scheme (because less oriented to market solutions) could require that alternative adoptive parents at least be sought in advance.

Because a pregnancy and a child's life are involved in the surrogacy interaction, rather than just one sexual encounter as with prostitution, "official" recognition of the interaction, with its contribution to commodification, will have to be tolerated, whether we choose market-inalienability or incomplete commodification. Decisions will have to be made about restitution in case of breach, about payment of the surrogate's expenses, and, above all, about care for the child if all parties fail to take responsibility. Even if we choose incomplete commodification, contract remedies should be avoided. Specific performance should be avoided because of the analogy to personal service agreements, and also because we should not conceive of children as unique goods. Damage remedies should be avoided because of the obvious "official" commodification involved in setting a dollar value on the loss.

We should be aware that the case for incomplete commodification is much more uneasy for surrogacy than for prostitution. The potential for commodification of women is deeper because, as with commissioned adoption in general, we risk conceiving of all of women's personal attributes in market rhetoric, and because paid surrogacy within the current gender structure may symbolize that women are fungible babymakers for men, whose seed must be carried on. Moreover, as with ordinary commissioned adoption, the interaction brings forth a new person who did not choose commodification and whose potential personal identity and contextuality must be respected even if the parties to the interaction fail to do so.

Because the double bind has similar force whether a woman wishes to be a paid surrogate or simply to create a baby for sale on demand, the magnitude of the difference between paid surrogacy and commissioned adoption is largely dependent on the weight we give to the father's genetic link to the baby. If we place enough weight on this distinction, then incomplete commodification for surrogacy, but not for baby-selling, will be justified. But we should be aware, if we choose incomplete commodification for surrogacy, that this choice might seriously weaken the general market-inalienability of babies, which prohibits commissioned adoptions.

For some people, incomplete commodification rather than market-inalienability on balance seems right for now. The reasons underlying such a judgment are these: evaluating the double bind to suggest that we should not completely foreclose women's choice of paid surrogacy, even though we foreclose ordinary commissioned adoptions; judging that people's (including women's) strong commitment to maintaining men's genetic lineage will ward off commodification and the domino effect, distinguishing paid surrogacy adequately from ordinary commissioned adoptions; and judging that that commitment cannot be overridden without harm to central aspects of people's self-conception.

In my opinion, however, market-inalienability is better for now, in spite of its difficulties. The reasons underlying this judgment are these: evaluating the double bind to suggest that poor women will be further disempowered if paid surrogacy becomes a middle-class option; and judging that people's commitment to men's genetic lineage is an artifact of gender ideology that can neither save us from commodification nor result in less harm to personhood than its reinforcement would now create. In addition, it seems significant that no grass-roots movement among women has coalesced to push for the right to engage in commissioned adoptions of any sort.

Feminism For and Against

Raising the issue of what women themselves are willing to struggle for politically suggests consideration of the feminist politics of commissioned adoption.[29] It should be clear that there are coherent feminist arguments on both sides of the general issue of baby-selling (commissioned adoption). By feminist arguments, I mean arguments advanced by those who wish primarily to make inroads against entrenched subordination of women, both conceptual and practical. By "conceptual," I mean subordination in what it now means, culturally, to be a woman, and by "practical," I mean subordination in how much money and power women now have.

One side would radically alter the status-quo regime in the name of market-based liberation. The feminist argument in favor of commissioned adoption, in favor of the full-blown market, is roughly that in this nonideal world of ours, power in the market is power, and power is liberating. Women, like men, the argument runs, should now be free to get out of their protected sphere and enter the market on an equal basis. Men in power should not tell them what to sell and what not to sell. Whatever is problematic in baby-selling (the dangers of commodification, the results for the women who do the selling and the children who are sold) should be for women to deal with as a matter of their own moral deliberation and choice.[30] Feminists who make the market-based liberation argument often apply it only to nonstandard reproduction, but the logic of the argument cannot be cabined on its own terms. If liberation requires that women themselves assess their own risks and decide what they will or will not commodify, it so requires however pregnancy is achieved.[31]

The other side would largely preserve the status-quo regime in the name of preventing harm to the personhood of women and children. The feminist argument against the market is roughly that in this nonideal world of ours, treating women like anonymous fungible breeders objectifies them and recreates subordination, and that in our culture of materialist fungible objects, children who know they have been bought will have difficulty forming a Kantian self-conception.[32] Entering the market by degrading oneself is not liberating under the circumstances; women have always both sold themselves and been degraded for it.

Neither of the coherent feminist arguments can find it an easy case to permit paid surrogacy but otherwise maintain the current "official" regime. The market-liberation position would validate paid surrogacy but also baby-selling in general; the personhood-preservation position would invalidate surrogacy along with baby-selling in general.

The difficult question for the feminist view of the situation in which we keep the status-quo regime, except permit surrogacy, is the one I described above. What makes surrogacy relevantly different from commissioned adoption, which our status-quo regime purports to abhor? Is it that a man is adopting a baby that carries on his genetic line? (Isn't that the symbolic way our culture as a whole is likely at this point in history to conceptualize the situation?) If *that* is what makes surrogacy an exception to our status-quo regime, then it appears that women are indeed fungible breeders.

In other words, from a feminist point of view, it appears that the symbolic result of an "official" regime in which surrogacy is recognized but all other paid adoptions decried is a reinforcement of aspects of the conceptual structure of sexual subordination. This regime, by keeping the status quo largely intact, denies women the liberating effect of the full-blown market that the first kind of feminist hopes for; and by making an exception that symbolically prefers the male genetic line, it reinforces the categories of subordination that the second kind of feminist fears.

It seems to me that if there is a good feminist argument for permitting surrogacy as an exception to the status-quo regime (rather than as part of a radical market-liberation approach that would permit all commissioned adoptions), it will probably start from the practice's possible effects on the traditional conception of the nuclear family. Perhaps the practice of surrogacy—in some respects like the widespread practice of divorce—can bring about new kinds of relationships of coparenting and new kinds of relationships between parents and children. This could perhaps be beneficial in transforming the traditional conception of the family as it has been in some respects oppressive for women (and children).[33] In order for this argument to be satisfying, one would want to know that these effects occurred in the practice of surrogacy, but not in ordinary commissioned adoption. Otherwise, by continuing to prohibit commissioned adoption we would still be symbolically preferring the male line if we permitted surrogacy.

It could be that if we allowed commissioned adoption, interesting relationships would develop among the various parents and the child; or it could be that commissioned adoptions would be more like arm's-length transactions. We will not be able to get empirical information about this unless we permit commissioned adoption in general. At the moment, therefore, my opinion is that if the state promotes surrogacy as an exception to the status-quo regime, not having sufficiently distinguished it from commissioned adoption in some way other than the one whose symbolism can be anguishing to feminists, feminists should remain quite troubled by the practice.

Race and Class

My discussion thus far has focused on surrogacy in the cross fire of issues raised by commodification and sexual subordination. It is necessary also to consider issues of race and class. Anita L. Allen makes the point that the practice of surrogacy does have connotations of the heritage of slavery for African-American women. Under slavery, white male owners impregnated their female slaves; slaves were surrogate mothers for their owners.[34] Allen also makes the point that if commercial surrogacy is legitimated, there is a very real danger that women of color will be used as gestational mothers to deliver white children to white genetic parents.[35]

Allen's concern is borne out by a California case, *Johnson v. Calvert*, in which an African-American woman, Anna Johnson, received both egg and sperm from the buyers, the adopting parents.[36] She changed her mind at birth about giving up the baby, but was forced to give it to the couple, a white man and an Asian woman. Unlike the *Baby M* case, in which a white surrogate mother retained parental rights even though custody was given to the buyers, the court in *Johnson v. Calvert* held that a woman in Johnson's position has no parental rights at all.

If we believe feminist market-liberationists (or for that matter free-market economists) that commissioned adoption benefits women, then it is necessary to notice that women of color do not participate much in these benefits, such as they are. The dangers that Allen points out might be less salient because of the exclusion of poor women and women of color from the practice of surrogacy, but then the double bind becomes more compelling. It appears so far that (mostly) fairly well-to-do white people engage the services of surrogates, and that surrogates themselves are (mostly) less well-to-do but not poverty-stricken white women. Legitimating surrogacy might reinforce the divisive injustices of class and race.

Now, one could respond to this situation by saying that surrogacy is just one more luxury that is available only to the rich, and, as we know, there is substantial overlap between the categories of "rich" and "white." After all, we haven't banned cosmetic surgery or moved to make it available to poor people. More to the point, we haven't banned *in vitro* fertilization and other expensive technological interventions to relieve infertility or yet moved to fund them for poor people.

We all understand already (this response continues) that in our culture the quality and extent of medical care depend upon one's place in the social hierarchy. Moreover, we know both that well to-do white couples will have an easier time obtaining a baby through "official" or "gray market" adoption channels, and that there is a tremendous demand for white infants because that is what these would-be parents desire. We all understand already that in our culture access to parenthood for those who cannot or choose not to bear their own children is biased in favor of those higher in the social hierarchy. Surrogacy is just more of the same.

I am not sure how to respond to this response. It seems despairing or uncaring just to say that one more expression and confirmation of existing patterns of subordination doesn't matter, given the existing pattern. At least we should be troubled about it; at least we should let our concern about it help us think about our culture as a whole, and about other practices that contribute to this pattern.

In our culture, the ability to become a parent seems to be important to self-conception. It seems analogous in some respects to the importance of education to self-development and full citizenship. Even though we do not ban private schools, no one welcomes the deterioration of public schools and the withdrawal from them of those privileged in the social hierarchy. Few are untroubled by white flight and what it means for the education of our young. Universal education is important to full citizenship, and many would say that a polity that does not take more care than ours to ensure equal distribution of quality education is reinforcing unjust subordination.

The parent-child relationship is important to the human form of life. All of us have had parents, and many of us make becoming parents ourselves important to our self-conception (personhood). Perhaps considerations analogous to those regarding education would imply that access to technological interventions to assist in procreation should be socially available. Some of these technological interventions could perhaps be made available to those of lower socioeconomic status without too much difficulty. But it seems that, as with private schools, it would be difficult under present social circumstances to create any regime of commissioned adoption (including surrogacy) that would be egalitarian in practice.

11

Commodification, Objectification, and Subordination

There are commodification debates—about the environment, notably—that are not centrally concerned with personhood, but in this book I have not focused on them. For those that are concerned with personhood, the reader will have noticed that worries about commodification seem to come to us linked with worries about other kinds of social oppression. If we are worried about people entering into "desperate exchanges"—poor people selling their kidneys—we are worried about maldistribution of wealth as well as commodification in the abstract. If we are worried that kidney-sellers will be disproportionately poor people of color, then we are worried about wrongful racial subordination as well. If we are worried about poor women selling their babies, then we may be worried about maldistribution of wealth and wrongful gender subordination as well as commodification in the abstract.

The question arises whether my main project in this book, to investigate commodification and personhood, isn't at least only secondary in its usefulness. Perhaps we should instead turn our attention directly to these other problems of social justice. Whether we should do so depends, among other things, on whether "mere" commodification can be usefully singled out for analysis. Whether commodification can be singled out depends in turn on the connections, if there are any, between commodification and the other kinds of social oppression, and how these connections work.

Does it make sense to consider commodification, subordination, and maldistribution separately, or are they interdependent? Is commodification worrisome only when it is coupled with subordination, or maldistribution, or both, and is it then worrisome not because of the mere fact of market pricing, but rather because of its linkage with sexism, poverty, or racism? One avenue of approach to these questions is to consider commodification as objectification. Are commodification, subordination, and maldistribution all usefully considered forms of objectification of persons?

Objectification

Consider the social "bad" of objectification. This concept derives from a Kantian worldview, in which persons are subjects and not objects. The person is a moral agent, autonomous and self-governing. An object is a nonperson, not treated as a self-governing moral agent. When we use the term "objectification" pejoratively, as in "objectification of persons," we mean, roughly, "what a Kantian moral reasoner would not want us to do." Whatever the more detailed content of this rough gloss—often it's not easy to figure out what a Kantian moral reasoner would say about a particular concrete problem—at minimum it means that objectification is failure to respect in theory and to make space in practice for the human subject. Objectification puts pressure on our conception of personhood.

The human subject—the Enlightenment person—has been problematized of late. I do not believe it is a category of understanding that we can give up, even though our understanding may (must) undergo transformation.[1] As long as we cannot give up the human subject, then its negation, objectification, also exists as a cultural category. If our understanding of subjectivity is conflicted or in process of transformation, then so is our understanding of objectification; but that doesn't mean that objectification is obliterated as a meaningful category.

If our culture changed enough to forget Kant, and agency, and intrinsic attributes entirely, and persons came to be elided with manipulable and exchangeable objects, the conception of the person would be different and perhaps no longer problematized. But that would be a culture so different from ours that it is hard to theorize about what it would be like. Maybe there would be no separate category of persons at all. In the meantime, the problematized conception of the person is associated with alienation, pain, degradation, and dissonance. That is the result of being caught in a crosscurrent. I do not mean to imply that the existence of objectification as a cultural category, which implies cultural recognizability of a distinction between persons and objects, means that the subject/object distinction must be thought of as a sharp disjunction, or one that is metaphysically grounded. As I discussed in Chapter 5, I believe, in fact, that certain kinds of relationships between persons and things tend to erode it.

In the culturally embedded Kantian worldview, persons have attributes, as part of their self-constitution as persons. Persons also possess objects that they may control or manipulate to achieve their ends as persons, the objects having no ends in themselves. (As I noted in Chapter 3, Kant would say they must control objects in order fully to constitute themselves as persons.) Objectification is improper treatment of persons because it makes them means, not ends (that is, treats them as available means, along with all other objects). As means, objects may be bought and sold in markets, to achieve satisfaction of persons' needs and desires. Objects, but not persons, may be commodified. Indeed, objectification is one of the indicia of complete commodification (see Chapter 8).

Objectification is a negative, a pejorative, when applied to persons. It operates to draw into question, or create a conflict within, our conception of personhood and our attributions of personhood. Objectification can come about in various ways. One is commodification. Objectification comes about through commodification when our cultural rhetoric conceives of certain attributes of the person as commodities that can be bought and sold. When attributes that are (or were) intrinsically part of the person come to be detached and thought of as objects of exchange, the conception of the person is problematized.

Subordination

Subordination of human beings to other human beings is a complex topic, as is the further question of under what circumstances it is wrongful. A rough formulation that will suit my purposes here is to say that wrongful subordination means unjustified dominance or exercise of power by one person or group over another. Wrongful subordination has these things in common with objectification: it is a form of improper treatment of persons that fails to recognize the other as bearing the same human status as oneself; it is a form of using others as means to one's own ends. At least in our culture, objectification may be one of the indicia of wrongful subordination, or of an important form of wrongful subordination. So, at least in our culture, wrongful subordination may be linked, through objectification, with commodification. This hypothesis is bolstered by the fact that in our culture slavery was—and symbolically remains—both the core instance of wrongful subordination and the core instance of commodification of persons.

Objectification comes about through wrongful subordination when our culture, or part of it, conceives of certain characteristics of persons—such as race, sex, or sexual orientation—as marks of lesser personhood. These marks license manipulation of those who bear the marks, that is, license treating them as means, not ends. They also license refusal to recognize in the bearers those rights and other indicia of respect otherwise conceived of as universally applicable to persons. One reason the culture of subordination is complex is that members of subordinated groups often partially internalize the prevalent rhetoric of subordination and develop a self-conception that partially reflects it, even as they seek to overcome it. Objectification can be internalized; as, for example, when women conceive of themselves in some respects as sex objects for men's use. Personhood is compromised from within as well as from without.

Another reason the culture of subordination is complex is that formal institutional structures are often at odds with social structures in practice. Women, people of color, gays and lesbians are in some respects (that is, in today's official "legal" institutions and distributions of power) conceived of as persons in the universal sense. It is possible to see Colorado's state constitutional amendment banning antidiscrimination redress for gays and lesbians as an exception, an extraordinary modern instance in which nonrecognition of universal personhood was inscribed in the official legal system itself.[2] At the same time, in other respects (that is, in today's unofficial "private" institutions and distributions of power), members of subordinated groups are conceived of or seen as less worthy than other persons.

They are caught in a conceptual/cultural crosscurrent. They are partially objectified, and our conception of the person is problematized.

In the framework of a liberal worldview, it is possible to think about wrongful subordination as a form of maldistribution. When a group of persons is wrongfully subordinated it lacks social recognition of the rights and other indicia of respect otherwise conceived of as universally applicable to persons. In a liberal worldview those rights and other indicia of respect are attributed to, allocated to, or distributed to all persons. Wrongful subordination can be thought of as a form of maldistribution because a just society *would* distribute to those in the subordinated position, as to all, equal opportunity and the bases of self-respect that would prevent their subordination. (The concept of distribution perhaps itself objectifies. Distribution assumes that persons are preexisting separate entities from the items being distributed; it presupposes a thin theory of the person, of the kind I criticized in Chapter 5. A thicker theory of the person would refer instead to attribution when dealing with core elements of personhood.)

There is much debate in social philosophy about whether maldistribution of wealth can count as the sort of maldistribution that wrongfully subordinates, and thereby diminishes, persons. Liberal theories such as those of John Rawls, Joseph Raz, and Martha Nussbaum[3] say the answer is yes. These theories conceive justice to require, at least in a culture committed as ours is to market society, that institutions be structured so as to keep people from sinking below the standard of living from which they could reasonably be able to compete on a fair basis with others and function well as citizens. For such theories of justice, self-constitution is not divorced from circumstances. Freedom and equal opportunity cannot be theorized without their socially structured enabling contexts.

Ours is a market culture with a history of racial and sexual subordination. So it is not surprising in practice that the various strands of objectification I have been discussing often come together. Commodification comes together with lingering institutional racism and sexism and with maldistribution of wealth. The market culture tends toward reductionism and measuring value in commensurable coin. This is the basis of commodification, and it makes the incommensurable, the nonreducible, the nonmonetizable, difficult to conceptualize. At the same time, the market culture also tends toward irregularities of "private" power, with the resulting subordination on the basis of wealth. And the "private" culture of lingering racism and patriarchy results in a state of affairs in which women and people of color are on the whole poorer than white men, hence more susceptible to subordination because of maldistribution of wealth as well as on the basis of race or sex.

If poor people in this social context find themselves seeking to enter into "desperate exchanges," such as selling their kidneys or their sexual services, some people will be troubled by their willingness to commodify attributes of self that our culture—our dominant culture—does not conceive of as fungible. But, as we must remind ourselves, we can hardly cure the problem of objectification by trying to ban the exchange without addressing the subordination that made the exchange seem desirable.

Thus, as we have seen in Chapter 4, trying to uncouple commodification from other kinds of objectification may sometimes result in regulation that is hypocritical. That hypocritical regulation may actually express and strengthen other forms of objectification (that is, the various forms of wrongful subordination). If many women and people of color are among those seeking to enter into "desperate exchanges," then if we ban these exchanges without changing the circumstances that led to their seeming desirable to the would-be sellers, we seem to deny freedom of choice to those who are already harmed in their freedom of choice by racism and sexism. At the same time we seem to close an avenue through which poor people would gain wealth when we prevent monetization of something that "belongs" to them.

As regards poor people, one horn of the double-bind dilemma always threatens subordination allied with maldistribution if commodification is denied. The other horn always threatens subordination allied with commodification if it is granted.

Commodification Linked to Other Forms of Objectification

What should we conclude from this? We can conclude that in a culture of commodification, sexism and racism, and great inequalities of wealth, the kinds of oppressive objectification corresponding to each "ism" often occur together. We can also conclude that we should problematize all of them, and not just commodification of persons and their attributes. We should not necessarily conclude that we should attack *only* the other forms of objectification, and not commodification along with them. Commodification can feed back into other forms of objectification of persons; the attack should begin anywhere a foothold in the feedback loop can be found.

Commodification can feed back into other forms of objectification through its rhetoric of objects traded in markets. For example, in the rhetoric of universal commodification often used by neoclassical economists to describe people's desires and values, to express one's racism or sexism in the marketplace is to manifest a "taste for discrimination." Such a "taste" is a preference to be monetized, no different from any others. In this rhetorical scheme, markets will overcome discrimination—unless market participants value discrimination enough to pay for it.[4] In this rhetorical scheme, subordination of others becomes a "product" we are purchasing, because we value it more in dollars than antisubordination, a "product" we choose not to purchase. If we view matters this way, through the rhetorical scheme of commodification, we foster subordination on the basis of race and sex because we legitimate discrimination as long as people are willing to purchase it. Moreover, viewing matters this way is at the same time a form of objectification because it doesn't recognize the personhood of those discriminated against; they are part of a "product" one purchases.

Is "Mere" Commodification Harmful?

The discourse and practice of commodification, and the conception of self and others it expresses, can also tend to be harmful in itself, at least if we do not abstract too much from our own discursive world. (Recognizing this tendency does not preclude the discourse and practice of commodification from being tolerable under certain circumstances. For example, under some circumstances we might decide that objectification in the form of wrongful subordination will be worse if we ban "desperate exchanges" than the objectification in the form of commodification we will see if we permit them.) Market discourse exists within a market culture. The cultural meaning (of course) is what renders worrisome the pricing of what we thought to be priceless. That cultural meaning has to do with our categories of severable, fungible "objects" as opposed to the realm of autonomous, self-governing "persons." Commodification of (attributes of) personhood implies objectification.

In our world there are contradictory tendencies about the meaning of pricing. As I argued in Chapter 7, the fact that money changes hands need not necessarily contaminate human interactions of sharing, although the market culture pushes in that direction. The fact that a social order makes nonmonetary sharing its norm—as in the prevalent conception of marriage—need not express subordination, although the market culture, in the context of the heritage of patriarchy, pushes in that direction. My point here is only that we should pay attention to both aspects, focusing on one or the other more sharply as the circumstances may demand. We should not limit our explorations by focusing on problems of subordination to the exclusion of problems of commodification.

But what about the issue of whether "pure" commodification, absent any other worrisome features such as maldistribution or wrongful subordination, would trouble us? That issue appears to be a professor's hypothetical. Commodification occurs in a market society, and market societies do not become fully developed in the real world without exhibiting at minimum serious wealth inequalities that problematize personhood for those at the bottom.

Much of the current debate about commodification has focused on surrogacy and sales of organs. Both of these are mixed cases; commodification is not the only worry they evoke. Third-party effects and issues of subordination and maldistribution are also involved. Still, the commodified conceptualizations at issue seem to stand out. The debate over whether people should be able to sell their kidneys or corneas raises the issue whether organs are or are not an aspect or attribute of personhood. It is not clear right now how this question should be resolved. The case of organ commodification is purer than the case of baby-selling, because babies do not choose their own commodification, as organ-sellers might. Still, we probably find it difficult to imagine, outside of professors' hypotheticals, that any comfortably well-off and unsubordinated person would be seeking to sell a kidney.

As I argued in Chapter 10, under current circumstances surrogacy can readily be culturally interpreted as reinforcing gender hierarchy, because it allows an exception to the general prohibition of commissioned adoption, and the exception privileges the male line. Like other pragmatists, I do not find it very useful to go too far into hypothetical realms unconnected to our own circumstances. But suppose the general prohibition of commissioned adoption were repealed. That would eliminate the symbolic thrust of selectively validating baby-selling only when the baby is sold to a genetic father, and gender subordination would be less clearly salient for our evaluation of the practice of baby-selling. Depending upon how we resolve remaining concerns about gender role subordination and wealth distribution, under such a regime we might think that some women's choices to sell their babies are not related to gender subordination,[5] but should instead be considered simple exercises of freedom. We might think their choices to conceive of themselves in the discourse of commodification, as traders in the market, represent expressive self-constitution on their part. Yet commodification in this case still has third-party effects on children. We might still think that the danger of promoting conceptualization of children as commodities outweighs concern for women's freedom and expressive self-constitution.

Go even further into hypothetical territory. In a case in which effects on third parties (especially children) were not directly in issue, and in which concerns about subordination or maldistribution were not present, would anticommodification regulation be an unwarranted curtailment of persons' autonomy? Perhaps so. We might imagine a world in which everyone is comfortably off, and no other factors of desperation or subordination are present. (As I said above, it is hard to get this hypothetical off the ground, because it is hard to imagine that this hypothetical society could exhibit the market structure and discourse that underwrite commodification.) Freedom of expression (to conceptualize oneself as a repository of fungible goods) might require us to permit commodification in such a hypothetical case. (See Chapter 12.) We might imagine that in such a world we could conclude that we must permit conceptualization of important aspects or attributes of personhood in the discourse of commodification, even though it tends to undermine the conception of personhood that is central to our political and moral culture. At present, perhaps, we cannot deny that it is *possible* that commodification by itself, without these other factors of social concern, would not seriously undermine personhood, even though that is its tendency, because in our world no unmixed cases of commodification of personhood seem to have arisen to trouble us.

But I suspect that this hypothetical disconnection of commodification from subordination is not a fruitful avenue of inquiry. It seems to me that wrongful subordination is going to be a worry anytime an aspect or attribute of personhood is commodified. Commodification implies objectification, and objectification, when it describes persons, seems to be one of the marks of subordination. An important issue in assessing worries about commodification is how we identify the salient aspects or attributes of personhood. I suspect the question is not separate from the question of how we define wrongful subordination of persons, although of course it is not the only issue involved in understanding wrongful subordination. If aspects or attributes of personhood that we understand to be salient become commodified, then persons are improperly objectified. If we fail to recognize and respect in other human beings any of those attributes or aspects of personhood that we understand as salient, and consequently exercise power over them as means, then, again, persons are improperly objectified; and, it seems, they are wrongful subordinated. Commodification of significant attributes of personhood cannot be easily uncoupled from wrongful subordination.

12

Free Expression

As one would expect, because of the discursive aspect of commodification there are a number of places where a legal and moral exploration of commodification intersects issues of freedom of expression. One area of exploration might be the range of ways in which expression itself is commodified: for example, advertising, and indeed the general structure of media and entertainment production; also campaign finance practices, the commodification of political candidates, and indeed the general structure of seeking and maintaining political power. These topics need book-length treatments of their own, and I will not go into them here.[1] Another area of exploration might be the complex issues of commodification raised by the pornography industry. That too is a book that I am not writing here,[2] although I will mention pornography and the social construction of gender in this chapter.

One question I do mean to explore is whether legal regulation aimed at forestalling commodification must be deemed to transgress freedom of expression insofar as discouraging commodification involves discouraging market rhetoric. It seems obvious, at least in our political culture, that even if it is wrong to sell babies, it is not wrong for Richard Posner or Gary Becker to conceive of children as commodities and speak of them in market rhetoric. But what is the status of this traditional stance once we recognize how indissoluble market rhetoric and reality are? Because social practices are at least partially constituted by our concepts and beliefs, Posner's and Becker's market conceptual scheme, if it becomes widespread, must structure, or help to structure, our relationships with our children.

Before I reconsider the traditional stance on protection of speech, I want to review the market metaphor that is central to the dominant way in which we have conceived of freedom of expression, at least in the context of liberal social thought and American constitutional law, and then contrast it with an alternative conception that better recognizes the interaction of discourse and practice and owes less to structures of commodification.

The Marketplace of Ideas

Liberal political life is sometimes conceived of in market rhetoric. In this worldview, a Leviathan is needed to overcome coordination problems and seek efficiency; Leviathan's subjects, unruly rent-seeking profit-maximizers, ceaselessly face prisoner's dilemmas and other transaction costs as they try to hold out and free-ride. But more than in the way liberalism itself is sometimes conceived, when it comes to freedom of expression a fabric of market rhetoric has been dominant, at least in the law. In the traditional legal view, freedom of expression protects a "marketplace of ideas." It promotes "free trade in ideas."

Some trace the notion of a marketplace of ideas to Mill's *On Liberty,* although that attribution can be disputed.[3] In its origin the metaphor appealed to the notion of objective truth, which could be pursued most effectively through a marketplace of ideas. It promised that we would converge on the truth through continuing arguments with our opponents. This rhetoric is still prevalent in legal discourse. At the same time, the metaphor has become more skeptical—less committed to the idea that objective truth exists—in the hands of some.[4] In their perspective, one idea is not intrinsically better or worth more than another; each idea's worth is measured only by its level of acceptance on the part of those who receive it. Indeed the value of a "value" is only the acceptance it can gain. The marketplace of ideas metaphor, once a commitment to convergence on objective truth no longer exists, signifies a laissez-faire theory of cultural development, a kind of "cultural drift" theory. Its skepticism—its aura of "Pushpin is as good as poetry"—does resonate with the skeptical reductionism of commodification.

The situation is much more ambiguous with regard to the market-place of ideas than with regard to the marketplace of economic goods, however. Although much that circulates in the laissez-faire market-place of ideas is commodified (governed by property and contract), there is also a great deal that is not, that is at least officially in the public domain. In contrast, a laissez-faire marketplace of goods consists en-tirely of commodified objects. In the contemporary era, the ideology of the laissez-faire market in economic goods has faded, and a broad range of governmental freedom to regulate is generally recognized. Yet, ironically, the ideology of the laissez-faire marketplace remains in full force when it comes to freedom of expression. Standard First Amend-ment rhetoric still has it that the marketplace of ideas must remain an inviolate laissez-faire realm. Just consider the American Civil Liberties Union's passionate defense of Nazis, Klansmen, and pornographers.

It is unclear why the market ideology has not faded with regard to expression as it has with regard to goods in general.[5] One reason for its staying power may be its ambiguity. Along with the contemporary skeptical connotations of laissez-faire, traces of the original theoreti-cal commitment to end-state truth remain.[6] The notion of (objective) truth is, unlike the notion of intrinsic economic value, something to which we keep returning.[7] Truth may not be some absolute value apart from the debate; but truth may still be conceived to be the end result of unconstrained conversation. In spite of the market rhetoric, then, it may be possible to reconceive the marketplace of ideas in terms of its role in achieving dialogic truth.[8]

At any rate, our situation is that freedom of expression, one of the core commitments of political liberalism, is conceived of primarily in market rhetoric. It is worth pausing to elaborate the metaphor, to reflect on what it means to think of ideas as commodities in a market. How does the power of this metaphor organize the way we under-stand creation and interaction of ideas?

First, objectification: Ideas are conceptually detached from the in-dividuals who have them, whether those who have them are creators and commentators—in market rhetoric, producers and sellers—or hearers and receivers—in market rhetoric, consumers or buyers. As long as ideas that meet the demand of the audience are produced, it doesn't matter how (if at all) committed to them their producers are, or how (if at all) the ideas are connected with the self-constitution of their producers. Nor does it matter who buys them or how they are connected with the buyers. It is as if buyers—people's minds—could be constituted wholly apart from the ideas that they are willing to buy from time to time. Nor does it matter where the demand comes from or how it is produced: just as in the market for goods, expenditures for advertising and packaging pay off in the marketplace of ideas.

Next, fungibility: Ideas are interchangeable, in the sense that for the purposes of the market, one idea is as good as another. In laissez-faire ideology, it doesn't matter if the market is flooded with ugly, unsafe, and degrading products, so long as people are willing to buy them. The notion of "sound bites" fits into the fungibility aspect of commodification. Moreover, one proponent of a given idea is as good as another; proponents are fungible too. Only if people are willing to buy it does it matter whether an idea is produced, and it doesn't matter who produces it—persons, groups, or corporations; advertising agencies; even the government.

In the marketplace of ideas, the government as idea-producer and disseminator is not functionally or normatively different from other idea-producers and disseminators. When it is understood as speaking, the government is just another speaker in the marketplace because, in laissez-faire ideology, the value of a commodity depends only upon the demand for it by buyers, and not upon who produces it or places it upon the market. Thus, the marketplace of ideas inscribes a public/private distinction, but it is not the one that locates the divide between the state and the free market. Instead it replicates the sovereign/proprietary distinction in the laissez-faire market for goods. When the state is acting in its sovereign capacity, it is supposed to be precluded from interfering with the natural forces of the free market, but when the state is acting as a property owner, it may become a player in the market on the same footing as everyone else.[9]

Next, commensurability: The rhetoric of the marketplace of ideas has not usually explicitly involved commensurability or money equivalence. Paeans to the marketplace of ideas do not usually declaim, "May the idea that commands the highest price win." They do in effect declaim, however, "May the idea that commands the greatest acceptance win," measured by number of adherents and intensity of commitment. This seems to be a thinly veiled commensurability: the value of ideas can be definitively ranked by their level of acceptance.

Also, of course, it is evident in practice that ideas as commodities are closely connected with dollars in a number of ways. In a marketplace the value of a commodity depends only on the demand for it, and the demand depends largely on how it is packaged and marketed. Does anyone doubt that as things stand, many ideas are accepted because of packaging and marketing? Or that major political candidates are aptly described as expensively designed, expensively packaged, and expensively marketed products? Media corporations are in the business of selling TV shows and print space to advertisers. Does anyone think it an accident that the news product they produce is not independent of the interests of those advertisers?[10]

Aligned with the reductionist aspect of commensurability, the marketplace of ideas involves a skepticism about values, as noted above. In the marketplace of ideas, the state cannot favor one group's value or expression over another's. In standard First Amendment rhetoric, state action that has an effect on expression must be viewed with intense suspicion unless it is content-neutral.[11] The worst evil is for the state to engage in viewpoint discrimination. Just as the minimal state is supposed to function only to prevent trespass and fraud so the laissez-faire market can work, in the marketplace of ideas, the state as sovereign (though not as speaker) can be only a traffic cop. If there is to be a laissez-faire market in ideas, it cannot be permissible free expression for persons or groups to drown out voices other than their own. Hence restrictions on time, place, and manner are uncontroversial in principle, on the ground of neutrality.

In other words, policing the ideas market, as in any laissez-faire market, involves only preserving competition among producers and sellers and voluntary transactions between sellers and buyers. People may not be coerced or deceived (either by sellers or by the government) into buying ideas. In the ideas market, perfect competition can be pursued by keeping barriers to entry for idea production low (for example, perhaps, by providing education so that the costs of thinking are reduced). If the cost of producing ideas remains low, the supply of them will be high. Domination of the marketplace by one kind of idea—high market share for one producer—is not necessarily a problem. Dominance of one idea need not mean that minds are monopolized in any worrisome sense. If barriers to entry are low, high market share may instead indicate market power resulting from successful product differentiation. That is, demand may be inelastic because of high consumer loyalty to one brand of ideas. Monolithic acceptance of certain ideas need not indicate market failure in the marketplace of ideas.

How do things stand with respect to the marketplace of ideas? Since the New Deal, there has been a disjunction between our level of commitment to the laissez-faire market in ideas versus the market in goods. Paralleling this disjunction is the distinction between speech and conduct that has been salient in the law (and philosophy) of freedom of expression.[12] The goods market represents the realm of acts (conduct) and the ideas market represents the realm of discourse (speech). At least in the post–New Deal era, freedom of expression uses this distinction to mark out its domain. In its stark form, the notion is that a broad range of state regulation of conduct is permissible, whereas state regulation of speech is presumptively impermissible. Only for the realm of conduct has the legal culture mitigated the extreme of commodification (laissez-faire ideology).[13] This means that judges often have to decide in particular cases whether government action is aimed at speech or conduct.

Cases of symbolic speech caused trouble for this model. Such problem cases refined the speech/conduct distinction, at least in theory, to distinguish between the relative importance of the communicative and noncommunicative aspects of people's activities, and/or between state action in which we can appropriately impute a state purpose to affect communication as opposed to state action in which communication is affected only indirectly.[14] I am not sure that these refinements have made great inroads on judges' commonsense acceptance of the stark distinction between speech and conduct. In any case, the refinements also rely on our being able to distinguish clearly between communicative impact and noncommunicative impact, and between state purpose to suppress communicative impact and other state purposes that merely suppress communicative impact indirectly. Perhaps the refinements are overly optimistic about how readily we can pull these strands apart. Or perhaps the refinements should be read as a kind of pragmatic reinterpretation of the traditional distinction, a topic I will consider below.

Liberal Legal Institutions and Culture-Shaping

The main traditional alternative to a market rhetoric conception of freedom of expression relates to a broadly republican conception of politics. This alternative understanding of freedom of expression gives primacy to political speech.[15] In this view, the purpose of freedom of expression is to foster self-government. Self-government can be narrowly or broadly conceived. If broadly conceived it involves a wide range of activities that foster appropriate self-constitution of persons as well-developed citizens.

In the political conception of freedom of expression, ideas are not conceived of as fungible market commodities. Public debate is not a process of letting the invisible hand validate a direction for the polity. Because it is not, the political conception does not stress content neutrality in the same way as the skeptical marketplace conception. When political expression has primacy, political expression must be distinguished from other kinds. This distinction requires a species of content preference. All that neutrality means in the political conception is that within the class of political speech we don't single out some as preferred and some as not: so that we know we're neutral if we give communists and fascists the same speaking rights that we give liberal democrats.

It is obvious that the political conception can be harnessed by conservative statists to curtail protection of important dissenting views or lifestyles, on the ground that they are not relevant to self-government.[16] But it need not be. It could also support a view that the commitment to self-government is vitiated unless there are pervasive cultural commitments to the bases of active citizenship (including education and economic well-being),[17] and that these commitments, among other things, involve the state in duties to foster empowerment of those who have been wrongfully subordinated or excluded.[18] The political conception of freedom of expression, in one guise, supports the view that the commitment to liberal polity is a commitment to protect certain particular values that create, enable, express, and maintain a culture of liberalism. The political conception of freedom of expression needs to select what is appropriately political, and in doing so it selects specific values that are thought necessary for liberal culture.

A number of recent theories of freedom of expression are more unambiguously committed to a family of liberal theories that are much less skeptical about values than the traditional understanding of the marketplace of ideas in legal culture (at least as I read it). In these theories, liberal institutions shape our culture.[19] The value of freedom of expression is connected to shaping and maintaining a liberal culture with particular characteristics. Debate shifts to the level of what those particular characteristics are or should be; the possibility of a neutral metalevel is denied. This is the way I see, for example, the argument that the law of freedom of expression is designed to create and maintain (against recurrent contradictory tendencies) a cultural character of tolerance.[20] This is also one way to see the argument that freedom of expression ought to protect and encourage (against recurring danger of being crushed by the status quo) "romance" or social destabilization by dissenters who are in some important sense outsiders.[21] One can also see as aimed at liberal culture-shaping the argument that freedom of expression ought to operate to create and maintain the fullest opportunities for self-actualization.[22]

In their frank recognition that liberal culture involves commitment to particular values by the state, these theories call to mind John Dewey (although their proponents are not Deweyans). Dewey thought of freedom of expression as central to developing the kind of culture that can support democracy. He explicitly recognized the interdependence of discourse and action, and the culture-shaping function of liberal institutions. Deweyan theory can still exemplify a way to conceive of the political role of freedom of expression, discursive construction and interchange, without invoking a metaphorical market.

Recall how Dewey thought of ideal democracy. First, from the standpoint of the individual, "it consists in having a responsible share according to capacity in forming and directing the activities of the groups to which one belongs and in participating according to need in the values which the groups sustain." Second, from the standpoint of groups, "it demands liberation of the potentialities of members of a group in harmony with the interests and goods which are common." Third, "[s]ince every individual is a member of many groups, this specification cannot be fulfilled except when different groups interact flexibly and fully in connection with other groups." This "free give-and-take" is related to persons' flourishing; it makes "fullness of integrated personality possible of achievement." Dewey disavowed the traditional dichotomy between individual and social values: self-constitution is possible only within a group. Indeed, the democratic ideal is nothing other than "the idea of community life itself."[23]

One reason groups are essential to individual self-development is that only in groups do we possess language and engage in communication; indeed, as Dewey argued in *Experience and Nature,* only in groups can we have mind and consciousness.[24] Groups allow us to make progress in knowledge by preserving previously acquired wisdom and tools and by allowing new insights and methods to be widely shared; and it is progress in knowledge that enables us to get closer to the democratic ideal of full development of human capacities. Thus there is a close connection between knowledge and democracy.[25]

A problem for democracy, then, is how to make all our various splintered interests and groups into one community in the sense requisite for progress in knowledge and full development of human capacities. It is clear at least that certain things are needed: unobstructed, genuine communication; open-ended experimental method; education and culture-creation to make these possible.[26] So the democratic ideal entails a democratic method. Dewey argued in *Freedom and Culture* that "democratic ends demand democratic methods for their realization."[27] An "obvious requirement" if the democratic ideal is to be fulfilled is "freedom of social inquiry and of distribution of its conclusions." Freedom of social inquiry in turn requires freedom of expression and, if it is to achieve any success in adding to the store of shared knowledge, "full publicity in respect to all consequences" that concern the public.[28] Precise knowledge of the factual details that are the consequences of social activity is needed, as well as willingness to try alternatives in order to alter the consequences. In other words, what is required is social inquiry that parallels modern scientific inquiry.

Thus, according to Dewey, experimental or scientific method as applied to social problems is the method of democracy. In order to make this method part of our social life we require education in its use, and we must use it to create a culture in which free inquiry—the method of "organized intelligence," "the procedure of organized cooperative inquiry"—is featured.[29] The culture that is needed to produce the method of cooperative inquiry is humanistic culture. Thus, for Dewey, "democracy means the belief that humanistic culture *should* prevail." The humanist view of democracy "tells us that we need to examine every one of the phases of human activity"—culture in general, education, science, art, morals, religion, industry and politics—"to ascertain what effects it has in release, maturing and fruition of the potentialities of human nature."[30] In the humanist view of democracy, freedom of expression is not a competitive marketplace but rather a cooperative pursuit of human flourishing.

Regulation and Conceptualization

What is the role of law in underwriting and expressing the humanistic culture that can support democracy? A pragmatist view focuses on the interdependence of discourse and action. Legal institutions can express culture, or they can help shape it. Where legal institutions help shape culture, they do so in part by instantiating and reinforcing particular conceptions of the nature of persons and their good. That is, they do so in part by means of discourse, by means of underwriting a conceptual scheme. Indeed it seems that the state is always involved in preferring one discourse to another. The liberal state prefers one conception of personhood, a conception involving equal status (one person, one vote). It has preferred one conception of the family, a conception involving heterosexual dyads and duties to support spouses and children.

Perhaps an obvious example for the point is the conception of gender. A conception of gender is a group possession. An individual cannot maintain and implement a conception of gender. If the legal system fails to regulate contracts and the labor market in ways that express and reinforce the conceptualization of women as beings belonging essentially to a separate "private" sphere—and even more so if it repeals previous regulation that did this—then the legal system discourages (and is openly understood as discouraging) the conception of women as belonging in a separate sphere. It promotes instead a conception of women in which their personhood in the economic aspects of life is (conceptually) indistinguishable from men's.[31] When it does this, the state makes it more difficult for dissenting groups (for example, certain fundamentalists) to maintain their previous conception of gender, even though this commitment may be at the heart of life from their point of view.

This position rejects any hard-and-fast distinction between public and private realms. It is not just that democratic government may appropriately play a part in promoting the good; it is also that, because of the cultural, symbolic nature of the government's activities, it is implicitly promoting some specific ("private") goods and discouraging others, whether it says so or not. Hence the position also implies that there cannot be any hard-and-fast distinction between government speech and the rest of government's activities. If this view of liberalism is accepted, the role of government speech in the discourse of the polity will require rethinking.

We see from this vantage point that in a legal system regulation of expression and regulation of action cannot be completely pulled apart. It is important not to move too quickly here. They can certainly be pulled apart in ordinary daily life; the speech/conduct distinction does remain useful for us. They can be pulled apart theoretically to some extent as well, in general, by refining the speech/conduct distinction with the postulate that action has a communicative aspect as well as some other, noncommunicative aspect(s). But in practice that postulate doesn't accomplish much when the issue is state structuring of important social conceptualizations such as gender or family. Not only is action communicative, but its communicative aspect (if such can be separated out) is often the main reason it is regulated.

Now I can return to the issue of how we should view the neoclassical economists' market rhetoric about babies. If we ban baby-selling, we are trying to prevent harm to babies and their parents, and to other children and their parents. That harm must be understood in terms of a conceptual structure that we find inappropriate. If commodification is the appropriate thought structure to associate with the perceived harm in baby-selling, then when we ban baby-selling we are trying to ban the communication of the idea that babies are commodities, and trying to forestall conceptualization of babies as commodities. The harm is forthrightly discursive, although our thought structure may tell us that the harm is much worse if a baby actually changes hands than if not. In this way of looking at matters, we permit the economists' market rhetoric because its harm is different in magnitude from that of consummated sales, not because it is different in kind.

One objection to this line of thought might be that I am overemphasizing the discursive element in the impulse to ban baby-selling. The objection would claim that major motivations for banning baby-selling are paternalism (rescuing sellers from decisions we think they will come to regret) and third-party effects (rescuing children from transactions that may harm them). Neither of these harms is primarily discursive, the objection might continue. Yet I would argue that both have a significant discursive aspect. It is true that sale transactions could harm children in a way not primarily related to what is communicated in the act of selling, if we find, for example, that buyers are more likely to abuse children than are nonbuyers. At least if sale transactions are prevalent, however, the harm of commodification is always there too, and the harm of commodification is contained in the socially constructed meaning of sale.[32]

It might seem that the objection to understanding a baby-selling ban at least partly in discursive terms is more solid when the issue is paternalism vis-à-vis the seller. If there are reasons to override someone's uncoerced choice to sell something, those reasons (it might be argued) need not relate primarily to what is communicated in the act of selling; they might relate instead, for example, to our estimates of how likely it is that the seller will regret selling because of her later unfulfilled need for the thing sold.

So it might be thought that our prohibition of baby-selling reflects a conviction that the mother will need the child. But we do not prohibit voluntary relinquishing of children for adoption. The worry that regret may set in is taken care of by a waiting period before adoption can become final. Any similar worry with baby-selling could be taken care of in the same way. Therefore, I do not think the paternalistic objection to baby-selling could be fully captured by the idea that we want to protect the seller from the type of regret having to do with future need. Instead I think the reasons for overriding someone's uncoerced choice to sell also relate significantly to the *meaning* of the sale. We might want to rescue the seller from communicating something she will regret. Or, in the broader version of paternalism that seems more apposite in this context, we might want to rescue her from doing wrong, where the wrong involved in the transaction simply is its effect on the conceptualization of persons; the wrong is communicative.

Pornography regulation is perhaps the best example from which to see that many battles over regulation are battles over what conceptualizations are going to be culturally reinforced by being underwritten by the law.[33] Traditional fundamentalists and some feminists both want to restrain pornography on the ground that it creates and maintains an undesirable conception of sexuality. Those feminists maintain that the undesirable conception of sexuality precludes equality for women throughout our culture, reinforcing a culture of domination and preventing the formation of a free and equal self-conception as persons.[34] Opponents who want to tolerate pornography do not dispute that law affects the discourse in which we conceive of ourselves, if they are judging that reinforcing a culture of tolerance outweighs whatever bad effects pornography has on the self-constitution of women as sexual beings, or on the conception of sexuality generally. Those who believe that pornography's effects on women's self-conception are not in fact bad still do not deny that the legal regime can affect self-conception. Only those who maintain that widespread sale of pornography has no effect at all on the common discursive framework that influences our self-conception join issue on terrain other than that of whose conceptualizations are going to get reinforced by law.

Not every legal enactment should be seen as significantly culture-shaping or culture-expressive. Yet I think those that engender divisive popular debates, such as abortion or pornography, most often should be. Regulation that discourages commodification of things important to human life readily fits into this picture. It discourages social construction, through the discourse of commodification, of something close to persons as a fungible object whose value is reducible to money or a common metric. The alternative nonregulation, omission to discourage commodification, is not neutral, if neutrality means not favoring one discursive construction over another. Either choice underwrites a conceptual structure.

Government "Speech" and Content Neutrality

If liberalism is understood in a way that recognizes the culture-shaping, discourse-structuring function of law, the role of government "speech" may well become central to the conception of freedom of expression in a way that hitherto it has not been. As long as the marketplace of ideas was conceptualized as a relatively self-contained arena in which objectified ideas competed for acceptance, the fact that the state itself put some ideas into play did not become a matter of central focus. The tendency to treat government as just another speaker in the marketplace seems to stem from the notion that people will buy commodities (ideas) in the marketplace on the basis of how much they value the commodities as compared to the competing ones available, and not on the basis of the identity or strength of whoever places them on the market.

In traditional thought about freedom of expression, state support for particular ideas has thus not been a paradigm case of impermissible market intervention, although it is understood that for the state to try to persuade an individual to espouse a particular view is impermissible if the persuasion amounts to force (just as duress would void a contract in the market for goods). Instead, as I noted earlier, the paradigm case of impermissible tampering with the marketplace of ideas has been state suppression of a particular view expressed by an individual or a group of individuals.

If we come to think that the role of the state, through its legal system, is much more far-reaching and direct in its structuring of culture and discourse than previous theory assumed, the issue of how a liberal government's expressive function itself ought to be structured should come to the fore. When it does, it will engender reconsideration of the notion of government neutrality. In the traditional conception of freedom of expression, the government is required to be neutral toward content when its regulations affect expression. This stance can be understood as the method of preventing state intervention in the self-contained marketplace of ideas; it reflects a conception of liberal neutrality. If we now believe there is no self-contained marketplace of ideas that can be walled off from state intervention, and if we now believe that the state cannot ultimately be neutral in the sense that whatever discursive structures it underwrites will exclude others, it will seem that the requirement of content neutrality at least cannot mean what it was formerly thought to mean.

In the culture-shaping conception of liberalism, many regulations further or hinder one or another possibly controversial conception of the good to some extent. Nevertheless, one possible reconsideration of the notion of content neutrality would start by noticing that pragmatically, some government actions do not affect conceptions of the good to any great extent; and pragmatically, some of them are in context completely uncontroversial. These are the ones we apprehend as neutral. To this we must add that there are excellent reasons that would support a rule—even if it would work well only in cases belonging to those pragmatically unproblematic categories—hindering government actors from purposefully suppressing views they don't like. A primary ideal reason is preservation of individual autonomy; a primary nonideal reason is keeping the power structure in check. It is not hard to see this rule as neutral or as aimed at promoting neutrality.

On the other hand, maybe a rule that broadly directs legislators and judges to be neutral with respect to people's ideological commitments is too broad to work in practice. Legislators and judges may too readily experience their own activities as neutral when in fact in context they are controversial and do substantially further their own commitments. Perhaps an example here is the Rehnquist Supreme Court's attitude about freedom of religion. A law that proscribed peyote use for everyone was seen as neutral, even though in practice it underwrote criminal penalties on Native American religion.[35] The general antidrug justification didn't single out anybody's religious commitments, and in practice the judges were willing to let the chips fall where they might. Supporting this willingness seems to be an understanding that the judges' own tacit commitment to mainstream religious culture is neutral. As various writers have noted, judges find it difficult to understand religious practices that do not incorporate Anglo-European traditions.[36]

The fact that the content-neutrality rule seems so porous to the commitments of the judges (the dominant culture) might make us think it not very effective, but all the more necessary; or it might make us think that we should seek more controllable subrules. The problems with the content-neutrality rule don't show that there cannot be pragmatic content to the notion of neutrality (quite the contrary, if we think we can perceive that legislators and judges violate it), but pragmatically it may be a notion that is too weak to accomplish much. Indeed it may be a notion that sanctions oppression.

On Pragmatism and Rules Governing Freedom of Expression

If liberalism is understood in a way that recognizes the culture-shaping, discourse-structuring function of law, regulation of social life that discourages market rhetoric—discourages the thought structure of commodification—poses no analytically special problem for the liberal commitment to freedom of expression. Nor does regulation that discourages any other conceptual structure. But this kind of regulation of course poses the same generic problems as any other regulation of social life. It may be unwise for various reasons.

Moreover, it may be unwise either in particular cases or in classes of cases. If we are able to say that such regulation is unwise in particular classes of cases, it is likely that we will also find it pragmatically desirable to have rules about those classes of cases. It is then possible that the classes of cases for which we find rules desirable will track the rejected artifacts of the marketplace-of-ideas metaphor. If the traditional distinction between content neutrality and viewpoint discrimination, for example, or the one between speech and conduct, animates a rule we find pragmatically desirable, then perhaps the change I am postulating in the philosophical underpinning of liberalism makes no difference at the level of doctrine and practice.

Some are attracted to this view.[37] Some might say, for example, that the distinction between speech and conduct remains just as firm whether it is thought ultimately to reflect practice or some "deeper" foundation. But some are attracted to an opposite view: when traditional formalism is rejected, they think, rules are impossible; everything is indeterminate or decision making is radically particularist.[38] Some might say, for example, that when the distinction between speech and conduct is shown to have no firmer foundation than practice, the logical consequence is that speech can be regulated just as readily as conduct (the marketplace of ideas should be treated exactly as the marketplace of everything else).[39]

I think that both of these extremes are unsatisfactory. Pragmatism does not preclude rules; how could it? Rules are a distinctive element of our form of life. Yet when we realize that rules are socially based we realize that the inescapable feeling of ruleness we experience when we are faced with what we recognize as a rule is culturally produced and maintained, and can be culturally changed. This realization must, I think, have some effect on our practice.

The effect could be a psychological awareness that some of the rules we confront are mutable. They respond to our work on them, in which we connect them with their underlying ground and with the surrounding culture of other rules that intersect them.[40] The effect could be that a rule stays in effect for us only so long as we think it useful with respect to its underlying ground, or only so long as we think it is useful to have a rule in this class of cases, or only so long as we think it is useful to have this particular rule in light of our need to have rules generally and to maintain the possibility of their implementation.

These reflections make me think that although rules are of course possible, and not only useful but indeed indispensable, still we may have to lower our expectations of what rules can accomplish.[41]

Speech and Conduct Revisited

The fuzzy speech/conduct distinction interests me because it parallels the (fuzzy) distinction between literal commodification (markets in reality) and commodification in discourse (market rhetoric). Even though there is no analytical bright line between speech and conduct, no one denies that there is a pragmatic distinction. In our form of life we readily recognize that certain behaviors count as speech and others do not. Moreover, for at least some category of harms (including inappropriate commodification), we can recognize that the harm is not separable from the thought structure that enables it, but still tend conventionally to perceive the harm as orders of magnitude worse when it is expressed in conduct than when it is not. As noted earlier, we might use this difference in magnitude of harm, if it exists, to rehabilitate the notion that regulation of speech is much harder to justify than regulation of conduct.

Although we do readily recognize that certain behaviors count as speech and others do not, we cannot use the distinction to give precise answers in cases in which dispute breaks out.[42] There is no a priori method for deciding that wearing armbands to protest the Vietnam War is speech,[43] but that burning one's draft card for the same reason is conduct.[44] Even if we refine the distinction to take into account that activities have both communicative and other aspects, there is no a priori method for deciding that one or the other will be paramount in a given case, with all its surrounding circumstances. There is no a priori method for deciding that prohibiting flag-burning is impermissible because it is aimed at communicative impact,[45] but that prohibiting political posters on utility poles is permissible because it is not aimed at communicative impact.[46] Moreover, the attempt to understand legislative action as directed solely toward either communicative or noncommunicative aspects of an activity seems to reinscribe a distinction between speech and conduct. In situations in which the strands cannot be pulled apart, then neither can the legislative motive be understood as directed at one or the other.

Because of this fuzziness, if there is a legal rule protecting speech but not conduct, judges are likely to use their estimate of how socially dangerous the behavior is in context to help them decide whether the behavior should be labeled speech (not too dangerous) or conduct (too dangerous). Likewise, if there is a legal rule that a state purpose to suppress communicative impact is impermissible, whereas some other state purpose having the "indirect" effect of suppressing communicative impact is permissible, judges are likely to use their estimate of how socially dangerous the behavior is in deciding whether what the government did should be considered to be aimed at communicative impact or found to affect it only indirectly. The Vietnam-era regulation prohibiting destroying one's draft card was not judged to be aimed at expression (or communicative impact). Neither were regulations from the era of the House Un-American Activities Committee directing that a resident alien who had formerly been a member of the Communist party, at a time when membership was not illegal, be deported and deprived of his social security benefits.[47]

Although we will thus be remanded pragmatically to the underlying substantive question of social dangerousness in certain kinds of disputed cases, this remand doesn't mean that rules or classifications must be useless in guiding decisions.[48] Suppose we decide that as a general matter, even when the harms of culture-creation through discourse are the issue, only those activities that count as normal everyday garden-variety conduct are ever likely to be dangerous enough to try to curtail. This kind of pragmatic rule seems, at least at first, to accord with intuition. Even if we decide that commodified conceptualizations of children should be discouraged, in other words, we would undoubtedly endorse the rule that the discouragement can take the form of trying to prohibit baby-selling but may not take the form of trying to prohibit reading of Posner's or Becker's writings.

Note, however, that the reason for considering regulating the reading of Posner's or Becker's writings and the reason for considering regulating baby-selling are the same. The reason is discouraging the conceptualization of children in the discourse of commodification because that is a harm to personhood. It would not be useful to try to characterize this reason as inherently aimed either at speech or at conduct. The pragmatic reinterpretation of the speech/conduct distinction has to stay at the level of concrete implementation of social purposes; it cannot serve a priori to weed out bad purposes from good ones.

In the preceding paragraphs I've suggested that the speech/conduct distinction could be reinterpreted at a broad pragmatic level: all speech (in our commonsense understanding of speech) is a lot less dangerous than all conduct (in our commonsense understanding of conduct). But once we think about it, the question is not so easy. A long-term media blitz reinforcing racist stereotypes (endlessly repeating that "they" are stupid, lazy, untrustworthy, and so on) seems a lot more dangerous to equality than, say, the unpublicized action of one prejudiced landlord who rejects a tenant for racist reasons. A full-blown free-market advertising structure for babies for adoption, even if they are not nominally being sold, may produce more harmful commodification than failure to prosecute consummated sales of babies so long as no channels of communication and no persons but the immediate parties are involved.

The standard answer to this kind of problem in the marketplace-of-ideas regime was that the remedy should be not suppression but more speech (known as the counterspeech argument). As long as there are no barriers to entry into the marketplace of ideas, opposing views will be expressed, and truth must eventually win out. There are various reasons why the counterspeech argument now seems unsatisfactory. One is that we, even those of us who are not skeptical about truth, are no longer so sure that truth will win out in a free market. Maybe people will not demand truth in the marketplace; we understand our response to media blitzes to be largely irrelevant to their truth or falsity. Moreover, those opposing a dominant position are unlikely to be able to mount media blitzes.[49]

One can seek to rehabilitate the counterspeech argument by arguing that irrespective of how dangerous speech (and counterspeech) is, a political commitment to reasoned public discourse requires that more speech be the only remedy, up to the point of imminent danger and no time for more speech.[50] This reasoning switches the argument from the marketplace of ideas to a species of republican political conception. It requires an ideal commitment to reasoned public discourse even in the face of what we pragmatically now know about media blitzes and the realities of power that decide who is able to mount them. The ideal of reasoned public discourse retains its appeal in liberal culture, but it is not clear today what pragmatic rules would best underwrite it.

Perhaps a generalization that speech is likely to be a lot less dangerous than conduct, even though not hard and fast, could be retained as a presumptive standard.[51] But maybe pragmatic reconsideration should proceed at a lower level of generality. Always understanding that speech and conduct cannot be firmly held apart when disputes arise, perhaps there are subcategories in which it makes sense to have a rule (and not just a presumptive standard) that speech is a lot less dangerous than conduct. Books, at least, would fall uncontroversially within such a subcategory, but certain kinds of advertising would not. The regulations against advertising that I suggested in aid of an incomplete commodification of sexuality (see Chapter 10) would remain controversial on free speech grounds, like proposed regulations that would suppress core categories of pornography. In these cases no rules can save us from having to assess the seriousness of the harm, including the likelihood of its occurrence.

13

Compensation

The practice of compensation is an obvious aspect of the law in which to investigate commodification. Compensation pays dollars "for" harms. Any time the harms are not merely dollar losses, but instead involve injury to attributes of personhood or to things close to the person, we can wonder whether compensation signals a troublesome commodification. In this chapter I will focus on compensation "for" personal injury, because that seems the obvious place to begin. The issue can be raised in many other legal realms: condemnation of property at the market price, if the property is personal rather than fungible; damages for invasion of civil rights by government actors; and even political reparations.[1]

When someone who has lost an arm in an accident receives $100,000 in compensation through the tort system, what does this transaction mean? Does it mean that an arm is "worth" $100,000? Our legal practice reflects conflict in how compensation for personal injury is understood—compensation is a contested concept. Commodified conceptions of compensation, in which harm to persons can be equated with a dollar value, coexist with noncommodified conceptions, in which harm cannot be equated with dollars. In a commodified conception, harm and dollars are commensurable, and in a noncommodified conception, they are incommensurable. Once we understand the relationship of commensurability to the issue of what

184

compensation means, we will be in a better position to understand the contemporary debate about whether the tort system should compensate for "nonpecuniary" harms.

Moreover, understanding the relevance of commensurability to this debate about compensation should shed light on the general problem of how to conceive of corrective justice. If we do not accept a commodified conception of compensation, in which harms and money are commensurable, then payment of money cannot restore persons to the status quo ante, and corrective justice will be impossible if that is what we demand of it. In this chapter I draw attention to an alternative conception of corrective justice. In the alternative conception, compensation is understood not as a commensurable quid pro quo for harm, but rather as a form of redress: affirming public respect for the existence of rights and public recognition of the transgressor's fault with regard to disrespecting rights.

Commodified Conceptions of Compensation

The proponents of law and economics conceive of tort law in market rhetoric. Tort law is an engine for accomplishing economic efficiency by maximizing the amount of dollar value in the world, given some set of entitlements as a starting point. A deterrence rationale most comfortably inhabits this market model. It tells us to perform a cost-benefit analysis: We should pay out damages as long as the cost to society of paying them will deter possible tortfeasors from imposing greater accident costs in the future.

In a pure deterrence model, can we even conceive of damages as "compensatory"? Perhaps not. If there is a core understanding in which "compensatory" denotes some direct relationship between the damages paid and the victim's loss and its magnitude, then, at least prima facie, damages are not "compensatory" in the pure deterrence model. Yet the deterrence model, at least when couched in market rhetoric, does equate the dollar value of damages with the dollar value of harm, and this is the equation that expresses commodification.

In the deterrence model, the equation comes about as follows. An economically rational tortfeasor would choose to implement safety measures that would prevent an accident if these measures cost it less than paying damages, and would choose to let an accident happen if the safety measures to prevent it would cost more than paying the damages. Society controls the level of safety measures, and thus the amount of harm from accidents, by the level at which it sets damages. The optimal level of safety measures for society, according to the model, is the level at which any further expenditures for safety would be more expensive than the "costs" of the harms that will occur without them. Thus, in this model, the harm to victims must be a known dollar value in order for the proper amount of damages to be set. Even if the reason the tortfeasor must pay is to achieve deterrence rather than to "compensate" the victim for her loss, in this model there is an equation between the value of harm and the value of damages.[2]

This view of damages conceives of harm to victims in market rhetoric. Injuries to life and health are "costs," just as the dollars expended for safety measures, against which they are balanced, are "costs." I call this a commodified conception because it conceives of the harm to the injured victim as commensurable with money, as if the victim's interest in being free of injury were the same as money or a fungible commodity she possessed. In this commodified conception, theoretically the harm is simply a cost to the victim. In market rhetoric, if I lose my arm or my car keys, either way it is simply a cost, although one cost may be greater than the other.

Many who are sympathetic to economic reasoning do not adopt this pure deterrence model. Instead, at least implicitly, they adopt a mixed view in which deterrence is consequentially important because it creates incentives for efficient activities and uses of resources, but rights like bodily integrity also are recognized. In the mixed view, rights are set by natural law, or by a rule-utilitarian precommitment procedure, or are simply presupposed, but in any event are set by other than the same consequentialist concerns that animate deterrence.

Even if we think a core requirement of compensation is that payment bear a direct relationship to the individual victim's harm (so that in a pure deterrence model damages are not compensatory), the mixed economic view leaves room for a quid pro quo conception of compensation that squarely meets the requirement. In a quid pro quo conception of compensation, payment is in return for rights that are violated. Compensation restores the dollar equivalent of wrongfully divested entitlements to their rightful holders. Compensation makes the victim completely whole; that is its theoretical aim, at least. In market rhetoric, the victim is conceived to be indifferent with respect to the alternatives of being harmed and getting the payment, and not being harmed at all. When the cost in dollars of the injury is paid, the victim is made whole.

The clearest form of a commodified conception of compensation appears in this mixed view, because the model treats injury and payment of damages exactly like the sale of a commodity the victim owns. I will refer to this as the core commodified conception. In a "transaction" between the injurer and the victim, the victim "trades" her bodily integrity for a suitable payment of money. In the economic pure deterrence model, the person's interest in bodily integrity is valued in dollars, as if it were a commodity the person owned; in the mixed view, in addition, the tortfeasor must pay in order to provide an equivalent in dollars to "compensate" for the divested commodity.

Noncommodified Conceptions of Compensation

The core noncommodified understanding of compensation relates, I believe, to a particular conception of corrective justice. There is no canonical conception of corrective justice. In a rough understanding that I find useful, "corrective justice" means to make required changes in an unjustified state of affairs between an injurer and a victim, when the injurer's activity has caused the injustice, so that such changes bring about a just state of affairs between them, and one that is related in a morally appropriate way to the status quo ante. A shorthand way of saying this is that corrective justice restores moral balance between the parties. From this perspective, tort law is an engine for bringing about corrective justice by requiring tortfeasors to make recompense to their victims. This view of tort law is not couched in market rhetoric. Its core concepts are rights and wrongs, not dollars and exchange.

Sometimes it appears that corrective justice can be accomplished by simply unwinding a wrongful interaction, restoring the parties to the status quo ante. Stolen money can be given back; goods obtained by fraud can be returned to the owner. Lawyers call this restitution. Some philosophers refer to rectification rather than restitution, and hold that rectification is what corrective justice requires.[3] "Rectification" means restoring the status quo ante or a state of affairs equivalent in moral value to the status quo ante. Thus, even when restitution of money or goods can be made, it may not amount to rectification.

Rectification may be incomplete without attention to other injuries brought about by the wrong, such as loss of use value, loss of opportunity to sell at a profit, or emotional distress.

In personal injury cases, rectification in the form of restitution is not possible, and compensation is used instead. Here the question arises, Can compensation serve as rectification? For the core commodified conception of compensation, the answer is yes. In that conception, the victim is by definition indifferent with respect to the alternatives of having been injured and having the money, on the one hand, and not having been injured but not having the money, on the other. The state of affairs after injury and compensation (having been injured and having the money) is identical with, or at least the moral equivalent of, the status quo ante (not having been injured but not having the money). But in other conceptions of compensation the answer is less clear that compensation can be rectification, or indeed clear that it cannot.

A noncommodified conception of compensation most comfortably inhabits a noncommodified view of torts in general, a view in which the central concepts are right and wrong, not "costs." In such a view, compensation does not imply commensurability between the harm and the payment; injuries and dollars are not ranked on a single scale of value. What else can compensation mean?

I want to call to mind the following possibility. Requiring payment is a way both to bring the wrongdoer to recognize that she has done wrong and to make redress to the victim. Redress is not restitution or rectification. "Redress" instead means showing the victim that her rights are taken seriously. It is accomplished by affirming that some action is required to symbolize public respect for the existence of certain rights and public recognition of the transgressor's fault in failing to respect those rights. In this conception of compensation, neither the harm to the victim nor the victim's right not to be harmed is commensurable with money. Neither is conceptually equated with fungible commodities. And this is—or might be—so even if, because of money's symbolic importance for us, large cash payments would be needed to symbolize a serious offense.

Many social democrats view the tort system not as an engine for delivering corrective justice, but rather as one aspect of a social insurance regime.[4] A different noncommodified conception of compensation can be part of such a view. In a social insurance regime, society makes payments to those in need for various reasons, including social disadvantage regardless of cause, and emotional, mental, or physical disabilities, whether congenital or caused by illness or accident.[5] In such a scheme, payments to accident victims are not compensatory in the two core senses I have described. They are not paid out to make the victim whole (core commodified conception) or to give the victim redress against someone whose activities have wronged her (core noncommodified conception). Payments may be compensatory in another sense, however, in that they are supposed to give the victim some needed wherewithal to lead a satisfactory life, thereby making up for—compensating for—the capabilities or advantages the victim lacks. This is a noncommodified conception because it does not suggest that the money payment is taken in trade for the harm or is equivalent to the harm in exchange value.

To summarize: Compensation seems to be a contested concept. Commodified and noncommodified conceptions are well crystallized, and they coexist. There is a core commodified conception, in which payment for an injury is like buying a commodity, and a less central commodified conception, in which harms are "costs" to be measured against the costs of avoiding them. There is also a core noncommodified conception, in which payment provides redress but not restitution or rectification, and a less central noncommodified conception, in which payment makes up for certain social disadvantages.

Compensation and Commensurability

How is value commensurability connected with the issue of compensation? At least at the theoretical level, if we think there are widespread areas of commensurability, we can be more confident that compensation, if calibrated correctly, can amount to rectification. If the fact that we see people making choices between a sum of money and someone's company means that money and company are ranked on a scale, then it should be possible to rank money and having one's limbs intact, money and having one's parent alive, or money and having the companionship of one's child. All we need for rectification in such a case is to pay the amount of money that is barely enough for the person to have chosen the money over the other thing she values. It may be true that in some cases no amount of money would satisfy this condition. There may be pockets of incommensurability.

But those whose intuitions run to inferring that many of our values can be scaled think that such cases are rare.

Both the reductionist and the scalar claims of commensurability can give rise to what I have called commodified conceptions of compensation. In the simplest case, the reductionist claim is put in monetary terms. That is, if it is claimed that there is some "stuff" in terms of which all other values can be expressed, and furthermore that the "stuff" is money, then all things one values reduce to commodities one owns, and compensation amounts to payment for the sale of one's commodity. The scalar claim also yields a commodified conception of compensation. If each thing someone values can be ranked as either better or worse than a sum of money, then, even if values do not reduce to money, there is in principle a sum of money that will provide rectification. In that case, it still appears that values are commodities that can be sold.

What about reductionism not involving money? Some utilitarians might claim that all values are reducible to one kind of "stuff"—utils, as time-honored convention would have it—but that utils cannot be made equivalent to money, perhaps because utils are wholly subjective. Clearly, then, interpersonal utility comparison becomes problematic,[6] and it might seem that this is a less clear case of commodification. Yet as long as utils can be scaled in theory, which seems to be implied in the claim that they are one kind of "stuff," this case is the same as the one involving the scalar assumption by itself.

Many utilitarians have the stubborn intuition that most values can be scaled. Perhaps that is what makes them utilitarians. Many economists have the same stubborn intuition, with the further unquestioned assumption that all values reduce to money. From this point of view, compensation is unproblematic, at least in theory, even if we believe that in order to satisfy the demands of corrective justice, compensation must amount to rectification. In practice, as I noted earlier, deterrence, rather than corrective justice, often fits better with economic views, so the question of rectification may not often come up for such theorists. Nevertheless, economists often have mixed views as I described, believing that some rights exist other than for consequentialist reasons. In such a view we are likely to find a version of corrective justice, conceived of as restoring wrongly divested entitlements or their equivalents to their rightful holders. In such a mixed economic view, compensation can substitute for the restoration of the entitlement.

Compensation poses a problem for those whose intuitions about commensurability run the other way. If corrective justice requires rectification, and if injury cannot be translated into money, how can payment of money ever amount to rectification, so as to satisfy the demands of corrective justice? The problem, an important one, has been too little noticed, perhaps because the connection between compensation and commensurability has been too little noticed. In my view, the problem will have to be dissolved rather than solved. That is, I think it most likely that the problem incommensurability poses for rectification as corrective justice will be solved only by developing an understanding of corrective justice that does not require rectification.

In other words, there must be some way to restore moral balance between the parties other than by putting the parties into the status quo ante, which may be irretrievable, or by putting them into a state equivalent in value to the status quo ante, which may be unachievable given the fact of incommensurability. As my earlier description of a core noncommodified conception of compensation reveals, I suggest that compensation can symbolize public respect for rights and public recognition of the transgressor's fault by requiring something important to be given up on one side and received on the other, even if there is no equivalence of value possible. Although I cannot now take on the task of trying to outline an appropriate theory of corrective justice, perhaps such a theory will conclude that this kind of redress is what corrective justice demands. At any rate, it is well to note the importance of incommensurability for the general theory of corrective justice.

The Pain and Suffering Debate

In tort law there is a debate in progress about whether compensation should be available for "noneconomic" or "nonpecuniary" harms such as pain and suffering or intense emotional distress. For these harms, the traditional common law position adheres by and large to a noncommodified conception of compensation. Yet the traditional position shows signs of commitment to internally conflicted (plural) meanings.

The *Second Restatement of Torts* draws a clear distinction between harm to "pecuniary interests" and "bodily harm or emotional distress." For pecuniary interests, "compensatory damages are designed to place the person in a position substantially equivalent in a pecuniary way to that which he would have occupied had no tort been committed." That is, for pecuniary interests, compensation is rectification. For other interests, however, compensation means something else. The *Restatement* goes on to say:

> When however, the tort causes bodily harm or emotional distress, the law cannot restore the injured person to his previous position. The sensations caused by harm to the body or by pain or humiliation are not in any way analogous to a pecuniary loss, and a sum of money is not the equivalent of peace of mind. Nevertheless, damages given for pain and humiliation are called compensatory. They give to the injured person some pecuniary return for what he has suffered or is likely to suffer. There is no scale by which the detriment caused by suffering can be measured and hence there can be only a very rough correspondence between the amount awarded as damages and the extent of the suffering.[7]

Thus, the traditional legal position on pain and suffering seems committed to incommensurability. Rectification is not possible ("the law cannot restore the injured person to his previous position" or to its equivalent), because the value to the victim of freedom from pain and suffering cannot be reduced to money (the harm is "not in any way analogous" to a loss of money, and the desirable state, "peace of mind," is "not the equivalent" of a sum of money), nor can amounts of suffering be arrayed on a scale ("there is no scale") so that they might be paired in parallel with amounts on the money scale.

What then does compensation mean, if it cannot be rectification? About this, the *Restatement* and the legal discourse it crystallizes supply little, and what they do supply seems to lean ambivalently back toward commensurability. The victim receives "some pecuniary return for what he has suffered"; the dollars awarded in damages do have a "very rough correspondence" to the extent of the harm. If the pecuniary return is "for" the suffering, if indeed it is a "return," the process can be understood in market rhetoric; suffering is an investment in exchange for which a return is received. If there is a "correspondence" between amounts of dollars and amounts of suffering, however "rough," suffering can be understood as scalable in the way that money is, and the earlier denial of commensurability ("there is no scale") is undercut.

The *Restatement* is accurate in conveying the traditional commitment to incommensurability, both in its ambivalence and in its inarticulateness about what compensation means when it does not mean rectification. Some courts say the purpose of compensation for pain and suffering is to come as close as possible to rectification, even while admitting that there is no way we could know what coming close would mean. The following is typical:

> An economic loss can be compensated in kind by an economic gain; but recovery for non-economic losses such as pain and suffering and loss of enjoyment of life rests on "the legal fiction that money damages can compensate for a victim's injury." We accept this fiction, knowing that although money will neither ease the pain nor restore the victim's abilities, this device is as close as the law can come in its effort to right the wrong. We have no hope of evaluating what has been lost, but a monetary award may provide a measure of solace for the condition created.[8]

This passage makes very clear the conflict in the traditional understanding of compensation. We are to come close to something amounting to rectification (aiming to ease the pain and restore the victim's abilities) while recognizing that we have no hope of evaluating what it is we are to come close to. This conflict may codify the conflicting intuitions about commensurability existing in our legal culture. One possible reason that legal discourse remains ambiguous, then, is that it reflects a conflict between different conceptions of compensation caused by different degrees of commitment to incommensurability. Another possible reason legal discourse has remained ambiguous or inarticulate about what compensation in such cases is for, and has kept making the rhetorical gesture of "coming close" to rectification, may be an effort to avoid implying a punitive meaning for compensation. One thing that compensation is not supposed to do in ordinary tort cases is punish the wrongdoer.

If compensation does not make the victim whole and does not punish the wrongdoer, what is left? One suggestion, as the last quoted passage mentions, is that money can provide solace for the victim. In a well-known article that marks the beginning of the contemporary debate about damages for pain and suffering, Louis Jaffe suggested that "though money is not an equivalent it may be a consolation, a solatium."[9] Yet the notion of solace, by itself, does not provide very strong support for a practice of compensation. It does not seem satisfactory from the point of view of corrective justice, since it does not seem to "right the wrong." And it causes problems for justifying any payment at all in cases in which the victim is in no condition to find any solace in money because she is dead or permanently comatose.

In fact, when incommensurability is assumed, there is a problem with payment on account of injuries to dead or comatose victims whatever the rationale for damages. In a case in which fungible property is wrongfully taken or destroyed, in which money damages can presumably make the victim whole, it is easy to understand the victim's rights to compensation not to depend at all on the victim's ability to receive it consciously; and it is easy to understand her compensation rights to pass to her successors just as the equivalent property rights would have. By contrast, if we do not conceive of bodily integrity as a property right—if we do not conceive of it in market rhetoric—it becomes harder to understand why the victim would have any rights to compensation unless she were conscious of suffering, and harder to understand why her compensation rights might inure to her surviving relatives.

Can my right to be free of pain and suffering be transgressed if I am rendered permanently unaware of pain? If not, it appears no damages should be paid to me. Is my right to be free of pain and suffering a "thing" I can will to my children? If not, it appears my surviving children should not be paid damages on account of my suffering. They might, of course, be paid on account of their own emotional distress.[10] They are in a condition to receive solace; but what sense does it make to pay them money intended to give me solace? Given incommensurability, solace is not a commodity. Solace is not transferable or inheritable like property.

These types of concerns may be reflected in traditional legal requirements that the victim be conscious of suffering,[11] and, in death cases, that no payment is available for death itself.[12] These types of concerns also may be reflected in varying legal responses to the issue of payments to survivors on account of the victim's suffering, as well as on account of their own suffering because of the victim's death.[13] Possibly the traditional limitations on recovery for pain and suffering in these situations reflected recognition of incommensurability.

Given incommensurability between injuries and dollars, another of Jaffe's proposals about what compensatory damages might mean in the context of pain and suffering seems promising. He suggested that "one who has suffered a violation of his bodily integrity may feel a sense of continuing outrage," and that the payment of money may somewhat "wipe out" this sense of outrage. Payment of money might succeed in mitigating the sense of outrage because it might make the victim feel that society really values her personality and bodily integrity. "[B]ecause our society sets a high value on money," Jaffe said, it can use "money or price as a means of recognizing the worth of non-economic as well as economic goods." Payment of money "will signify society's sincerity."[14] This formulation is similar to the conception of redress to which I earlier correlated a core noncommodified conception of compensation.

Jaffe's suggestion resonates with the noncommodified conception of compensation because it attributes a plausible meaning to compensation other than punishment or quid pro quo: recognizing the wrong and signifying its weightiness. Weightiness is signified by something of great importance in our society—money. It need not be of overwhelming significance that this thing, money, is unrelated to the harm suffered, although exactly what the significance of that unrelatedness is remains to be investigated. The claim is that money may serve as a form of redress, though not rectification, because of its importance in our culture. Moreover, when the wrongdoer is a business entity, as is often the case, money is the only thing important to it, and thus the only significant thing it can yield up. Money is the only thing it can give to a person in recognition of the wrong for which it is responsible.

In spite of his suggested rationale, Jaffe found the case for damages for pain and suffering to be uneasy. In a consequentialist move that I think is empirically doubtful, he suggested that damages for past pain might not be appropriate, because past pain is unlikely to be causing present outrage; presumably, therefore, payment is not needed to relieve outrage. He also was troubled by the very intractability—one might say the very incommensurability!—of incommensurability, which he thought counted as a reason not to pay anything: "And even granting these arguments there must be set over against them the arbitrary indeterminateness of the evaluation." He also thought that, leaving aside insurance, "doing honor to plaintiff's pain" might be an injustice in light of the "real economic loss" to the negligent defendant; and that, taking insurance into account, "it is doubtful that the pooled social fund of saving should be charged with sums of indeterminate amount when compensation performs no specific economic function."[15]

We see here the germ of an argument that the mere fact of incommensurability means we should not pay. To Jaffe, the twin earmarks of incommensurability—"indeterminacy" and "no specific economic function"—were enough to render the case for compensation very dubious. By finding the earmarks of incommensurability to be reason enough that no payment should be made, Jaffe's argument denies the significance of incommensurability. Indeed, by treating "honor to plaintiff's pain" as capable of being outweighed by defendant's economic loss, the argument ambivalently reinscribes commensurability. In a sense, Jaffe faithfully tracked the traditional legal position, even as far as encapsulating its ambivalence.

Some of Jaffe's contemporary successors are pressing these arguments against compensation for pain and suffering ever more forcefully. In order to understand the vehemence of these arguments, it is necessary to switch to realpolitik. The backdrop of these debates is a "crisis" in tort liability, in which there have been persistent perceptions that juries are awarding "too much" to injured plaintiffs. Insurers and their sympathizers, doctors and their sympathizers, product manufacturers and their sympathizers—all agree that damage awards are too high. Only plaintiffs and their attorneys contend otherwise. Compensation for pain and suffering becomes a focal point because it is claimed that allowing it gives juries too much discretion to implement their sympathies with injured plaintiffs at the expense of (what the defense advocates fear that jurors perceive as) corporate deep pockets.

Incommensurability gives defendants and insurers an argumentative handle. They say that damages for pain and suffering are indeterminate, that there is no way to evaluate their appropriateness, that there is no serious check on the jury's discretion. Many, like Jaffe, have the intuition that the mere fact of indeterminateness is an argument against compensation. Incommensurability is evidently worth big bucks to defendants.

Moreover, there is an ironic way in which incommensurability links the interests of defendants, especially insurers and product manufacturers, with the theoretical view of certain economists. In what has become a standard economic view, put forward in the legal literature by Alan Schwartz, manufacturers of defective products should not have to pay those pain and suffering damages that would not have been part of a rational bargain between the manufacturer and the buyer of the product.[16] That is, unless the product buyer has bargained and paid for insurance against her own pain and suffering should an accident occur, it is inefficient for tort law to insure her against her loss. I will call this the optimal-insurance view.

The proponents of the optimal-insurance view argue that it is irrational to insure oneself against future losses of this kind, because of the expected diminished value of one's wealth in an injured state. The optimal-insurance view is part of a larger economic worldview in which it is given that persons are maximizers of dollars or utils, and rationality is maximization. Given the model's assumptions about how much people value their dollars when they are healthy versus how much they value them when they are impaired or in pain, a rational calculus shows that it is wealth- or welfare-maximizing not to insure. Thus, it would be irrational to purchase insurance. Proponents of the optimal-insurance view also argue empirically that people's rationality is borne out by their failure to insure. They argue that because we do not see separate insurance markets in which people insure themselves against the risk of future pain and suffering (or loss of quality of life, or loss of consortium, or intense emotional distress), we should infer that people in fact are unwilling to insure themselves against these losses. Because people are unwilling to insure themselves against these losses, the argument proceeds, we should assume that the prices people pay for products do not include payment for implied warranties against such losses. The contract between consumer and manufacturer should be assumed not to include a bargained-for insurance provision, both because such a provision would be theoretically irrational and because the absence of actual insurance markets for pain and suffering counsels us not to assume such a provision. In the absence of such a bargained-for provision, the argument concludes, no damages should be available for pain and suffering. It would be inefficient for the law to give consumers something they themselves will not pay for.[17]

But what precludes purchase of insurance may be not irrationality but incommensurability. If it is empirically true that consumers do not insure themselves against their own pain and suffering, the best interpretation of their failure to insure may be not that they are maximizing how much they value their money over different possible states of their health, but rather that they are affirming the incommensurability between pain and suffering and dollars. Perhaps the purchase of pain-and-suffering insurance would signify to people that their own pain and suffering is a commodity replaceable with money. Perhaps people reject this conception of their own pain and its connection to themselves. It may be that when it comes to their own pain and suffering, people do not conceive of themselves as wealth-maximizers. It may be that they avoid conceiving of their own pain and suffering as commensurable either with money or with other commodities that money might buy. In other words, it may be that people reject the idea of purchasing insurance because they reject the symbolism of the transaction. They may reject the meaning it would have for their selfhood.

The economic worldview of which the optimal-insurance argument is a part is a commodified conceptual scheme. Motivations are conceived of in market rhetoric, rationality is conceived of as maximizing profit or welfare, and justice is conceived of as efficiency. Rationality thus conceived seems to imply an assumption—a model—of widespread commensurability. The economic worldview does not recommend that we determine empirically whether people really do conceive of rationality and justice in market rhetoric, and whether people really do understand values as widely commensurable. As a theoretical model, it is not put forward to track people's conventional understandings. As its adherents make clear, its value as a theoretical model is supposed to lie in its explanatory and predictive force, not in the extent to which it tracks cultural or individual self-understandings about the meaning of transactions.[18] Proponents of the economic worldview cannot consistently hold that the model's general assumption of commensurability can be disconfirmed for specific kinds of cases if we discover that in practice people accept incommensurability in those cases.

Yet the optimal-insurance view on compensation for pain and suffering seems to want it both ways. The view stops short of supposing that people's valuation of their own bodily integrity or freedom from pain should simply be understood on its general theoretical economic market model; instead, the view tells us that here we look and see what people's conventional understanding is by observing whether insurance is purchased, and here we attach importance to that conventional understanding. The argument asks us to attach importance to conventional self-understandings just at the point where incommensurability gets in the way of damage recovery, but no further—not enough to look for widespread incommensurability, which, if its significance were similarly treated, could undermine the overall theoretical assumptions of economic analysis.

One way to correct the inconsistency would be forthrightly to assimilate pain and suffering to the market model. That is, in an economic analysis that postulates that all things people value are goods with prices, one could bite the bullet and postulate as well that bodily integrity and freedom from pain are also goods with prices. This is a form of simple reductionism, which assimilates to the view I call universal commodification.

In simple reductionism, bodily integrity is just one more good that people value, and every value is reducible to dollars. Since people are assumed to value their bodily integrity directly in dollars, when injured they can be made whole by paying them the appropriate number of dollars. Thus, simple reductionism leads easily to the core commodified conception of compensation, reflecting the reductionist claim of commensurability. In fact, for simple reductionists the next step would be for the law to admit that pain and suffering is simply another kind of economic loss.[19]

An economic argument about compensation for pain and suffering that is often put forward in opposition to the optimal-insurance view may rely on simple reductionism. The argument claims that consumers are willing to pay to avoid pain and suffering, even if they do not explicitly insure against it. In such an economic view, the implicit contract between manufacturer and consumer should be understood to include, at the appropriate price, compensation for such harms, in order to achieve optimal precautions against accidents. I will call this the optimal-precautions view. Thus, Judge Richard Posner opines:

> We disagree with those students of tort law who believe that pain and suffering are not real costs and should not be allowable items of damages in a tort suit. No one likes pain and suffering and most people would pay a good deal of money to be free of them. If they were not recoverable in damages, the cost of negligence would be less to the tortfeasors and there would be more negligence, more accidents, more pain and suffering, and hence higher social costs.[20]

The optimal-precautions view is embedded in a deterrence view of torts in general, in which the purpose of paying damages is to deter accidents that would otherwise cost more.

Judge Posner may be a simple reductionist. Although he does not flatly say that injuries reduce to dollars, he does say that pain and suffering are "real costs." In any case, as we can see from his remark, he assumes commensurability between the cost of paying damages (dollars) and those other social costs (pain and suffering) if the dollars are not paid. This is the crux of the optimal-precautions view; it must assume that we can tell which costs are "higher." Thus, although the optimal-precautions view need not explicitly reduce injuries to dollars, it is committed to the possibility of ranking injuries on a scale with dollars so that we can determine at what point the dollars are equal to or greater than the value of not being injured.[21] This view reflects at least the scalar claim of commensurability, if not the reductionist claim. It arrives at the conclusion that damages for pain and suffering ought to be paid, but it does so by committing itself to a commodified conception of compensation.

Another way to deal with the apparent inconsistency in the economic optimal-insurance argument is to investigate in a much broader way what our actual understandings of compensation are. What would such an investigation reveal? We could take our understanding to be the somewhat ambiguous traditional conception, reflected in the passage from the *Restatement* quoted above, that compensation for pain and suffering provides redress in some way other than by making freedom from injury commensurable with money. We could recognize that corrective justice is at least an important basis for tort law, and try to develop a view of corrective justice that does not require the rectification that incommensurability precludes.

We could also take it to be the case, as I suggest, that there is no one understanding of compensation that is "ours." The *Restatement's* ambivalence may faithfully mirror conflict. Intuitions are divided about commensurability, and so are intuitions about what compensation means. Our practice of compensation is conflicted; commodified and noncommodified understandings coexist. What should we make of the conflict, practically speaking?

One suggestion for alleviating the "crisis" in tort liability seems to be to ignore the conflict. We should bypass conflicting theories of tort and compensation prevalent in legal rhetoric and look more system-

atically at the bottom line in practice. How much money is being paid
for what? Two recurrent complaints about awards for pain and
suffering are that they are indeterminate, causing perceptions of un-
fairness and causing deterrence theory not to work, and that they
leave it open to juries to give plaintiffs the moon. The suggestion is
that the way to alleviate both worries is to compile extensive data on
awards in specific categories of cases and to require future awards
presumptively to adhere to a schedule based on these data.[22] Outliers
will be prevented, or at least juries will have to justify them.

I am sympathetic with the pragmatic methodology that would
counsel us to work around our conflicts by paying closer attention to
concrete practice rather than attempting to resolve them a priori in
theory. At first glance, therefore, the suggestion that the tort "crisis"
can be alleviated by legislating schedules based upon past awards
seems promising.[23] Yet I think it is especially important for a pragmatic approach to try to find out how much incommensurability
actually exists and whether we need it for anything significant. I
believe we ought not to beg the questions whether people have
significant commitments to incommensurability and, if so, whether
such commitments are important to human flourishing.

It seems to me that the suggestion that we legislate schedules based
upon past awards does risk begging these questions by assuming a
species of commensurability. A tendency to assume commensurability
can be seen in the way these reformers approach the issue of how the
law should delineate the specific categories in which damage awards
should be made comparable. One suggestion is that severity of injury
and age of the injured party are the main relevant factors, with the
implication that severity of injury is something that can at least be
roughly scaled or placed in categories ranging from least to most
severe.[24] By linking such a scale to ranges of dollar amounts, this
approach asks the law to institutionalize a scalar version of commensurability, though not one that is outright reductionist in equating
freedom from injury with dollars.

One group of researchers finds useful a scale of severity developed
by insurers to evaluate malpractice cases.[25] Another researcher simply
lists eighteen types of injury and sets out data showing how the legal
system has compensated for them.[26] According to his research, cancer
and burn victims are most likely to receive some award for pain and
suffering, and people who suffer paraplegia, quadriplegia, or brain

damage are likely to receive the largest pain and suffering awards.[27] Assuming this research is valid, what should we do with it? The researchers advocate, in essence, that the law should adopt a species of commensurability by enacting a schedule that makes these trends into legal rules. Such rules would make the harm of various injuries into a linear, algorithmic scale.

Whether we should declare a species of commensurability in this way is unclear. If we think incommensurability is an important commitment in self-constitution and in life as we know it, then before enacting such legal rules we at least would like to know whether the law itself has any effect on the existence of incommensurability. This is to ask about the culture-shaping function of law as it relates to incommensurability. How deep and how extensive are people's commitments to incommensurability? If the law does declare commensurability, will it cause people's commitment to incommensurability to fade?

Compensation Practice and the Culture-Shaping Function of Law

Is the existence of incommensurability something that can vary depending upon the state of the legal system? The answer is yes, if (1) incommensurability is part of the conventional cultural system of meaning, and if (2) the state of the legal system affects that system of meaning. With respect to (1), I believe that incommensurability is an artifact of our form of life and its shared discourse. (What else could it be?) With respect to (2), as I have argued throughout this book, I also think that the law matters for that shared discourse. But the details of how it matters are not easy to specify.

In the view that I find attractive, law not only reflects culture but also shapes it. The law is a powerful conceptual—rhetorical, discursive—force. It expresses conventional understandings of value and at the same time influences conventional understandings of value. Yet mere recognition of this reciprocal process is too general to be useful. It is not easy to say when we should view the law as predominantly reflecting background culture and when we should view it as a moving force in changing that culture. Nevertheless, it seems in general that, at least sometimes, the law can be a cultural moving force. If this is a useful way to see the function of law, then the law indeed influences how we understand ourselves and our values and, in particular, whether we understand certain aspects of ourselves, such as bodily integrity and freedom from pain, to be incommensurable with money.

I have said that our conventional understanding of what compensation means is conflicted, that compensation is a contested concept. Suppose, however, that someone believes that because we inhabit a market society, the main meaning of paying money for injuries is that money and injuries are exchangeable commodities. The observer might believe that our compensation practice directly reflects a commodified conception of compensation; we really are saying that injuries are reducible to dollars or can be placed on a scale with dollars. Or, more subtly, the observer might espouse a domino theory. She might believe that even if our compensation practice is primarily meant, as traditional legal discourse would have it, not to equate injuries and dollars, but rather to provide a different sort of redress, nevertheless, since the practice is located in a market society, the practice will come to be interpreted as commodification and indeed will create commodification. That is, when we live in a world in which many or most things people need and want are routinely traded as commodities, and when we see dollars systematically being paid to people after they are injured, and in some way "for" or "on account of" the injury, we are likely to come to conceive of freedom from injury as another commodity bearing exchange value, even if we do not now conceive of it that way. If such an observer holds that conceiving of bodily integrity and freedom from pain as commodities leads to a degradation of personhood and an inferior conception of human flourishing, then he may argue that compensation for pain and suffering should be abolished.

This is one way to read the arguments of Richard Abel, who advocates a social insurance scheme. He would replace the tort system with one that grants money to people regardless of whether their misfortunes are caused by their own fault, other people's fault, an unavoidable accident, an illness, or a congenital disability. Abel's ideal system would not compensate for pain and suffering; such damages "commodify our unique experience." Nor would it compensate for loss of consortium or witnessing injury to a loved one; such damages "commodify love."[28] In saying that damages operate to "commodify," Abel implies either that our shared understanding of compensation is a commodified conception or that the practice of payment, in our market social context, can make it so.

Another observer of our discursive practice of compensation might not be so ready to think that the commodified conception prevails or will come to prevail.[29] Perhaps, even though market rhetoric is an important conceptual scheme in our culture, and even though we are influenced in our conceptualization of compensation by a legal system that pays people dollars in a context that expresses that the payment is "for" the injury, we can still maintain a noncommodified conception of compensation. Perhaps the noncommodified conception is robust; perhaps incommensurability is robust.

The issue is very similar to the question whether a noncommodified conception of children can withstand the onslaught of an explicit market in adoption. I can restate it as follows. If we do conceive of compensation in primarily a noncommodified way—if we are clear that it is not a quid pro quo, but rather a symbolic action that reinforces our commitments about rights and wrongs—then the practice of paying compensation does not signify that we conceive of the harms to persons for which we pay it as commodities. Yet one who values noncommodified understandings of human attributes, quality of life, and bodily integrity might still fear that the noncommodified conception of compensation is in danger of giving way sooner or later to the commodified conception, under the onslaught of constant payment "for" injuries in the context of a culture that readily understands analogous interactions as market exchanges, perhaps helped along by the rhetoric of economic analysis. How should we evaluate this fear? How robust is the noncommodified conception?

One thing we can do is look and see how prevalent the noncommodified conception is in legal discourse, and try to evaluate whether it is becoming weaker or more questionable. The investigation could pursue a "thick description" of arguments in tort cases, jury instructions, and trial and appellate court opinions. My supposition is that this investigation would show that the traditional noncommodified conception, albeit ambiguous and conflicted, is holding firm. Or the investigation could pursue an analysis of the rhetoric of tort scholarship. My supposition is that this investigation would show that the commodified conception is gaining ground.

We also could try to evaluate just how deeply entrenched our intuitions of incommensurability are, for those of us who have them, although I do not know how such an investigation would proceed. Perhaps understandings involving incommensurability are so deeply entrenched that no amount of market rhetoric can dislodge them or the conceptions of human values they underwrite. If this is how things are, then commodified and noncommodified conceptions will simply continue to coexist as they do now, and they will pretty well track people's commitments about incommensurability. People who accept incommensurability will tend to have a noncommodified conception of compensation, and people who do not accept incommensurability will tend to have a commodified conception of compensation. On the other hand, perhaps our intuitions of incommensurability will turn out to be more fragile—perhaps the conventional discursive system that underwrites them will turn out to be more malleable—in which case incommensurability may tend to disappear under the continued influence of surrounding market discourse and practice. For now, though, it remains unclear how we should evaluate the effect of the law's own symbolic force in maintaining the existence of incommensurability, and hence the noncommodified conception of compensation.

14

Democracy

Certain liberal views of democratic politics, and of culture generally, are couched in the discourse of commodification. These views carry out in detail the market metaphor of social "contract." Rational choice contractarianism, at least as it is understood by many legal writers, conceives of politics in the discourse of commodification.[1] Its proponents often think of themselves as Hobbes's intellectual descendants. In this conception, politics is a competitive market. Rationality is maximizing profits and rational actors are profit-maximizers. All deviations from competitive markets are attributable to (or justified by) market failure. Political theory is a species of economics. The reasons for rational actors to leave the prepolitical condition and institute a state amount to an economic calculation demonstrating that the benefits of doing so exceed the costs.

Rational choice contractarianism is often presented as completely commodified in rhetoric because the payoffs—welfare gains to individuals that add up to more welfare for society as a whole—are conceived of in terms of money. Sometimes the view is presented as incompletely commodified, in that welfare gains are not conceived of as monetizable. As I argued in Chapter 8, even if welfare gains are not reduced to money, where commensurability is assumed (that is, if welfare is all one kind of "stuff"), the view is still usefully considered a variety of market rhetoric. Just as market rhetoric is pervasive in how we conceive of the central liberal commitment of freedom of expression (the marketplace of ideas), so is it pervasive in how we consider the justification for the liberal state itself (social contract).

Public Choice Theory

The economic theory of democracy, otherwise known as public choice theory or positive political theory, applies the postulates and reasoning of neoclassical economics to politics. "The basic behavioral postulate of public choice, as for economics, is that man is an egoistic, rational, utility maximizer."[2] The basic methodological premise, as for economics, is a rigorous atomistic individualism. The basic moral stance, as for much of economics, is that the theory doesn't need one. This is "positive" theory, unconcerned with the goodness or badness of political actors and institutions, seeking only to observe how incentives and institutional structures interact to produce empirical consequences.

Rather than focusing primarily on the original social "contract," the public choice theorist focuses primarily on the instability of the "contract" once instituted. In the simplest form of this theory, political struggles reflect an *n*-person prisoner's dilemma game.[3] Everyone's first choice is to try to be a predator ("defect") while everyone else follows the rules. If everyone succeeds in pursuing this first-choice strategy, the system reverts to the prepolitical state (Hobbes's war of all against all). The job of the state is to keep everyone pursuing a second-best strategy, considered from the standpoint of self-interest. In the second-best strategy, each person follows the rules, in return for a guarantee that everyone else will. This system has two problems. One is that everyone is always trying to defect, giving rise to the need for a state. The other is overreaching by the state. Given the premise of atomistic individualism, the state consists only of a group of individuals given power to enforce the rules for the benefit of all. It, too, will always be trying instead to serve the interest of that group of individuals rather than of society as a whole—assuming that the group called the state is able to cooperate and doesn't disintegrate because of internal conflicts.

For the functioning of democratic institutions—legislatures, administrative bodies, courts—the main predicted empirical consequence of all this individual maximization behavior by political actors—legislators, administrators, judges—is that there is massive rent-seeking going on. Rent-seeking means manipulating wealth transfers away from the unorganized public in favor of well-organized interest groups. Public choice theorists use two different aspects of social scientific methodology, which I can characterize as deductive and inductive, to study these phenomena. In deductive research, public choice theorists use formal models to draw out in detail exactly how we should expect to see all this profit-seeking do its work on various aspects of the body politic. In inductive research, they use statistical analysis of data to give us the details of how the profit-seeking postulate fits the facts of democratic institutions, their process and output.

Public choice theory presents a bleak picture for any sanguine believer in high-school civics. Instead of being committed to dialogue, deliberation, and ideals of public betterment, politicians are committed to collecting as much campaign money as possible so that they can be reelected. In this bleak picture it's a paradox why voters even vote, because it is an irrational act, economically speaking. Maybe votes are just commodities that are bought by interest groups for politicians "in exchange for higher probability of seeing a favorite bill passed."[4]

Many legal writers are attracted to public choice theory.[5] Many judges are attracted to it as well. Justice Antonin Scalia, in his decisions involving "takings" of private property, tends to assume that state and local governmental bodies are engaging in rent-seeking.[6] As a land use teacher, I can say that the model seems to describe pretty well a lot of the interactions between developers and local planning and zoning officials. Attorneys who practice in the field are quite open about the need to have their developer clients make large campaign contributions to the city council member in whose district a proposed project is located.

But if this is the truth about politics, what can we make of the ideal of deliberative self-government? What can we make of the ideal of a polity whose whole is more than the sum of its parts? Must we conclude that these ideals are merely obfuscatory rhetoric, used only because such rhetoric is welfare-maximizing for some powerful group? I will return below to the challenge of public choice theory for these democratic ideals. First I want to explore, more speculatively, the reach of market rhetoric in political theory beyond the obvious cases of rational choice contractarianism and public choice theory.

Liberal Neutrality

The liberal view that government must remain neutral on the good life is less committed to explicit market rhetoric than rational choice contractarianism and public choice theory are. Proponents of liberal neutrality do not speak so univocally as public choice theorists of market failures (freeriders and holdouts, information costs, and so on). They do not so readily speak of bodily integrity and friendship in terms of quantities demanded at a given price. Yet liberal neutrality, at least in a guise that is widespread in contemporary legal culture, also might be thought of as a species of incomplete commodification. Thinking of liberal neutrality this way involves linking the notion of incomplete commodification with skepticism about values, through the skeptical overtones of fungibility and commensurability.

Liberal neutrality, in the prevalent legal view, is a species of skepticism. Consider Robert Bork:

There is no principled way to decide that one man's gratifications are more deserving of respect than another's or that one form of gratification is more worthy than another. [Footnote: "The impossibility is related to that of making interpersonal comparisons of utilities."] Why is sexual gratification [for those who wish to use contraceptives] more worthy than moral gratification [for those who condemn contraception]? Why is sexual gratification nobler than economic gratification? There is no way of deciding these matters other than by reference to some system of moral or ethical values that has no objective or intrinsic validity of its own. . . .[7]

This legal view of liberal neutrality submerges the traditional priority of the right over the good in Kantian political theory by equating the notion of neutrality with the idea that any value commitment is as good as any other. (Many liberal social philosophers find this prevalent legal view simplistic or misguided. Nevertheless, its prevalence in legal discourse has significance for the culture-shaping function of law.) In this reductionist notion of neutrality, people's value commitments are fungible. Interchangeability is a feature that values have in common with objects traded in laissez-faire markets.

The skeptical conception of liberal neutrality coheres with a broader ordinary conception of liberal culture, bearing an analogous skeptical resonance, that I have called cultural laissez-faire. In this conception, cultural groups, like political interest groups, struggle with one another. Whatever cultural outcome achieves or retains a firm social entrenchment is by definition to be tolerated if not indeed celebrated—until it is replaced by something else.

The laissez-faire conception of culture has by no means been monolithic in our intellectual life. Although many people are willing to espouse skeptical political and cultural laissez-faire in some moods or in some contexts, perhaps few are unwaveringly committed to them. Most want to be able to say that getting rid of slavery was *right* in some higher sense than just that the political struggle came out that way. As we saw in Chapter 12, however, cultural laissez-faire became (and has remained) important in the legal conceptualization of freedom of expression, especially through the influential opinions of Oliver Wendell Holmes, Jr.[8] It thus remains an important strand in legal liberalism.

In an intellectual trend that can be characterized as a countercurrent to market rhetoric, the skeptical view of liberal neutrality is now being largely rejected by liberal social philosophers. Some argue that neutrality is impossible even when this coarse skeptical view is refined, but that neutrality is not a core commitment of liberalism. (Their view is sympathetic to the Deweyan culture-shaping view of law that I described in Chapter 12, and to which I will return shortly.)

Other liberals stick with a refined notion of neutrality. They deny that liberal neutrality involves skepticism about values. They point out, at minimum, that requiring the *state* to be neutral on the merits of pushpin versus poetry does not imply that there is no truth of the matter about which pursuit is better for human beings.[9] Neutrality is merely a procedure for maintaining a stable political order in the face of people's deeply conflicting value commitments, mistaken though they may be.[10]

The refined view of liberal neutrality reemphasizes a distinction between public and private realms of argument and action. If individual liberty requires that political action maintain neutrality among individuals' conceptions of the good, that requirement can be extrapolated to the idea that political debate also be neutrally structured. Thus, it is argued that given the fact of pluralism and its significance for liberty, the procedure for stable political coexistence requires that certain kinds of arguments be excluded from the arena of public reason.

In my view, liberal writers who have rejected liberal neutrality have more thoroughly escaped the aura of skepticism, with its overtones of market rhetoric, than those who have merely refined it. To underwrite a social structure in which freedom is possible, in which liberal citizenship is possible, in which equal concern and respect are possible, must involve the state in furthering some version of the good life and excluding opposing ones.[11] At least in the minds of some, denial that values are fungible means that liberals must own up to affirmative liberal values. At least in the minds of some, the political and cultural commitment to liberalism commits us to certain values that rule out others, and this does indeed choose among conceptions of the good for human beings. Tolerance, secularism, and public education are among the values to which the political culture of liberalism is committed. They rule out their cultural opposites.

As liberals come to adopt this position, they return to (or reinvent) the commitment of John Dewey, who was its most passionate exponent.[12] This view tends to deemphasize the traditional distinction between the public realm (in which the social structure is supposed to be maintained) and the private realm (in which people are supposed to make and live out commitments to a particular conception of the good).[13] In this view the social structure underwrites and enables certain kinds of individual commitments and discourages or precludes others, and at the same time people's commitments create and maintain the social structure. Deweyan thought about liberal democracy can, I believe, give us a fruitful way to think about public choice theory and the conception of polity in market rhetoric.

Deweyan Democracy and Public Choice Theory

Dewey was passionately committed to the democratic ideal. But he was also a passionate critic of democracy-as-we-know-it, political democracy in practice. Our institutions of government, and our society as a whole, he viewed as falling far short of the democratic ideal. Many of his criticisms seem apt today as well. As I will show, they are related to the problem of conceiving of social life in market rhetoric.

In *Liberalism and Social Action,* Dewey outlined a "crisis in liberalism," connected with "failure to develop and lay hold of an adequate conception of intelligence integrated with social movements."

This is in large part a failure of social science, Dewey argued, which has not matured to the point where it can improve our day-to-day existence; it has not developed to parallel physical science. Whereas "every discovery in physical knowledge signifies . . . a change in the processes of production," because "there are countless persons whose business it is to see that these discoveries take effect" in practical operations, there is "next to nothing of the same sort with respect to knowledge of man and human affairs."[14] Thus, "The prime condition of a democratically organized public is a kind of knowledge and insight which does not yet exist."[15]

Cooperative experimental intelligence as applied to human affairs is the systematic exploration of how to achieve human flourishing within a culture and community. According to Dewey, our approach to education reflects the primitive state of our grasp of this method. Science is taught in school as simply another subject, where it "signifies one more opportunity for the mechanization of the material and methods of study." In contrast, "If it were treated as what it is, the method of intelligence itself in action, then the method of science would be incarnate in every branch of study and every detail of learning. Thought would be connected with the possibility of action, and every mode of action would be reviewed to see its bearing upon the habits and ideas from which it sprang."[16]

Partly because of our undeveloped approach to education, Dewey argued, the needed widespread cultural commitment to the scientific attitude does not exist. For the same reason, the kind of genuine communication needed in order to understand the consequences of social action and increase shared knowledge of the effectiveness of various social tools also does not exist.

Rapid progress in communications technology might have provided an opportunity for real cooperative interchange and augmentation of knowledge; instead, Dewey said, we have a flood of propaganda and a concomitant skepticism about voting and the process of government.[17] A large percentage of voters doesn't bother to vote at all, and people think their vote doesn't matter, doesn't change anything.[18] Politics is dominated by factions (parties) run by machines. According to Dewey, the public is unorganized and diffuse. The theory that elected representatives are responsible to the electorate has broken down; it works best in describing politicians' behavior in response to local pressure groups.[19]

Likewise, our process of formation of social policies in legislation reflects our lack of grasp of the method of intelligence, which is the democratic method. According to Dewey, the democratic method exerts far less force in politics than do "the interest of individuals and parties in capturing and retaining office and power," and "the propaganda of publicity agents," and "organized pressure groups." "Our times," Dewey said, are characterized by a "corrosive 'materialism,' " which "springs from the notion, sedulously cultivated by the class in power, that the creative capacities of individuals can be evoked and developed only in a struggle for material possessions and material gain."[20]

Moreover, Dewey argued insistently, part of the reason for people's preoccupation with material gain is that many of them are still wanting in the basic necessities of life. Dewey believed that the chance to make progress toward the democratic ideal will be "lost for a considerable period" if we are not willing to "socialize the forces of production . . . so that the liberty of individuals will be supported by the very structure of economic organization." For "liberation of the capacities of individuals for free, self-initiated expression is an essential part of the creed of liberalism,"[21] and to achieve this end, liberalism must adopt cooperative means; socialized economy is necessary.[22] Laissez-faire individualism hindered progress toward the democratic ideal by mistaking progress in technological control over the physical environment for progress in freedom:

> It failed to see that the great expansion which was occurring [in industrialization] was in fact due to release of *physical* energies; that as far as human action and human freedom is concerned, a problem, not a solution, was thereby instituted: the problem, namely, of management and direction of the new physical energies so they would contribute to realization of human possibilities.[23]

In sum, the task for liberalism, the task for progress toward ideal democracy, is to apply the method of experimental intelligence, not dogma or a priori broad generalizations.[24] "[U]ntil the method of intelligence and experimental control is the rule in social relations and social direction," we will find "that the problem of social organization in behalf of human liberty and the flowering of human capacities is insoluble."[25]

The problems Dewey observed with political democracy in its nonideal state—as he saw it in his day and as we still see it today—resonate interestingly with the postulates of public choice theory. People are acting as isolated individuals, he said, as though intelligence were entirely atomistic; this correlates with the premise of methodological individualism. People are acting from self-regarding motives, he said; this correlates with the premise of "rational" welfare-maximization. Paralleling the premises of public choice theory, Dewey argued, as we have seen, that in fact, as things stand in practice, the public is unorganized and uncommitted, whereas interest groups wield power. Legislators are responsible to interest groups and not to the public. Burgeoning communications technology, rather than making real communication possible, increases the power to win votes by advertising and packaging. Voters are skeptical, apathetic, and undereducated. The interest of politicians is in capturing and retaining office, not in engaging in deliberative democracy.

Insofar as public choice theory is an attempt to apply genuine scientific method to observing and understanding the particular facts of this situation, I am sure Dewey would approve. He would approve of the air public choice has of debunking tired old ideology with hard facts. Even if the picture is bleak, I imagine he'd say, if these are the facts, we should straightforwardly name them and disseminate them; we shouldn't take refuge in vague, self-deluding, high-minded rhetoric.

Moreover, both the deductive and inductive strands of public choice methodology might represent at least an early stage of an appropriate scientific attitude toward understanding political practice as we now know it. For such an appropriate (quintessentially Deweyan) scientific attitude, the crucial idea is to achieve a detailed, articulated understanding of the particular consequences of particular institutional forms and incentive structures as they exist in the real world. Both inductive research (painstaking empirical observation and data recordation) and deductive research (thoughtful formalization of variables and predicted results) are appropriate in the attempt to create such a detailed understanding.

A Critique of Public Choice Theory

I want to conclude this chapter, and this book, by offering a critique of public choice theory—commodified political theory—in a Deweyan spirit. Although I believe Dewey might find the meticulous dissection of institutional workings a plus of public choice theory, I believe he would also find its tendency to reify its behavioral premises a significant minus. To repeat what I pointed out above, Dewey's observations about political democracy *in its current nonideal state* resonate interestingly with the *postulates* of public choice theory: isolated individuals acting from self-regarding motives, an organized and uncommitted public, power wielded by interest groups, politicians motivated by seeking and keeping office. A satisfactory critique of public choice theory will, I believe, start by noticing the difference in epistemic status of these behavioral observations.

The epistemic status of Dewey's observations about political democracy-as-we-know-it is contingent and relative. The characteristic motivations and responses of political actors are mutable. They depend upon the particular historical events and circumstances that have brought us to where we are. The epistemic status of the methodological and behavioral postulates of public choice theory is, on the other hand, more foundational. For the economic analyst, these are the "laws" of human nature. They are not relative to time and place; they are independent of history and culture.[26]

In other words, Dewey had a dynamic model of human behavior. According to Dewey, we can change the sorry state of democracy-as-we know-it, or at least he had faith that we can, and accordingly he argued that we must. In contrast, public choice theorists assume a static model of human behavior. On the whole, they don't think we can change the sorry state of democracy-as-we-know-it. Some think we can manipulate it to some extent to achieve relatively better policy results in this nonideal world, and some think, skeptically, that we can do no more than understand just how nonideal it is.

I believe we can be confident that a Deweyan critique of public choice theory would begin by criticizing its reification of premises, because dislodging presupposed absolutes and turning them into contingent intellectual consequences is a consistent Deweyan theme. Dewey argued in many contexts that philosophical premises taken to be absolute truths of human nature and the good are instead only the consequential reflections, in intellectual life, of the historical and cultural circumstances that gave them birth.[27]

In this vein, Dewey set out with some care what he took to be the historical origins of the foundational premises of liberalism. The premise of atomistic rights-bearing individuals he took to be the result of the need to throw off institutional ties, especially to the church, that hindered progress:

> Since it was necessary, upon the intellectual side, to find justification for the movements of revolt, and since established authority was upon the side of institutional life, the natural recourse was appeal to some inalienable sacred authority resident in the protesting individuals. Thus "individualism" was born, a theory which endowed singular persons in isolation from any associations, except those which they deliberately formed for their own ends, with native or natural rights. The revolt against old and limiting associations was converted, intellectually, into the doctrine of independence of any and all associations.[28]

There is nothing inherently logical or transcendentally right about the philosophical doctrines of individualism, Dewey continued. Had circumstances been otherwise, had the problems facing the beginning of the industrial era been other than they were, so would our philosophical commitments have been different:

> It is now easy for the imagination to conceive circumstances under which revolts against prior governmental forms would have found its theoretical formulation in an assertion of the rights of groups, of other associations than those of a political nature. There was no logic which rendered necessary the appeal to the individual as an independent and isolated being. . . . But, as we have already remarked, the obnoxious state was closely bound up in fact and in tradition with other associations, ecclesiastic (and through its influence with the family), and economic . . . The easiest way out was to go back to the naked individual, to sweep away all associations as foreign to his nature and rights save as they proceeded from his own voluntary choice, and guaranteed his own private ends.[29]

An analogous Deweyan critique applies to economic analysis, as represented by Bentham. Dewey admired Bentham for his view that "all organized action is to be judged by its consequences," for his rejection of natural rights and of "Reason as a remote majestic power that discloses ultimate truths," and for his fertile invention of detailed legal and administrative devices designed, in a scientific spirit, to remedy specific evils and abuses.[30] Dewey called Bentham "the first great muck-raker in the field of law."[31] Nevertheless, it was naive to suppose that the *nature* of man, everywhere and anywhere, was that of a mercantile reckoner, just because the circumstances of the rising mercantile society brought forth these characteristics.

Dewey's judgment on Bentham and on liberalism's fundamental premises turns on the usefulness—the consequences—of these ideas. And although Bentham's (and his followers') reformist zeal and meticulous systematic attention to consequences had positive social consequences, so the liberals' naiveté about the foundational status of their premises was not without harmful consequences. On the plus side, Dewey said that "in spite of fundamental defects in his underlying theory of human nature," "the history of the legal and administrative changes in Great Britain during the first half of the nineteenth century is chiefly the history of Bentham and his school." These reforms are "proof that liberalism can be a power in bringing about radical social changes," when (as Bentham did) it "combine[s] capacity for bold and comprehensive social invention with detailed study of particulars and with courage in action."[32]

But the ultimate consequence of liberalism's reification of individualism was tragic. Liberals "put forward their ideas as immutable truths good at all times and places; they had no idea of historic relativity, either in general or in its application to themselves."[33] Liberals could not recognize that their interpretations of liberty, individuality, and intelligence were historically conditioned and relevant only to their own time. By the middle of the nineteenth century, laissez-faire liberalism, rather than being a radical reform doctrine, provided the intellectual justification of the status quo. Indeed, it provides the basis for the largely conservative agenda of law-and-economics, including public choice theory, today.

The consequences of liberalism's reification of individualism, with its intellectual justification of the status quo, carried over into court decisions in which judges "destroy social legislation passed in the interest of a real, instead of purely formal, liberty of contract." The decisions of the *Lochner* era[34] could have been deprived of their intellectual and moral support, according to Dewey, if only liberals had appreciated the historical relativity of their own interpretation of the meaning of liberty, and thus had understood that new economic and social conditions called for a new conception. "If the early liberals had put forth their special interpretation of liberty as something subject to historical relativity," Dewey said, "they would not have frozen it into a doctrine to be applied at all times under all social circumstances."35 Had they not frozen it in this way, bad consequences (to be discussed shortly) might have been avoided.

Public choice theory reifies a Hobbesian conception of human nature. The individual of public choice theory is the Hobbesian mechanistic self-interest maximizer in a laissez-faire market. This model was called forth by historical circumstances that no longer obtain, among them the need to undermine the divine right of kings. Moreover, public choice theory also reifies the notion that all these atomistic individuals have given "preferences" that they are trying to satisfy, and that these "preferences" are independent of the "preferences" of others. This model may be adequate for the purest of market interactions but is obfuscatory when it comes to other kinds of human interactions. In democracy-as-we-know-it, with imperfect freedom and undeveloped intelligence, people's behavior largely follows habit and custom (as Dewey recognized) rather than the method of intelligence, and thus, in democracy-as-we-know-it, the public choice model of striving to satisfy preferences, without questioning how we came by them, may approximate social reality. But, as Dewey might say, that is no reason to freeze the model and call it eternal human nature.

Finally, public choice theory also reifies the means/ends dichotomy. Economic analysis takes it to be foundational that people engage in social activities only instrumentally, as a means toward the end of achieving maximum satisfaction of their preferences. Again, although it may be true that under current conditions many people engage in political activities purely instrumentally with regard to their own goals, this need not necessarily be the case. Moreover, I think Dewey would also say, even in democracy-as-we-know-it, the rigid means/ends dichotomy misdescribes how people act and understand their actions. Every end is also a means to some other end; no action is purely a means, and no end is purely an end.36

Having argued that the premises of economic analysis are reifications, I believe a Deweyan critique would go on to say that these reifications are not only intellectually wrong; they may cause real pain for real people. By analogy, in Dewey's critique of the reifications of liberalism, he argued that if only liberals had not frozen their historically contingent conceptions of liberty and intelligence into immutable, transcendental laws, they would have recognized that effective liberty is a function of the social conditions existing at any time. If they had done this, they would have known that as economic relations became dominantly controlling forces in setting the pattern of human relations, the necessity of liberty for individuals which they proclaimed will require social control of economic forces in the interest of the great mass of individuals.[37]

This failure of liberalism was a tragedy for human beings and for their social progress: "Because the liberals failed to make a distinction between purely formal or legal liberty and effective liberty of thought and action, the history of the last one hundred years is the history of non-fulfillment of their predictions."[38]

Public choice political theorists—positive political theorists—tend to be resolutely non-normative; most do not put forth their work primarily as a basis for policy recommendations. In contrast, the point of Dewey's insistence on a scientific attitude toward understanding the consequences of various social practices and institutional designs was that only with such an understanding can we hope to be more than hit-or-miss at achieving the policy results we desire. For Dewey, policy results were what mattered. It is not enough to understand the world as it is; the point is to change it. Knowledge is valuable not for its own sake but for its use in improving the lives of all human beings. The reason for acquiring an accurate understanding of the world, in ever-increasing detail and capabilities for control of consequences, is so that we can change the world for the better.

Thus I believe Dewey would object to the resolute non-normativity of pure public choice theory. Even retaining the reified premises of economics, one could still adopt the stance Dewey praised in Bentham: one could concentrate on using the information to improve nonideal democracy. We could use it to make new institutions or to revise old ones, without challenging the premises of economic man. If the findings of public choice theorists represent scientific facts and causal linkages, it may be argued that their findings can be the backdrop of policy choices exactly as Dewey envisioned.

For example, we might avoid structuring regulatory commissions in such a way that the members hold tenure at the will of one legislator. That structure tends to result in decisions in favor of whatever applicants give the most money to that legislator's campaign fund, because the legislator will fire any commissioner who doesn't behave this way.[39] For another example, we might insist on campaign finance reform and campaign spending control to make it more difficult for legislators to succumb to maximizing their own war chests.[40] One of the big pluses of public choice theory, from this point of view, is that it can tell us which forms of institutional design ought to be avoided because they are most vulnerable to corruption.

Does this mean, then, that Dewey would approve of the conservative agenda of much law-and-economics scholarship? After all, we can hardly fail to notice that the impact of public choice theory on the legal world is not non-normative at all. Lawyers and judges who admire this kind of scholarship tend to want to consider economic regulation as rent-seeking,[41] and hence tend to want to implement laissez-faire markets,[42] and even tend to want to bring back *Lochner*.[43] In this commodified scheme, regulation is presumptively illegitimate and can be validated only if market failure is shown.

I believe Dewey would approve of any insights public choice can give us into designing institutions to avoid corruption, given the nonideal state of democracy-as-we-know-it. Yet it seems clear he would deplore the broader law-and-economics agenda. *Lochner*-like reasoning would not seem any better to him now than it did in its first flowering. The reason he would deplore it, again, is that this agenda just deepens the reification of the outmoded conceptions of liberal individualism. Thus, I believe Dewey would want to find a way to explore in detail how we can *change* these premises—make them less true of us—so that we can get closer to ideal democracy.

To summarize so far: public choice theory is praiseworthy insofar as it seeks scientific facts about democracy-as-we-know-it, looking to intricate causal relationships between institutional design and political consequences; and insofar as it eschews soothing rhetoric to "tell it like it is." Public choice theory falls far short of Dewey's vision for the method of democracy, however, because it reifies its premises, and is thus largely disabled from using its accumulated knowledge to make progress toward ideal (or less nonideal) democracy. Although we could use public choice theory to redesign institutions in light of its commodified premises (in the manner of Bentham), we can't use it to make progress toward ideal democracy, because of the reification of its commodified premises.

What would a more satisfactory democratic theory in a Deweyan spirit now look like? I believe it would have to incorporate all the tools of public choice theory for detailing the sad state of democracy-as-we-know-it, but in addition, it would have to have two other salient features: (1) it would not reify human-nature-as-we-know-it, nor any of the commodified conceptions of human-motivations-as-we-know-them that drive the machinery of democracy-as-we-know-it; (2) it would try to theorize how the method of intelligence, suitably construed, can be used to push nonideal democracy toward ideal democracy. Any such progressive agenda, of course, would have to take the double bind seriously (see Chapter 9). Even if we can formulate a view of ideal democracy, it need not follow that steps taken toward it would improve our situation.

In constructing the method of intelligence, the Deweyan scientific attitude, I believe Dewey would wish to heal the modern split between "science" and the "humanities." He would caution us, I believe, to avoid the overidentification of science with number-crunching. The power and elegance of commensurability can lead us astray in science as elsewhere. Just as Dewey would not equate rationality with profit-maximizing, so he would not equate rationality with quantification. He would not suggest that the scientific attitude in social value choices means we should regard everything human beings value as commensurable, so that they can all be weighed in a giant cost-benefit analysis.[44] He would not equate science with commodification.

At the same time Dewey would also caution us, I believe, against glorifying the irrational in ethics and cultural studies. He would not give up on the idea of a knowing subject in the context of other knowing subjects, and he would not give up on the idea of progress. For a Deweyan pragmatist, the deconstructive moment is important, but it cannot displace reconstructive work.[45] Both criticism (of the nonideal) and vision (of the ideal) are necessary.

What can be accomplished if we both reconstruct the method of intelligence and take care not to reify human nature? We will understand that human nature will change as culture changes and, in turn, that culture will change as human nature changes. We will come to a better understanding of human dynamism and contextuality (see Chapter 5). The relationship between culture and human nature suggests that, if we want to apply scientific knowledge and imagination to the problem in a Deweyan spirit, what we need is an evolutionary model—that is, a dynamic systems model designed to take account of feedback. Such models have been developed in evolutionary biology, population dynamics, organic systems development, and other fields of inquiry. They are beginning to be applied to economics, where they are displacing the assumptions of the neoclassical model that is the basis of much of public choice theory.[46] I imagine that Dewey would hope—just as he hoped with earlier scientific models—that these intellectual discoveries will also prove useful in the study of culture and its complex of interlocking processes.

At least at this point we can name the processes; it's clearer to us than it was in Dewey's time that they can be characterized as forming a complex feedback system. Culture and material conditions interact with each other. In particular, the scientific attitude that Dewey commends needs to be created by culture; the ability to create it presupposes certain material conditions, and once we have created it, it will operate to change material conditions. The ability to create it also presupposes certain commitments and self-understandings. Culture and people's commitments and self-understandings—their "human nature," their "preferences"—also interact with each other. These self-understandings evolve in response to changes in culture; they also change the culture.

Culture and the law also interact with each other. The law both expresses and works to form and evolve cultural commitments and characteristics. As Dewey would be the first to point out, this statement is too wholesale to be of much use. What is needed is a more concrete analysis of how the interaction between law and culture works. I hope my discussions in this book of tort damages for pain and suffering and of markets in adoption can provide starting points.

Because these processes—law, culture, human nature, material conditions—are involved in interlocking feedback relationships, it is easy to mistake cause for effect. It's not true, for example, that law always "causes" cultural shifts, but neither is it true that law always is merely a "consequence" of culture. So Dewey's exhortation that we try to become ever more sophisticated in our understanding of consequences, if we want to improve society and democracy, is difficult to fulfill.

People's commitments and self-understandings interact with the law. "Preferences" bring law into being, but law also makes and changes "preferences." Because public choice defines this particular feedback loop out of existence, it is much too crude; it is retarded science at best. Dewey would want us to ask a question that public choice is not formulated to ask, because it is a question about feedback: If we conceive of democracy solely in terms of self-interested profit-maximizers, what does this conceptual scheme do to our culture? What does it do to our selves?

It might be that the practice of conceiving of politics in market rhetoric is actively bringing about in us those very motivations and characteristics it presupposes and reifies. Then, the more we suppose that government consists of politicians lining their own pockets or those of their supporters, the more it is so. The more we conceive of all things that people value as mere preferences that can be expressed in dollars and traded off against other dollar values, the more it is so. Public choice is a commodities model of politics; it uses the conceptual scheme of market exchange of commodities to characterize the entire realm of political activity. It might be that the more we presuppose a model of commodification in politics, the more we help create a commodified social world.

To deny this link between market rhetoric and our political life is to suppose that the commodified model of politics can coexist indefinitely with noncommodified ideals of political life, of social value, of self-constitution in a social context, without making significant inroads on them. To suppose such a stable coexistence we must believe that our commitments to those noncommodified ideals are very stubborn. Possibly they are. But I don't know right now how this stubbornness of commitment could be shown. Those of us for whom these ideals are precious should not be content with just assuming it.

Notes

1. Commodification as a Worldview

1. See Gary S. Becker, *A Treatise on the Family* 108 (enl. ed. 1991): "an efficient marriage market usually has positive assortative mating, where high-quality men are matched with high-quality women and low-quality men with low-quality women, although negative assortative mating is sometimes important."

2. Indeed, there is a conceptual difficulty with universal commodification that at least shows that it cannot exist in the real world and probably not hypothetically without contradiction. See Chapter 8.

3. Even when a difference between "objective" and "subjective" value is recognized, universal commodification tends to presume that the two measures of "subjective" value are equivalent. The possible divergence between what an entitled holder would demand to relinquish something and what an unentitled potential holder would pay to acquire it is sometimes called by critics "the offer-asking problem." See C. Edwin Baker, "The Ideology of the Economic Analysis of Law," 5 *Philosophy and Public Affairs* 3, 32–41 (1975); Duncan Kennedy, "Cost-Benefit Analysis of Entitlement Problems: A Critique," 33 *Stanford Law Review* 387, 401–421 (1981).

4. See Richard A. Posner, *Economic Analysis of Law* 31–35 (4th ed. 1992).

5. Id. at 34.

6. Elisabeth M. Landes and Richard A. Posner, "The Economics of the Baby Shortage," 7 *Journal of Legal Studies* 323, 347 (1978); see also Posner, *Economic Analysis of Law* at 150–154.

7. Posner, *Economic Analysis of Law* at 154. After publishing the article in which these remarks first appeared, Posner said, however, that he "did not advocate a free market in babies"; Richard A. Posner, "Mischaracterized Views," 69 *Judicature* 321 (1986).

8. Posner, *Economic Analysis of Law* at 12–13. See also Richard A. Posner, *The Economics of Justice* 115 (1981), defending wealth maximization as "the criterion for judging whether acts and institutions are just or good."

225

9. Posner, *Economic Analysis of Law* at 27; see also id. at 266 (stating that the threat of liability promised by "corrective justice" is a "kind of price"). Lest it appear that Becker and Posner occupy the entire field, for other applications of economic analysis to spheres that are not conventionally considered economic, see, for example, Margaret F. Brinig, "Rings and Promises," 6 *Journal of Law, Economics and Organizations* 203 (1990); Lloyd Cohen, "Marriage, Divorce, and Quasi-Rents; or, 'I Gave Him the Best Years of My Life,' " 16 *Journal of Legal Studies* 267 (1987); Martin Zelder, "The Economic Analysis of the Effect of No-Fault Divorce Law on the Divorce Rate," 22 *Harvard Journal of Law & Public Policy* 241 (1993); Paula England and George Farkas, *Households, Employment and Gender* (1986). Legal academics and policy analysts will recognize how pervasive the rhetoric of economic analysis is even where practitioners do not mean to embrace its deeper implications.

10. Posner, *Economic Analysis of Law* at 3; note also idem, *The Economics of Justice* at 1–5 (defending the application of economics to all fields of human activity).

11. Richard A. Posner, *Sex and Reason* (1992). For lively responses to *Sex and Reason* setting forth objections to conceiving of sexuality in this way, see, among others, Gillian K. Hadfield, "Flirting with Science: Richard Posner on the Biomechanics of Sexual Man," 106 *Harvard Law Review* 479 (1992); Martha Nussbaum, " 'Only Grey Matter?' Richard Posner's Cost-Benefit Analysis of Sex," 59 *University of Chicago Law Review* 1689 (1992).

12. Proponents of law and economics often note that they do not endorse the view that efficiency equals justice, because an efficient state (however efficiency is defined) is always efficient relative to an initial wealth distribution, and the initial distribution may be unjust. See, for example, Posner, *Economic Analysis of Law* at 14. But many of them ignore their caveat. See id. at 27, stating that efficiency is "perhaps the most common" meaning of "justice."

13. See, for example, Robert C. Ellickson, "Adverse Possession and Perpetuities Law: Two Dents in the Libertarian Model of Property Rights," 64 *Washington University Law Quarterly* 723, 737 (1986) (finding, with approval, that "the deep structure of property law has traditionally been . . . transaction-cost utilitarianism"); idem, Round Table Discussion, "Time, Property Rights, and the Common Law," 64 *Washington University Law Quarterly* 793, 796 (1986) (suspecting that "most of us" law-and-economics scholars are utilitarians at bottom).

14. See, for example, James M. Buchanan, *The Limits of Liberty: Between Anarchy and Leviathan* (1975); Richard Epstein, *Takings: Private Property and the Power of Eminent Domain* 331–350 (1985). Epstein seems to have undergone an odyssey from libertarianism to utilitarianism, passing through a stage in which he tried to embrace both at once. (See Chapter 2, note 28.)

The utilitarian consequentialist commitment to rest rightness on prediction is, in my view, ultimately at odds with the libertarian deontological commitment to preexisting and immutable natural property rights. See Margaret Jane Radin, "Problems for the Theory of Absolute Property Rights," in *Reinterpreting Property* 98–119 (1993).

15. See generally Amartya K. Sen, *Inequality Reexamined* (1992); idem, *Choice, Welfare, and Measurement* (1982).

16. Thus, economists who accept the possibility of judgments calculating Kaldor-Hicks efficiency are closer to universal commodification than those who do not. Kaldor-Hicks efficiency is the state of affairs obtaining when all "winners" (from any particular course of action) *could* compensate all "losers" and still have the action register a net gain. The compensation need not be carried out. In order for the comparison to be made at all, though, we need to assume that the "losers" value their dollars the same way the "winners" do, or at least in some functional relationship that can be definitely ascertained. See, for example, Posner, *Economic Analysis of Law* at 13–16.

17. Thomas Hobbes, *Leviathan, or the Matter, Forme, and Power of a Common Wealth, Ecclesiastical and Civil* 10, 16, 42 (1651). C. B. Macpherson reads Hobbes as reflecting the worldview of commodification; *The Political Theory of Possessive Individualism* 17–87 (1962).

18. See, for example, James M. Buchanan, Robert D. Tollison, and Gordon Tullock, eds., *Toward a Theory of the Rent-Seeking Society* (1980).

19. Becker, *A Treatise on the Family* at 138–139.

20. See Posener, *Economic Analysis of Law* at 261–266.

21. Id. at 150–151; Richard A. Posner, "The Regulation of the Market in Adoptions," 67 *Boston University Law Review* 59 (1987).

22. Becker, *A Treatise on the Family* at 45.

23. Jeremy Bentham, *Principles of the Civil Code,* chap. 6 (trans. Richard Hildreth 1840).

24. See, for example, Robert Nozick, *Philosophical Explanations* 2 (1981), stating that "[n]o philosophical argument forces us to accept its (unpleasant) conclusion."

25. See, for example, the essays collected in Michael Krausz, ed., *Relativism: Interpretation and Confrontation* (1989); and in Michael Krausz and Jack W. Meil, eds., *Relativism: Cognitive and Moral* (1982).

26. Thomas S. Kuhn, *The Structure of Scientific Revolutions* 142–144 (2d rev. ed. 1970).

27. Id. at 206.

28. Id. at 206–207. In my view Kuhn's rejoinder just pushes the question back a stage. For some time our paradigms have been subsumed by a larger one in which puzzle-solving is what science is *for,* but what if some other group has an entirely different view of the point of science? (Maybe in that case we'd say they didn't have the concept of "science"?)

29. Donald Davidson, "On the Very Idea of a Conceptual Scheme," in *Inquiries into Truth and Interpretation* 183 (1984).

30. Hilary Putnam, *Reason, Truth, and History* 113–126 (1981).

31. Legal scholars have begun to notice that this kind of incommensurability, debated for some time in the philosophical literature, might be important for law, and there is an ever-expanding body of writing on the subject by legal scholars. See Frederick Schauer, "Commensurability and Its Constitutional Consequences," 45 *Hastings Law Journal* 785 (1994); Cass R. Sunstein, "Incommensurability and Valuation in Law," 92 *Michigan Law Review* 779 (1994); Jeremy Waldron, "Fake Incommensurability: A Response to Professor Schauer," 45 *Hastings Law Journal* 813 (1994); Elizabeth Anderson, *Value in Ethics and Economics* (1993); Margaret Jane Radin, "Compensation and Commensurability," 1993 *Duke Law Journal* 56; Donald T. Hornstein, "Reclaiming Environmental Law: A Normative Critique of Comparative Risk Analysis," 92 *Columbia Law Review* 562 (1992); Donald R. Korobkin, "Value and Rationality in Bankruptcy Decisionmaking," 33 *William and Mary Law Review* 333 (1992); Richard Warner, "Incommensurability as a Jurisprudential Puzzle," 68 *Chicago-Kent Law Review* 147 (1992); Scott Altman, "(Com)modifying Experience," 65 *Southern California Law Review* 2121 (1990); Michael J. Perry, "Some Notes on Absolutism, Consequentialism, and Incommensurability," 79 *Northwestern University Law Review* 967 (1984–1985).

32. Martha Nussbaum makes clear that the incommensurability debate in ethics is much older than controversies over utilitarianism. According to Nussbaum, Plato argued for "an ethical 'science of measurement,' at the heart of which is the belief in commensurability"; "Plato on Commensurability and Desire," in *Love's Knowledge* 106 (1992).

33. James Griffin, *Well-Being: Its Meanings, Measurement and Moral Importance* 75–92 (1986); idem, "Are There Incommensurable Values?" 47 *Philosophy & Public Affairs* 39 (1977).

34. Joseph Raz, *The Morality of Freedom* 321–366 (1986); idem, "Value Incommensurability: Some Preliminaries," 86 *Proceedings of the Aristotelian Society* 117 (1985–86).

35. Raz, *The Morality of Freedom* at 345–352.

36. See, for example, Griffin, *Well-Being*. A similar position is presented in Gerald F. Gaus, "Does Compensation Restore Equality?" in 33 *NOMOS: Compensatory Justice* 45 (ed. John W. Chapman 1991).

37. Raz, "Value Incommensurability" at 128–134; see also Anderson, *Value in Ethics and Economics* at 44–64; Sunstein, "Incommensurability and Valuation in Law" at 805–812.

38. Ludwig Wittgenstein, *Philosophical Investigations* 30–34 (2d ed., trans. G. E. M. Anscombe 1958).

39. Thus the puns possible on the word "property" disappear; one's

properties as a person are merely one's property. The ambiguity in the word "property"—for example, in the way Locke used it—may be related to market rhetoric at a deeper level. See Margaret Jane Radin, "The Rhetoric of Alienation," in *Reinterpreting Property.*

40. Becker, *A Treatise on the Family* at 145.

41. As we have seen, Posner did take some steps in that direction. See Posner, *Economic Analysis of Law* at 152–154; Landes and Posner, "The Economics of the Baby Shortage"; Posner, "The Regulation of the Market in Adoptions."

42. This is no doubt particularly true for African-American women involved in such transactions. See Anita L. Allen, "The Black Surrogate Mother," 8 *Harvard Blackletter Law Journal* 17 (1991); idem, "Surrogacy, Slavery, and the Ownership of Life," 13 *Harvard Journal of Law & Public Policy* 139 (1990).

2. Market-Inalienability

1. For a sampling of views at and between these poles, see Elizabeth S. Anderson, *Value in Ethics and Economics* 67–68 (1993) (describing inalienabilities as a form of "lexical preference ordering" in which trade-offs between certain goods—for example, a trade-off between rights to basic liberties and economic benefit—are prohibited); Randy E. Barnett, "Contract Remedies and Inalienable Rights," 4 *Social Philosophy and Policy* 179, 185 (1986) ("To characterize a right as inalienable is to claim that the consent of the right-holder is insufficient to extinguish the right or to transfer it to another"); Guido Calabresi and A. Douglas Melamed, "Property Rules, Liability Rules, and Inalienability: One View of the Cathedral," 85 *Harvard Law Review* 1089, 1092 (1972) ("An entitlement is inalienable to the extent that its transfer is not permitted between a willing buyer and a willing seller"); Arthur Kuflik, "The Utilitarian Logic of Inalienable Rights," 97 *Ethics* 75, 75 (1986) ("An inalienable right is a right that a person has no right to give up or trade away"); Michael W. McConnell, "The Nature and Basis of Inalienable Rights," 3 *Law and Philosophy* 25, 27 (1984) ("That which is inalienable . . . is not transferable to the ownership of another"); Diana T. Meyers, *Inalienable Rights: A Defense* 4 (1985) ("an inalienable right is one that the right-holder cannot lose regardless of what he does or how others treat him and even if others are justified in declining to grant him what he demands in exercising his right"); idem, "The Rationale for Inalienable Rights in Moral Systems," 7 *Social Theory and Practice* 127, 127 (1981) ("Inalienable rights are rights that cannot be relinquished by the individuals who possess them").

2. In addition to transfer by gift and sale, barter represents a theoretically possible means of transfer. I do not consider barter, however, because it is not a widespread method of exchange in our culture.

3. We might think of assets held in trust for a minor, for example.

4. There are also subsets of gift transfer: transfer *inter vivos,* and bequest or devise. In this book I do not pursue the varieties of gift transmission.

5. See National Organ Transplant Act, 42 U.S.C. §274(e) (1984) (banning organ sales in interstate commerce). (Organ transfer is discussed further in Chapter 7.)

6. See, for example, Block v. Hirsh, 256 U.S. 135, 159 (1921) (McKenna, J., dissenting) (protesting that rent control "is contrary to every conception of leases that the world has ever entertained").

7. See Calabresi and Melamed, "Property Rules, Liability Rules, and Inalienability" at 1111–15.

8. See id. at 1106–10. Although they do not elaborate the point, Calabresi and Melamed think that the same regime is justified from a libertarian point of view. Property rules best satisfy libertarian concerns because they generally require the least state intervention, but liability rules might serve libertarian interests better in certain circumstances, for example, where property rules are especially difficult to enforce. See id. at 1092, n. 7. Such a convergence of efficiency and liberty is often claimed by free-market apologists.

9. Id. at 1092.

10. Id. at 1111.

11. Id. at 1112.

12. See id. at 1113–15.

13. See id. at 1113.

14. Id. at 1114.

15. Id. at 1113.

16. Id. at 1115.

17. Id. at 1114.

18. Id. at 1102, 1104.

19. See Guido Calabresi, "Thoughts on the Future of Economics in Legal Education," 33 *Journal of Legal Education* 359, 363–364 (1983). I believe that Calabresi would now disapprove of market rhetoric to consider the legal or moral treatment of baby-selling, as in the passage quoted in the text, or to consider the treatment of rape, which I discuss in Chapter 6.

20. Richard A. Epstein, "Why Restrain Alienation?" 85 *Columbia Law Review* 970, 990 (1985).

21. Id. at 970.

22. See Harold Demsetz, "Toward a Theory of Property Rights," 57 *American Economic Review* 347 (1967); Garrett Hardin, "The Tragedy of the Commons," 162 *Science* 1243 (1968).

23. See Epstein, "Why Restrain Alienation?" at 978. The assumption that people cannot restrain themselves from wrecking commonses arises from the conception of the person as a Hobbesian self-interested profit-maximizer. In real life, many commonses survive (for example, joint property ownership).

See Elinor Ostrom, *Governing the Commons* (1990); Carol Rose, "The Comedy of the Commons: Custom, Commerce, and Inherently Public Property," 53 *University of Chicago Law Review* 711 (1986).

24. See Epstein, "Why Restrain Alienation?" at 979–982, 984–988.

25. Id. at 981.

26. Id. at 988.

27. To see the extent of Epstein's market rhetoric, consider his opinion that the most likely motive for buying votes "is to obtain control of the public machinery, in ways that allow a person to recover, at the very least, the money that was paid out to the individuals who sold their votes, with something left to compensate the buyer for the labor and entrepreneurial risk." Id. at 987–988. Someone whose rhetoric is less thoroughly market oriented might surely conceive the motive for buying votes to be advancing one's unmonetized political, social, religious, or moral ideas.

28. Id. at 971. In earlier work, Epstein stressed libertarian rights. See, for example, Richard A. Epstein, "Possession as the Root of Title," 13 *Georgia Law Review* 1221 (1979). Then he claimed that libertarian rights and utilitarian reasoning lead to the same institutional rules. See idem, "Past and Future: The Temporal Dimension in the Law of Property," 64 *Washington University Law Quarterly* 667 (1986); idem, Round Table Discussion, "Time, Property Rights, and the Common Law," 64 *Washington University Law Quarterly* 793, 793 (1986) ("my long-term campaign . . . is to explain why libertarian rules are the first approximation of a decent set of rights in the utilitarian world"). Robert Ellickson and I demonstrated that it is not as easy as Epstein claims to be simultaneously a libertarian and a utilitarian. See Robert C. Ellickson, "Adverse Possession and Perpetuities Law: Two Dents in the Libertarian Model of Property Rights," 64 *Washington University Law Quarterly* 723, 737 (1986); Margaret Jane Radin, "Time, Possession and Alienation," 64 *Washington University Law Quarterly* 739, 743–745 (1986); See also idem, "Problems for the Theory of Absolute Property Rights," in *Reinterpreting Property* (1993). Later Epstein seemed to affirm that his foundational normative principle is indeed efficiency and not libertarian natural rights. He says, for example, that the traditionally recognized natural rights evolved instrumentally to serve efficiency before people were able to theorize explicitly about efficiency. See "Remarks of Richard Epstein," in "Proceedings of the Conference on Takings of Property and the Constitution," 41 *University of Miami Law Review* 49, 125–127 (1986).

29. See Susan Rose-Ackerman, "Inalienability and the Theory of Property Rights," 85 *Columbia Law Review* 931, 932–933 (1985).

30. See id. at 932.

31. See id. at 938.

32. Id. at 932.

33. See id. at 935.

34. "If policymakers wish to benefit a particular sort of person but cannot easily identify these people ex ante, they may be able to impose restrictions on the entitlement that are less onerous for the worthy group than for others who are nominally eligible." Id. at 940.

35. Id. at 942, 948–949.

36. See id. at 941.

37. Rose-Ackerman's conclusion that "it is generally possible to conceive of an alternative policy that would be superior [to inalienability] if transaction costs were lower" seems to indicate that efficiency—even if it is efficiency in achieving aims that are "distributive"—is her main concern. To this conclusion there is a "major exception" involving the "ideal of citizenship, where insulation from market forces may be desirable in principle." Id. at 969.

38. Id. at 931.

3. Problems for the Idea of a Market Domain

1. Robert Nozick, *Anarchy, State, and Utopia* 150–151, 230–231 (1974). Nozick provides a third part: rectification of past injustices in the two main categories. Nozick suggests that rectification is necessary to translate his ideal theory to the nonideal world.

2. See, for example, Northwest Real Estate Co. v. Serio, 114 A. 245, 246 (Md. 1929) (holding as repugnant to the fee simple title a clause preventing the property from being sold or rented before a designated date without the consent of the grantor).

3. See, for example, Wellenkamp v. Bank of America, 582 P.2d 970 (Cal. 1978) (holding that a due-on-sale clause in a deed of trust constituted an unreasonable restraint on alienation).

4. See Jeremy Bentham, "Theory of Legislation," in *Principles of the Civil Code,* pt. 1, chaps. 6–12 (trans. Richard Hildreth 1840).

5. Richard A. Epstein, *Takings: Private Property and the Power of Eminent Domain* 74, 304 (1985). Conceptualism is not necessarily linked with the views of those who espouse commodification. Marx's "bourgeois property" is a similar concept meaning ownership plus free alienability, that is, commodification. See, for example, Karl Marx, *The Communist Manifesto* (trans. Paul M. Sweezey 1964); idem, "The German Ideology," in *The Marx-Engels Reader* 186–193 (ed. Robert C. Tucker, 2d ed. 1984). Marx presumably would not have accepted any view that ownership might be justified if separated from market alienability, since he asserted that bourgeois property could not coexist with other kinds. See id. at 505–519.

6. John Stuart Mill, *Principles of Political Economy,* bk. 2, chap. 2 at 218, 220, 221 (ed. W. J. Ashley 1909).

7. Id., bk. 3, chap. 1 at 208. Political theorists who explain and justify capitalist private property must address the issue of human commodification. Their problem is to condemn slavery while justifying the sale of one's labor on the market model—that is, to distinguish worker commodification under slavery from the (alleged) worker commodification under (alleged) wage slavery. The sociologist Orlando Patterson argues that there is no intrinsic difference between "property" in the work of slaves and in the work of employees or of divorced spouses with legally enforced support obligations. See Orlando Patterson, *Slavery and Social Death* 21–27 (1982). Patterson's main point is that slavery is not tied to the notion of property in human beings; it exists under many kinds of social structures that do not include property. For those who wished to affirm the liberal market society and its pervasive property relations, while rejecting slavery, however, distinguishing between market property in human beings' labor and slave property in human beings' labor was crucial.

8. Mill, *Principles* at 229–231.

9. Id. at 226–229. The U.S. Supreme Court has held that the right to pass on property at death is so central a component of ownership that any governmental attempt to undercut it can be per se an unconstitutional taking of property. See Hodel v. Irving, 481 U.S. 704, 716 (1987) (right to pass on property at death "has been part of the Anglo-American legal system since feudal times").

10. We should not attribute such a position to Mill himself. Mill thought that land ownership yielded only "qualified" property because its importance and scarcity resulted in a duty of stewardship owed to society by its owners. See Mill, *Principles* at 229–235. As we have seen, he also thought that landed property was less justifiable than property in things created by one's own faculties, and hence gave rise to weaker or fewer rights. He might well have rejected the idea that the bad consequences of allowing land to be exclusively controlled by its owners should be characterized as external costs; he might also have rejected the idea that his qualifications were only exceptions in aid of market results.

11. See Immanuel Kant, "The Doctrine of Right" ("Rechtslehre," 1797), in Kant, *The Metaphysics of Morals* 50 (trans. Mary Gregor 1991) ("A *person* is a subject whose actions can be *imputed* to him. *Moral* personality is therefore nothing other than the freedom of a rational being under moral laws"); G. W. F. Hegel, *Philosophy of Right,* §41 (trans. T. M. Knox 1952) ("Personality is the first, still wholly abstract, delineation of the absolute and infinite will"), §35 ("The universality of [the] consciously free will is abstract universality, the self-conscious but otherwise contentless and simple relation of itself to itself in its individuality, and from this point of view the subject is a person").

12. If the person is simply pure subjectivity empty of individuating characteristics and personal attributes, then these characteristics and attributes may

be readily conceived of as separate from the person and possessed by the person. From the view that attributes and characteristics are separate possessions, it is an easy step to conceptualize them as lying on the object side of the subject/object divide. This conceptualization as objects eliminates inalienabilities based on things internal to the person, because nothing is internal to the person considered as an abstract, subjective unit. Once individuating characteristics and personal attributes are conceptualized as possessions situated in the object realm, it is another easy step to conceive of them as separable from the person through alienation. Finally, once characteristics and attributes are seen as alienable objects, it is not difficult to see them as fungible and bearing implicit money value.

13. See Kant, "The Doctrine of Right" at 68–71; Hegel, *Philosophy of Right,* §§41–71.

14. Hegel, *Philosophy of Right,* §65.

15. Id., §§66, 66R.

16. See Kant, "The Doctrine of Right" at 68.

17. Hegel, *Philosophy of Right,* §44.

18. Immanuel Kant, *Lectures on Ethics* 165 (trans. Louis Infield, ed. J. Macmurray, rev. ed. 1930). Kant's argument here was in the form of a contradiction, a form of argument that Hegel also used. From this contradiction, which seems to rule out voluntary enslavement (although Kant did not mention it here), Kant purported to deduce not only that sexual services cannot be marketed, but also that a person is not entitled to sell one of her teeth. If nothing else, this deduction can serve as a warning that the internal/external or subject/object distinction does not generate noncontroversial particular consequences.

19. See Hegel, *Philosophy of Right,* §42: "What is immediately different from free mind is that which, both for mind and in itself, is the external pure and simple, a thing, something not free, not personal, without rights."

20. See id., §44.

21. See Kant, "The Doctrine of Right" at 68.

22. Hegel, *Philosophy of Right,* §67.

23. See id., §69.

24. See, for example, Ethan Katsh, *Law in a Digital World* (1995).

25. Id., §39.

26. See Hegel, *Philosophy of Right,* §66R.

27. See id., §65. But note that Hegel thought that a landed aristocracy with entailed estates was most qualified to govern the properly developed state. See id., §§305–307 and also 180R: "In the higher sphere of the state, a right of primogeniture arises together with estates rigidly entailed; it arises, however, not arbitrarily but as the inevitable outcome of the Idea of the state."

28. Id., §73. Something exists according to its concept *(Begriff)* when it is

fully actualized in accord with mind or spirit *(Geist)*.

29. Id., §71R.

30. Id., §74.

31. See Karl Marx, *Capital* 84–85 (ed. Friedrich Engels 1894, trans. Samuel Moore and Edward Aveling 1984).

32. See Hegel, *Philosophy of Right,* §75R.

33. See id., §§75R, 158–169, 261.

34. See id., §§183R, 257, 260.

35. Id., §66R.

36. Id.

37. Nevertheless, the distinction and its consequences still seem obvious to some. For a discussion of inalienability that relies on an intuitive subject/object distinction, see Randy E. Barnett, "Contract Remedies and Inalienable Rights," 4 *Social Philosophy and Policy* 179, 195 (1986), in which the author states that "rights to possess, use, and control resources external to one's person are (generally) alienable, and . . . the right to possess, use, and control one's person is inalienable."

38. See Thomas S. Kuhn, *The Structure of Scientific Revolutions* 6 (2d rev. ed. 1970) (arguing that the adoption of scientific theories has both reflected and transformed "the world within which scientific work was done"); and Richard Rorty, *Philosophy and the Mirror of Nature* 378–379 (1979).

39. See Isaiah Berlin, "Two Concepts of Liberty," in *Four Essays on Liberty* 122 (1969) ("Political liberty in this sense is simply the area within which a man can act unobstructed by others"); and Quentin Skinner, "The Idea of Negative Liberty: Philosophical and Historical Perspectives," in *Philosophy in History* 193, 197 (ed. Richard Rorty, J. B. Schneewind, and Quentin Skinner 1984) (defining negative liberty as "the mere nonobstruction of individual agents in the pursuit of their chosen ends").

40. Kant, "The Doctrine of Right" at 52.

41. See Duncan Kennedy, "Distributive and Paternalist Motives in Contract and Tort Law, with Special Reference to Compulsory Terms and Unequal Bargaining Power," 41 *Maryland Law Review* 563, 626–629, 631–649 (1982).

42. Perhaps it is possible to refine the notion of paternalism to avoid the stark conflict with negative liberty. Donald Regan, "Paternalism, Freedom, Identity, and Commitment," in *Paternalism,* 113–117 (ed. Rolf E. Sartorius 1983), argues that paternalism might be justified in some cases by converting the notion of freedom into a teleological principle (maximizing freedom), and that this is still a notion of negative freedom. Regan also proposes a form of justification based upon avoiding harm to someone's later self. This form of justification implicitly relies upon a notion of fostering personhood or self-development that may be inconsistent with negative liberty. For similar views

close to Regan's see John Kleinig, "Argument from Personal Integrity," in *Paternalism* 67–73; and Anthony T. Kronman, "Paternalism and the Law of Contracts," 92 *Yale Law Journal* 763, 786–797 (1983).

43. See Joel Feinberg, "Voluntary Euthanasia and the Inalienable Right to Life," 7 *Philosophy & Public Affairs* 93, 120–123 (1978).

44. See id. at 120–121.

45. See id. at 121. Feinberg understands "inalienable" to mean prohibition of voluntary relinquishment. See id. at 112: "an *inalienable right* is one that a person cannot give away or dispense with through his own deliberate choice." As I mentioned in Chapter 2, there is no firm agreement on what is meant by "inalienable." In order to avoid unnecessary confusion, the discussion in the text substitutes "nonrelinquishable" for Feinberg's use of "inalienable."

46. See id. at 115–116.

47. Id. at 121.

48. Whether Feinberg is committed to negative liberty is unstated in the article under consideration, although that seems fairly inferable from his declaration of "doubts about the theory of inalienable rights in any case" (id. at 94) and his characterization of mandatory rights as "smug paternalism" (id. at 122) and "offensively demeaning" (id. at 106). A commitment to negative liberty is clear in Joel Feinberg, *Harm to Self* 62–66 (1986), in which Feinberg distinguishes among autonomy, liberty, and freedom and defines both liberty and freedom in terms of absence of constraint.

49. John Stuart Mill, *On Liberty,* in *Three Essays* 126 (1975).

50. See, for example, Feinberg, "Voluntary Euthanasia" at 75–79.

51. Mill, *On Liberty* at 117.

52. Id.

53. Id. A modern version of this argument is found in C. Edwin Baker, "Counting Preferences in Collective Situations," 25 *UCLA Law Review* 381 (1978), in which the author defends a distinction between regulation and prohibition that parallels Mill's.

54. Nozick, *Anarchy, State, and Utopia* at 331, takes the extreme view: a "free system" will allow an individual "to sell himself into slavery."

55. See Harold Demsetz, "Toward a Theory of Property Rights," 57 *American Economics Review* 348–349 (1967).

4. Compartmentalization

1. Michael Walzer, *Spheres of Justice* (1983). See also idem, "Liberalism and the Art of Separation," 12 *Political Theory* 315 (1984); criticized in Thomas Morawetz, "Tension in 'The Art of Separation,' " 13 *Political Theory* 599 (1985). For another prominent example of compartmentaliza-

tion, see Elizabeth S. Anderson, "The Ethical Limitations of the Market," in *Value in Ethics and Economics* (1993). See also Judith Andre, "Blocked Exchanges: A Taxonomy," 103 *Ethics* 29 (1992).

2. Although this is Walzer's theoretical assumption, in practice there would not be a very large free-market sphere left after all the various kinds of welfare regulation he recommends were implemented. Thus, in a sense, a theory of incomplete commodification would have served Walzer's purposes better than the spatial metaphor.

3. Walzer, *Spheres of Justice* at 120.

4. Although this boundary is described as a moral matter, and the market exceeding its bounds is—in a nice phrase—"moral irredentism," Walzer says that the issue of what things cannot be bought and sold, because we do not want certain values to be priced, is "an empirical matter." But surely this issue too is a moral matter, since it involves the containment of the market within its proper sphere, necessary for justice as complex equality. Walzer says as much when he says that these "blocked exchanges" "set limits on the dominance of wealth." See Walzer, *Spheres of Justice* at 100.

The puzzle is resolved to some extent when one takes into account that Walzer is at least sometimes a moral conventionalist. What *is* right is what the relevant social group *thinks* is right. Thus, if his list coincides with social practice, no further argument is needed to convince us of its moral rightness. Walzer's critics have taken him to task for his conventionalism. See, for example, Elizabeth S. Anderson, *Value in Ethics and Economics* 143 (1993); Brian Barry, "Intimations of Justice," 84 *Columbia Law Review* 806 (1984) (book review); James S. Fishkin, "Defending Equality: A View from the Cave," 82 *Michigan Law Review* 755 (1984) (book review). To be fair, however, it should be noted that Walzer is only sometimes merely a conventionalist; sometimes he is a pragmatist refusing to accept the positive/normative distinction (that is, the fact/value dichotomy).

5. The fourteen things are: human beings; political power and influence; criminal justice; freedom of speech, press, religion, assembly; marriage and procreation rights; emigration rights; exemptions from military service, jury duty, and "any other form of communally imposed work"; political offices and professional standing; the minimum level of "basic welfare services like police protection or primary and secondary schooling"; "desperate exchanges"; public and private prizes and honors; divine grace; love and friendship; and, finally, "a long series of criminal sales." See Walzer, *Spheres of Justice* at 100–103. In this list, all different kinds of inalienabilities are lumped together under a general ban on buying and selling. To speak only of sale when a particular kind of inalienability is broader than that distorts its political and social significance and reflects a tendency toward universal commodification, at least in rhetoric.

6. Walzer, *Spheres of Justice* at 100–103. See also Cass R. Sunstein, "Incommensurability and Valuation in Law," 92 *Michigan Law Review* 779, 787 (1994): "There is often a connection between blocked exchanges and ideas about equal citizenship. The exchange may be barred by social norms or law because of a perception that, while there may be disparities in social wealth, the spheres in which people are very unequal ought not to invade realms of social life in which equality is a social goal."

7. Joel Feinberg, *Harm to Self* 80–81 (1986).

8. Richard A. Posner, *Economic Analysis of Law* 261–266 (4th ed. 1992).

9. The concept of coercion—in particular the issue of what factors of power we should characterize as negating free choice—is a philosophical dispute I cannot review more deeply here. See, for example, Richard E. Flathman, *The Philosophy and Politics of Freedom* 180–220 (1987); Robert Nozick, "Coercion," in *Philosophy, Science, and Method* 440 (ed. Sidney Morgenbesser, Patrick Suppes, and Morton White 1969).

5. Personhood and the Dialectic of Contextuality

1. Immanuel Kant, "The Doctrine of Right" ("Rechtshlehre," 1797), in Kant, *The Metaphysics of Morals* 82–95 (trans. Mary Gregor 1991). See also Barbara Herman, *The Practice of Moral Judgment* (1993).

2. See, for example, Viviana Zelizer, *The Social Meaning of Money* (1994).

3. See Margaret Jane Radin, "Property and Personhood," in *Reinterpreting Property* 35–71 (1993).

4. Perhaps what remains could be thought of as mere undifferentiated Kantian moral agency. Thus in the thinnest theory of the self we have the power of conceiving the good and the power of choice, but nothing is "attached" to this that makes us concretely unique as individuals.

5. A deeply entrenched tic or vice, nail biting or cigarette smoking, can be part of one's character, and yet to separate it from oneself may be deeply wished, even if doing so requires reconstruction of the self.

6. Compare, for example, Margaret Jane Radin, "Residential Rent Control," in *Reinterpreting Property* 72–97; with Robert C. Ellickson, "Rent Control: A Comment on Olsen," 67 *Chicago-Kent Law Review* 947 (1991); or Richard A. Epstein, "Rent Control and the Theory of Regulation," 54 *Brooklyn Law Review* 741 (1988).

7. Radin, "Residential Rent Control."

8. Ellickson, "Rent Control"; Roberto M. Unger, *Plasticity into Power: Variations on Themes of Politics. A Work in Constructive Social Theory* (1987).

9. See Amartya K. Sen, "Functionings and Capability," in *Inequality Reexamined* (1992). In an earlier work, Sen calls to task students of Chicago

economics for their assumption, "the first principle of Economics," that "every agent is actuated only by self-interest." Amartya K. Sen, "Rational Fools: A Critique of the Behavioral Foundations of Economic Theory," 6 *Philosophy and Public Affairs* 317, 317 (1976). Sen notes that neoclassical economics' exclusive focus on self-interest as the sole motivator of action fails to account both for sympathy ("[i]f the knowledge of torture of others makes you sick, it is a case of sympathy") and for commitment ("if it does not make you feel personally worse off, but you think it is wrong and you are ready to do something to stop it, it is a case of commitment"). Id. at 326. Sen asserts that in failing to account for commitment, indeed, in accusing those motivated by it of irrationality, neoclassical economists may in many fields be misapprehending what they observe.

10. Sen, *Inequality Reexamined* at 39, n. 3.

11. Martha C. Nussbaum, "Nature, Function, and Capability: Aristotle on Political Distribution," in *Oxford Studies in Ancient Philosophy* 145 (ed. Julia Annas and Robert H. Grimm 1988).

12. Id. at 145–146.

13. Id. at 146.

14. Martha C. Nussbaum, "Human Functioning and Social Justice: In Defense of Aristotelian Essentialism," 20 *Political Theory* 202, 205–207 (1992).

15. Hilary Putnam, *The Many Faces of Realism* 17 (1987).

16. Nussbaum, "Nature, Function, and Capability" at 174–175.

17. Id. at 175–176.

18. Martha C. Nussbaum, "Aristotelian Social Democracy," in *Liberalism and the Good* 217–226 (ed. R. Bruce Douglas et al. 1990).

19. Nussbaum, "Human Functioning and Social Justice" at 216; idem, "Aristotelian Social Democracy" at 219.

20. Nussbaum, "Human Functioning and Social Justice" at 222; idem, "Aristotelian Social Democracy" at 225.

21. The list occurs in Nussbaum, "Human Functioning and Social Justice" at 216–220; and idem, "Aristotelian Social Democracy" at 219–223; in "Non-Relative Virtues: An Aristotelian Approach," in *Midwest Studies in Philosophy* 262–264 (ed. Peter A. French et al. 1988), the list consists of eight items.

22. The entire list appears in Nussbaum, "Human Functioning and Social Justice" at 222; idem, "Aristotelian Social Democracy" at 225.

23. Nussbaum, "Human Functioning and Social Justice" at 215.

24. Nussbaum, "Non-Relative Virtues" at 265.

25. Nussbaum, "Human Functioning and Social Justice" at 219.

26. Nussbaum, "Aristotelian Social Democracy" at 233.

27. Nussbaum, "Non-Relative Virtues" at 266; idem, "Human Functioning and Social Justice" at 222–223; idem, "Aristotelian Social Democracy" at 226 (quoting Marx).

28. Nussbaum, "Non-Relative Virtues" at 266.

29. Nussbaum, "Aristotelian Social Democracy" at 226.

30. Id. at 229.

31. Id.

32. As Nussbaum says, too abstractly for a pragmatic lawyer's taste: "The idea is that the entire structure of the polity will be designed with a view to these functions. Not only programs of allocation, but also the division of land, the arrangement for forms of ownership, the structure of labor relations, institutional support for forms of family and social affiliation, ecological policy and policy toward animals, institutions of political participation, recreational institutions—all these, as well as more concrete programs within these areas, will be chosen with a view to good human functioning." Id. at 230.

33. Id.

34. Id. at 231.

35. Id. at 233–234.

36. See Chapters 12 and 14.

37. Nussbaum, "Aristotelian Social Democracy" at 233.

38. Nussbaum, "Human Functioning and Social Justice" at 231.

39. Id.

40. Nussbaum, "Aristotelian Social Democracy" at 232.

41. Continuing, Marx elaborated: "when it exists for us as capital, or when it is directly possessed, eaten, drunk, worn, inhabited, etc.—in short, when it is *used* by us." "Economic and Philosophic Manuscripts of 1844," in *The Marx-Engels Reader* 73 (1972).

42. It is open to argue that my understanding is parochial. "Some people take the stages of the journey and its destination as prearranged: a pilgrimage toward salvation. Others deny the journey picture and insist that their job is to occupy their allotted station and perform its duties faithfully." Don Herzog, personal communication.

6. Human Flourishing and Market Rhetoric

1. See Margaret Jane Radin, "The Rhetoric of Alienation," in *Reinterpreting Property* 191–202 (1993).

2. Karl Marx, "Economic and Philosophic Manuscripts of 1844," in *The Marx-Engels Reader* 70, 71 (ed. R. Tucker, 2d ed. 1984).

3. Karl Marx, "The German Ideology: Part I," in *The Marx-Engels Reader* 193.

4. See Karl Marx, *Capital* 71–83 (ed. Friedrich Engels ed. 1894, trans. Samuel Moore and Edward Aveling 1984). For essays relating the theory of commodity fetishism to legal studies, see Isaac Balbus, "Commodity Form

and Legal Form: An Essay on the 'Relative Autonomy of the Law,' " 11 *Law and Sociology Review* 571, 573–575 (1977); and Duncan Kennedy, "The Role of Law in Economic Thought: Essays on the Fetishism of Commodities," 34 *American University Law Review* 939 (1985).

5. Thoroughgoing reification, with its ramifications for the disempowerment of human beings, is the classical meaning of commodity fetishism. There are other meanings as well. One refers to the surface phenomena of rampant consumerism or crass devotion to material possessions. To be a commodity fetishist in this newer and less technical sense is simply to have one's identity too tied to possessions, to be too dependent upon thing-ownership for pleasure and a sense of self-worth. This meaning does not correspond to commodity fetishism in the classical Marxist sense, because it does not refer specifically to the nature of the things possessed as capitalist market trade artifacts. Nevertheless, it is a form of fetishism (projection onto objects), and it is certainly compatible with some Marxist views of the world. Another meaning is what Fred Hirsch calls "the new commodity fetishism," the idea that "an excessive proportion of individual activity is channeled through the market so that the commercialized sector of our lives is unduly large." Fred Hirsch, *Social Limits to Growth* 84 (1976). This "new commodity fetishism" sticks to the technical meaning of "commodity" and is thus different from the commonsense view I have just described, which is more truly fetishist.

6. What we now call market value, Marx thought of as "exchange value," which he contrasted with "use value" (the worth of something to consumers) and "value" (the amount of labor socially necessary to produce something). See Marx, *Capital* at 84–93. For explication and criticism of Marx's theories of value, see, for example, Gerald A. Cohen, "Labor, Leisure, and a Distinctive Contradiction of Advanced Capitalism", in *Markets and Morals* 107 (ed. Gerald Dworkin, Gordon Bermant, and Peter Brown 1977); and Jon Elster, *Making Sense of Marx* 119–165 (1985).

7. Marx, *Capital* at 79; see also C. Edwin Baker, "Property and Its Relation to Constitutionally Protected Liberty," 134 *University of Pennsylvania Law Review* 741 (1986), arguing that "market oriented liberty"—as opposed to individual liberty defined as self-determination and self-realization—is not conducive to the autonomy of either producers or consumers.

8. Georg Lukács, "Reification and the Consciousness of the Proletariat," in *History and Class-Consciousness* 83 (trans. Rodney Livingstone 1971).

9. Id. at 170, 198.

10. See id. at 88–92. "Rationalization" is Max Weber's term for the development of the economic system toward achieving ever greater profit at less cost. See, for example, Anthony T. Kronman, *Max Weber* 130–137 (1982), discussing the formal rationality of economic action.

11. Lukács, "Reification and Consciousness of Proletariat" at 91.

12. Id. at 100.

13. Id. at 184.

14. Id. at 116. See 114–117.

15. "Only by conceiving of thought as a form of reality, as a factor in the total process can philosophy overcome its own rigidity dialectically and take on the quality of Becoming." Id. at 203.

16. Id. at 204.

17. See, for example, E. B. Pashukanis, *Law and Marxism* (1989); George M. Armstrong Jr., "From the Fetishism of Commodities to the Regulated Market: The Rise and Decline of Property," 82 *Northwestern University Law Review* 79 (1987); Csaba Varga, *The Place of Things in Lukács' World Concept* (1985).

18. Clifford Geertz, "Thick Description: Toward an Interpretive Theory of Culture," in *The Interpretation of Cultures* 1–30 (1973); Frank I. Michelman, "Saving Old Glory: On Constitutional Iconography," 42 *Stanford Law Review* 1337 (1990). See also Richard Bernstein, *Objectivity, Relativism, and Beyond* (1983); Robert M. Cover, "Nomos and Narrative," 97 *Harvard Law Review* 4 (1983); Jonathan Culler, *On Deconstruction: Theory and Criticism after Structuralism* 107–134 (1989); Michel Foucault, "Two Lectures," in *Power/Knowledge: Selected Interviews and Other Writings* 78–108 (trans. Colin Gordon et al., ed. Colin Gordon, 1980).

19. This slogan seems to have been popularized by Samuel Hayakawa. See Samuel Hayakawa, *Language in Thought and Action* 24–25 (4th ed. 1978). It and a companion "extensionalist" slogan, "A map is not the territory," apparently stem from the work of Alfred Korzybski. See, for example, Alfred Korzybski, *Science and Sanity* 750 (4th ed. 1958).

20. For a typical economic analysis, see Werner Z. Hirsch, "From 'Food for Thought' to 'Empirical Evidence' about Consequences of Landlord-Tenant Laws," 69 *Cornell Law Review* 604 (1984).

21. Richard A. Posner, *Economic Analysis of Law* 218 (4th ed. 1992).

22. Id. Not until the fourth edition of his *Economic Analysis of Law* does Posner acknowledge that "the fact that some sort of rape license is even thinkable within the framework of the wealth-maximization theory that guides so much of the analysis in this book will strike many readers as a limitation on the usefulness of that theory." Id.

23. Id. at 219.

24. Birendranath Ganguli, *Emma Goldman: Portrait of a Rebel Woman* (1979); Bonnie Haaland, *Emma Goldman: Sexuality and the Impurity of the State* (1993).

25. See, e.g., Victor Fuchs, *Women's Quest for Economic Equality* (1988); Virginia Held, "Noncontractual Society: A Feminist View," in *Feminism* 405 (ed. Susan Moller Okin and Jane Mansbridge 1994); Susan Moller Okin,

Justice, Gender, and the Family 134–169 (1989); Hanna Papanek, "To Each Less than She Needs, From Each More than She Can Do: Allocations, Settlements, and Value," in *Persistent Inequalities* (1990); Carol M. Rose, "Women and Property: Gaining and Losing Ground," 78 *Virginia Law Review* 421 (1992).

26. See Guido Calabresi and A. Douglas Melamed, "Property Rules, Liability Rules, and Inalienability: One View of the Cathedral," 85 *Harvard Law Review* 1089, 1124–27 (1972), applying their framework to criminal sanctions.

27. Although the article by Calabresi and Melamed has a strong tendency to talk in monetized efficiency terms, there is a hint of compartmentalization in this passage, which must be quoted at some length in order to convey the rhetorical flavor:

"The question remains, however, why *not* convert all property rules into liability rules? The answer is, of course, obvious. Liability rules represent only an approximation of the value of the object to its original owner and willingness to pay such an approximate value is no indication that it is worth more to the thief than to the owner. . . . If this is so with property, it is all the more so with bodily integrity, and we would not presume collectively and objectively to value the cost of a rape to a victim against the benefit to the rapist even if economic efficiency is our sole motive. Indeed when we approach bodily integrity we are getting close to areas where we do not let the entitlement be sold at all and where economic efficiency enters in, if at all, in a more complex way. . . . The first year student might push on, however, and ask why we treat the thief or rapist differently from the injurer in an auto accident or the polluter in a nuisance case. Why do we allow liability rules there? In a sense, we have already answered the question. The only level at which, before the accident, the driver can negotiate for the value of what he might take from his potential victim is one at which transactions are too costly. The thief or rapist, on the other hand, could have negotiated without undue expense (at least if the good was one which we allowed to be sold at all) because we assume he knew what he was going to do and to whom he would do it." Id. at 1125–27. Recall that Calabresi and Melamed also hint at compartmentalization in their mention of "other justice reasons" for setting entitlements, but they find it difficult to flesh out this idea, in my view because of their commitment to market rhetoric in that article. (See Chapter 2.) Calabresi has since modified his views and probably no longer conceives of rape in market rhetoric.

28. Id. at 1125.

29. See John Rawls, *Political Liberalism* 8 (1993); idem, *A Theory of Justice* 48–51 (1971).

30. See W. V. O. Quine, "Two Dogmas of Empiricism," in *From a Logical Point of View* 20, 42 (2d ed. 1980). As Quine recognized, the coherence view

tends toward pragmatism. See id. at 42–46. There are some knotty problems with coherence theory that cause some pragmatists to deny that pragmatism is a coherence theory. See Margaret Jane Radin, "The Pragmatist and the Feminist," 63 *Southern California Law Review* 1699 (1990). See also Joseph Raz, "The Relevance of Coherence," 72 *Boston University Law Review* 273 (1992).

31. See Ludwig Wittgenstein, *Philosophical Investigations* (3d ed. 1958); Thomas S. Kuhn, *The Structure of Scientific Revolutions* (2d ed. 1970).

32. Kuhn, *The Structure of Scientific Revolutions* at 128. Several schools of thought converge with modern pragmatism on the issue of the theory-or discourse-dependence of reality, including critical theory, hermeneutics, the sociology of knowledge, and perhaps poststructuralism. These thought traditions diverge on the issue of whether discourses can be judged as better or worse, which is one reason I pursue only the antifoundationalist pragmatist view.

33. The sweeping implications of rejecting traditional dichotomies between language and reality and between fact and value may be difficult to imagine. They would infuse and transform our everyday discourse. The vocabulary of our conversation always presupposes certain categories and foundational principles while we are in the process of philosophically rejecting them. See, for example, Richard Rorty, "Pragmatism, Relativism, and Irrationalism," in *Consequences of Pragmatism* 160 (1982).

34. See Hilary Putnam, *Reason, Truth, and History* 139–141 (1981). What is at issue both for Putnam and for me is not any kind of directional causal chain but the interdependence of values, facts, and discourse. See, for example, id. at 132–135, 201–203, 215.

35. See id. at 139–140.

36. Id. at 140. Extreme utilitarians ("super-Benthamites") would in fact be led to argue for punishment of innocent people on consequentialist grounds. See, for example, J. J. C. Smart, "Extreme and Restricted Utilitarianism," 6 *Philosophical Quarterly* 344 (1956). Because we are not super-Benthamites, the idea of punishment of the innocent has been an embarrassment for most utilitarians, a problem to be solved. See John Rawls, "Two Concepts of Rules," 64 *Philosophical Review* 3 (1955).

37. Putnam, *Reason, Truth, and History* at 141.

38. See id. at 140.

39. Id. at 141.

40. The issue of commensurability is complicated, and incommensurability may be a contested concept. See Chapters 1 and 13.

41. Martha C. Nussbaum, "Plato on Commensurability and Desire," in *Love's Knowledge* 106, 123 (1990).

42. Richard A. Posner, "An Economic Analysis of the Criminal Law," 85 *Columbia Law Review* 1193 (1985).

43. See Posner, *Economic Analysis of Law* at 217.

44. Perhaps Robert Frank's studies are suggestive here. He found that economics students come to behave as economistic profit-maximizers more than do students in other disciplines. See Robert H. Frank, Thomas Gilovich, and Dennis T. Regan, "Does Studying Economics Inhibit Cooperation?" *Journal of Economic Perspectives* Spring 1993.

45. See Lewis Hyde, *The Gift: Imagination and the Erotic Life of Property* 56 (1983) ("It is the cardinal difference between gift and commodity exchange that a gift establishes a feeling-bond between two people, while the sale of a commodity leaves no necessary connection"). See also Richard M. Titmuss, *The Gift Relationship: From Human Blood to Social Policy* 71 (1971) ("Within all . . . gift transactions of a personal face-to-face nature lie embedded some elements of moral enforcement or bond"). In the same vein, gifts are characterized by John Noonan as "given in a context created by personal relations to convey a personal feeling." John T. Noonan, *Bribes* 695 (1984). Elizabeth Anderson states that "[g]ift exchange affirms and perpetuates the ties that bind the donor and the recipient." Elizabeth S. Anderson, *Value in Ethics and Economics* 151 (1993).

46. See, for example, Fred Hirsch, *Social Limits to Growth* app., 95–101 (1976).

47. See Michael Shapiro, "Regulation as Language: Communicating Values by Altering the Contingencies of Choice," 55 *University of Pittsburgh Law Review* 681, 760–790 (1994).

48. This point is made by writers as disparate as Georg Lukács and Peter Singer. See, for example, Lukács, "Reification and Consciousness of Proletariat" 83; Peter Singer, "Freedom and Utilities in the Distribution of Health Care," in *Markets and Morals* 149 (ed. Gordon Bermant, Peter Brown, and Gerald Dworkin 1977).

49. In fact utopian noncommodifiers, who think that commodification is inherently wrong, also tend to think that commodified and noncommodified forms of human interactions cannot coexist. In his view that "bourgeois property" cannot coexist with other kinds of property, Marx may be understood to have meant that market and nonmarket forms cannot coexist.

50. See Titmuss, *The Gift Relationship*. Peter Singer uses the form of argument I call the domino theory in his defense of Titmuss against the liberal view that both gifts and sales should be permitted. See generally Singer, "Freedom and Utilities in Distribution of Health Care."

51. In *The Social Meaning of Money* (1994), Viviana Zelizer provides evidence that the second premise of the domino theory may be shaky. Her study of the ways in which people "earmark" monies (a complicated weave of Christmas clubs, pin money, allowances, "clean" and "dirty" money, etc.), partitioning them according to source, intended use, and the like, shows a resistance on the part of "money-marking" people to the "standardizing, depersonalizing effects of state-homogenized money." Id. at 201–202.

7. Incomplete Commodification

1. On the use of suspect "cognitive ability" tests in the workplace see Mark Kelman, "Concepts of Discrimination in 'General Ability' Job Testing," 104 *Harvard Law Review* 1157 (1991). On the preference for statistical measures of ability in education even when such measures do not accurately predict grade performance see James Crouse and Dale Trusheim, "The Case against the SAT," 93 *Public Interest* 97, 102 (1988).

2. See Margaret Jane Radin, "Justice and the Market Domain," in 31 *NOMOS: Markets and Justice* 165 (ed. John W. Chapman 1989); see also Elizabeth S. Anderson, "The Ethical Limitations of the Market," in *Value in Ethics and Economics* (1993).

3. See Hannah Arendt, *The Human Condition* (1958). Arendt noted that many languages have two words corresponding to "work" and "labor," and that only "work," understood as a noun, designates a finished product. Labor, on the other hand, remains a verbal noun. Id. at 80. For her, labor meant the kind of activity necessary to sustain life. It is ephemeral and leaves no traces on the environment; and it does not distinguish human beings from animals, since they too must labor in this sense. Work, on the other hand, lives after us and changes the world in which we live. Id. at 79–93. (This seems to me similar to Marx's notion of "working up" our world.) See also André Gorz, *Critique of Economic Reason* (trans. Gillian Handyside and Chris Turner 1988).

4. A balanced and thoughtful presentation of this concern is found in Dan W. Brock and Allen E. Buchanan, "The Profit Motive in Medicine," 12 *Journal of Medicine and Philosophy* 1 (1987).

5. Thus, to think of our labor power only as a commodity separate from ourselves is, as Marx thought, to do violence to our ideal of personhood. In supposing that for some of us work is incompletely commodified, I am supposing—perhaps contrary to Marxists—that unalienated work exists to some extent. I am not supposing that no alienated labor exists, nor am I supposing that unalienated work is not correlated with class.

6. See, for example, Richard A. Posner, *Economic Analysis of Law* 332–340 (4th ed. 1992) (discussing inefficiencies resulting from regulation of the employment relationship); id. at 470–474 (discussing inefficiencies resulting from housing code enforcement); Richard Epstein, "A Common Law for Labor Relations: A Critique of the New Deal Labor Legislation," 92 *Yale Law Journal* 1357 (1983); idem, "In Defense of the Contract at Will," 51 *University of Chicago Law Review* 947 (1984). But compare John J. Donohue III, "Is Title VII Efficient?" 134 *University of Pennsylvania Law Review* 1411 (1986) (using an economic model to argue that antidiscrimination legislation might enhance economic efficiency).

7. See Robert Nozick, *Anarchy, State, and Utopia* (1974).

8. See, for example, James M. Buchanan, *The Limits of Liberty* (1975); David Gauthier, *The Logic of Leviathan* (1969); idem, "The Social Contract as Ideology," 6 *Philosophy & Public Affairs* 130–164 (1977); Russell Hardin, *Collective Action* (1982); Gregory Kavka, "Hobbes' War of All against All," 93 *Ethics* 291–310 (1983); idem, "Rule by Fear," 17 *Nous* 601–620 (1983).

9. John Rawls, *A Theory of Justice* 274 (1971). John Stick argues interestingly that Rawls's methodology readily leads to Nozickian results. See John Stick, "Turning Rawls into Nozick and Back Again," 81 *Northwestern Law Review* 363 (1987).

10. Indeed, it is difficult to find a substitute rhetoric—and "good" is significantly ambiguous itself (one might almost say incompletely commodified). Yet it does seem that some of the bases of self-respect may be more perspicuously conceived of as attributes or elements of self-constitution.

11. For example, T. M. Scanlon's influential essay, "Contractualism and Utilitarianism," in *Utilitarianism and Beyond* 103–128 (ed. Amartya Sen and Bernard Williams 1981), cogently argues in favor of a moral methodology based on hypothetical uncoerced agreement. The market metaphor of contract is not a necessary part of this argument, and may in fact detract from its breadth and force.

12. See Michael Walzer, *Spheres of Justice,* chap. 3 (1983) (discussed in Chapter 4 above).

13. Susan Okin, *Justice, Gender, and the Family* (1989).

14. A well-known version of this critique is found in Roberto M. Unger, *Knowledge and Politics* 1 (1975).

15. Note, for example, Rawls's reference to "Hobbes's thesis" in his defense of the liberal ideal of the rule of law, in *A Theory of Justice* at 240–241.

8. Conceptual Recapitulation

1. See, for example, David H. Gauthier, *Morals by Agreement* (1986); Kurt Baier, "Obligation: Political and Moral," 12 *NOMOS: Political and Legal Obligation* 116 (ed. J. Ronald Pennock and John W. Chapman 1970).

2. Where regulation of literal markets represents incomplete commodification in the stronger sense, this continuum of commodification in rhetoric is analogous to the continuum in literal markets from those that are completely laissez-faire to those that are heavily regulated (sense 1 in the discussion in the text).

3. See Chapter 6. See also Joseph Raz, *The Morality of Freedom* 321–366 (1986), especially §5 on constitutive incommensurabilities.

4. This point is felicitously made in Frank I. Michelman, "Ethics, Economics, and the Law of Property," in 22 *NOMOS: Property* 3, 30–31 (ed.

J. Ronald Pennock and John W. Chapman 1980). See also Jules L. Coleman, *Risks and Wrongs* (1992).

5. See, for example, Jean Hampton, "Rational Choice and the Law," 15 *Harvard Journal of Law and Public Policy* 649 (1992).

9. The Double Bind

1. See Margaret Jane Radin, "Market-Inalienability," 100 *Harvard Law Review,* 1849, 1921–25 (1987). See also, for example, Elizabeth S. Anderson, *Value in Ethics and Economics* 156 (1993) ("If the prohibition of prostitution is to serve women's interests in freedom and autonomy, it should not function so as to drive them to starvation"); and Debra Satz, "Markets in Women's Sexual Labor," 106 *Ethics* 63, 83 (1995).

2. For an overview of the special treatment/equal treatment debate, see Herma H. Kay, "Text Note: Ensuring Non-Discrimination," in *Text, Cases, and Materials on Sex-Based Discrimination* 566–572 (3d ed. 1988).

3. California Fed. S & L Assn. v. Guerra, 479 U.S. 272, 288–289 (1987).

4. See Margaret Jane Radin, "Affirmative Action Rhetoric," 8 *Social Philosophy and Policy* 130 (1991).

5. My colleague Barbara A. Babcock served as deputy attorney general of the United States in the Carter administration. When reporters asked how she felt about getting the job because she is a woman, she replied that it was better than not getting the job because she is a woman.

6. See Catharine MacKinnon, *Feminism Unmodified* 85–92 (1987); idem, "Feminism, Marxism, Method, and the State: An Agenda for Theory," 7 *Signs: Journal of Women in Culture and Society* 515, 532 (1982).

7. MacKinnon, *Feminism Unmodified;* idem, "Feminism, Marxism, Method, and the State" at 533–542.

8. Nevertheless, in our current nonideal circumstances, "just say no" may be the best legal standard to adopt. See Susan Estrich, *Real Rape* 29, 38, 101 (1987).

9. See Robin L. West, "The Difference in Women's Hedonic Lives: A Phenomenological Critique of Feminist Legal Theory," 3 *Wisconsin Women's Law Journal* 81 (1987).

10. A related instance of the double bind is our attitude toward battered women. Are they weak-willed victims of false consciousness? If so, we view them as degraded selves, so how will they find the self-esteem to free themselves? Or (the other side of the double bind) do we view their situation as one that they are choosing? If so, we risk trying to bring about empowerment by pretending it is already present. See Christine A. Littleton, "Women's Experience and the Problem of Transition: Perspectives on Male Battering of Women," 1989 *University of Chicago Legal Forum* 23.

11. See, for example, Marjorie M. Shultz, "Contractual Ordering of Marriage," 70 *Columbia Law Review* 207 (1982).

12. See, for example, Susan Prager, "Sharing Principles and the Future of Marital Property Law," 25 *UCLA Law Review* 1 (1977).

13. Clare Dalton has expressed well the "heads the man wins, tails the woman loses" irony of the double bind. Dalton relates how patriarchal judges can deny the claims of women in palimony suits either by deciding that no contractual relationship exists because the state presumes that these kinds of relationships are too intimate to be touched by contract, or else by deciding that no contractual relationship exists because the state presumes that these kinds of relationships are too distant to be included in the contractual model. See Clare Dalton, "An Essay in the Deconstruction of Contract Doctrine," 94 *Yale Law Journal* 997, 1106–13 (1985).

10. Prostitution and Baby-Selling

1. I am confining the present discussion to traditional male-female prostitution because I am considering a set of would-be commodities that women would control. Gay male prostitution is an important separate topic requiring an analysis of its own.

2. For various views on prostitution, see, for example, Debra Satz, "Markets in Women's Sexual Labor," 106 *Ethics* 63 (1995); Stephen J. Schnably, "Property and Pragmatism: A Critique of Radin's Theory of Property and Personhood," 45 *Stanford Law Review* 347, 359–360 (1993); Robin L. West, "Legitimating the Illegitimate: A Comment on 'Beyond Rape,'" 93 *Columbia Law Review* 1442, 1449 (1993); Lars O. Ericsson, "Charges against Prostitution: An Attempt at a Philosophical Assessment," 90 *Ethics* 335, 337–357 (1980); Carole Pateman, "Defending Prostitution: Charges against Ericsson," 93 *Ethics* 561, 563 (1983); Alison M. Jaggar, "Prostitution," in *The Philosophy of Sex* (ed. Alan Soble 1980); David A. J. Richards, "Commercial Sex and the Rights of the Person: A Moral Argument for the Decriminalization of Prostitution," 127 *University of Pennsylvania Law Review* 1195 (1979).

3. See, for example, Scott Altman, "(Com)modifying Experience," 65 *Southern California Law Review* 293 (1991).

4. See, for example, Catharine Mackinnon, *Feminism Unmodified: Discourses on Life and Law* (1987); idem, "Feminism, Marxism, Method, and the State: Toward Feminist Jurisprudence," 8 *Signs: Journal of Women in Culture and Society* 635 (1983); idem, "Feminism, Marxism, Method, and the State: An Agenda for Theory," 7 *Signs: Journal of Women in Culture and Society* 515 (1982); Rhonda Gottlieb, "The Political Economy of Sexuality," 16 *Review of Radical Political Economics* 143 (1984); Catharine Wells

(formerly Hantzis), "Is Gender Justice a Completed Agenda?" 100 *Harvard Law Review* 690 (1987).

5. See, for example, Alison M. Jaggar, *Feminist Politics and Human Nature* (1983); Patricia A. Roos, *Gender and Work* 119–154 (1985); Gayle Rubin, "The Traffic in Women: Notes on the 'Political Economy' of Sex," in *Toward an Anthropology of Women* 157 (ed. Rayna R. Reiter 1975). Insistence on continued noncommodification of homemaker services of a wife is also problematic. The context of current sexual politics makes both commodification and noncommodification seem generally disempowering to women. Assimilation to the market paradigm seems defeating for personhood, relationships, and political identity, but given economic and cultural realities, so does continued insistence on a realm of nonmarket interpersonal sharing. On the history of this debate, see Reva Siegel, "Home as Work: The First Women's Rights Claims concerning Wives' Household Labor, 1850–1880," 103 *Yale Law Journal* 1073 (1994). The additional argument that the commodity form of a thing might drive out the noncommodified version of the 'same' thing does not seem at present a great threat to nonmarketized homemaker services. A domestic services market (though not one that is in full bloom) does coexist with a parallel class of unpaid providers. It does not appear that, as a result, we have implicitly come to think of homemaker services in market rhetoric. And if we had—here is the double bind again—many women would be better off at divorce, when money is all that is left at stake. See Lenore J. Weitzman, *The Divorce Revolution* 323–401 (1985), describing the disastrous economic consequences to women and children of the present system of divorce.

6. See generally Elaine Landau, *Black Market Adoption and the Sale of Children* (1990); Nancy C. Baker, *Babyselling: The Scandal of Black-Market Adoptions* (1978), and id. at 43, suggesting that most birth mothers who give up babies for adoption on the black market are 13-to-14-year-old girls. In the past decade, the black market for children has become an international problem. Whites from wealthy nations are buying babies from poor non-whites in less developed countries. In these transactions the problem of the double bind is especially evident. Babies are sold for thousands of dollars (anywhere from $7,000 to $20,000), but mothers receive only a tiny portion of the sale price after the commissions of intermediaries are extracted. See Holly C. Kennard, "Curtailing the Sale and Trafficking of Children: A Discussion of the Hague Conference Convention in Respect of Intercountry Adoptions," 14 *University of Pennsylvania Journal of International Business Law* 623 (1994); Kristina Wilken, "Controlling Improper Financial Gain in International Adoptions," 2 *Duke Journal of Gender Law and Policy* 85 (1995). See also Lisa Swenarski, "In Honduras, a Black Market for Babies," *Christian Science Monitor,* May 13, 1993, p. 12.

7. See Gary S. Becker, *A Treatise on the Family* 140–141 (enl. ed. 1991).

8. See, e.g., Harry D. Krause, *Family Law* 1275 (3d ed. 1990), stating that "in 1984, the 'black market' price for a healthy white infant was reported to be $50,000." Contrast this with figures for nonwhite babies in note 6 above.

9. As Lewis Hyde recounts: "In 1980 a New Jersey couple tried to exchange their baby for a secondhand Corvette worth $8,800. The used-car dealer (who had been tempted into the deal after the loss of his own family in a fire) later told the newspapers why he changed his mind: 'My first impression was to swap the car for the kid. I knew moments later that it would be wrong—not so much wrong for me or the expense of it, but what would this baby do when he's not a baby anymore? How could this boy cope with life knowing he was traded for a car?' " Lewis Hyde, *The Gift: Imagination and the Erotic Life of Property* 96 n. (1979).

10. It is sometimes argued that baby-selling violates the Thirteenth Amendment. See, for example, Angela R. Holder, "Surrogate Motherhood: Babies for Fun and Profit," 12 *Law, Medicine and Health Care* 115 (1984); Anita L. Allen, "Surrogacy, Slavery, and the Ownership of Life," 13 *Harvard Journal of Law and Public Policy* 139, 147–148 (1990) ("One strains to see female liberation in a practice that pays so little, capitalizes on the traditionally female virtues of self-sacrifice and care-taking, and enables men to have biologically related children without the burden of marriage"); idem, "Privacy, Surrogacy, and the *Baby M* Case," 76 *Georgetown Law Journal* 1759 (1988). For a summary of various arguments leveled against baby-selling, see Robert S. Prichard, "A Market for Babies?" 34 *University of Toronto Law Journal* 341 (1984).

11. But perhaps we should prophylactically decline to trust any parents wishing to give a child away for "frivolous" reasons to raise a child adequately if forced to keep her.

12. See, for example, "The Pain of Infertility: One Couple's Choices," *Los Angeles Times,* March 22, 1987, §6 at 12, col. 1. One adopting father remarked: "We felt, in the case of surrogates, we would be involved from the beginning: conception, monitoring the fetus." The couple said they "would have adopted had the surrogate option not been available."

13. See, for example, Joan H. Hollinger, "From Coitus to Commerce: Legal and Social Consequences of Noncoital Reproduction," 18 *University of Michigan Journal of Legal Reform* 865, 893 (1985) ("The payments are not to purchase a child, but to compensate for personal services"). See also Note, "Baby-Sitting Consideration: Surrogate Mother's Right to 'Rent Her Womb' for a Fee," 18 *Gonzaga Law Review* 539, 549 (1983) (arguing that a surrogate mother is not selling her baby, but rather is "provid[ing] a home in her womb for the child of another").

14. In the Matter of Baby "M," 525 A.2d 1128, 1157 (N.J. Super. 1987).

15. Biblical "surrogate" interactions may be seen in this way. See Genesis 16 (Abraham, Sarah, and Hagar) and 30 (Jacob, Rachel, and Bilhah).

16. See, for example, Helena Ragoné, *Surrogate Motherhood: Conception in the Heart* 54 (1994), reporting that "surrogates are predominantly white, working class, of Protestant or Catholic background; approximately 30 percent are full-time homemakers, married with an average of three children; high school graduates, with an average age of twenty-seven years. In addition, 98 percent report that they have completed their own families." See also "Surrogate Motherhood: A Practice That's Still Undergoing Birth Pangs," *Los Angeles Times,* March 22, 1987, §6 at 12, col. 2, citing research finding that "[t]he average surrogate mother is white, attended two years of college, married young and has all the children she and her husband want."

17. Id. at col. 1.

18. See, for example, Ann G. Dally, *Inventing Motherhood: The Consequences of an Ideal* (1982); Adrienne C. Rich, *Of Woman Born: Motherhood as Experience and Institution* (1976); Wells, "Is Gender Justice a Completed Agenda?"

19. There has been relatively little study, however, of the emotional aftermath of adoption. See Eva Y. Deykin, Lee Campbell, and Patricia Patti, "The Post-Adoption Experience of Surrendering Parents," 54 *American Journal of Orthopsychiatry* 271 (1984); Caleb Foote, Robert J. Levy, and Frank E. A. Sander, *Cases and Materials on Family Law* 404–424 (3d ed. 1985); Rynearson, "Relinquishment and Its Material Complications: A Preliminary Study," 139 *American Journal of Psychiatry* 338–339 (1982). As we can recognize from the widespread incidence of child abuse and neglect, not all genetic parents are bonded to their children in any ideal sense.

20. See Janet F. Smith, "Parenting and Property," in *Mothering: Essays in Feminist Theory* 199 (ed. Joyce Trebilcot 1983).

21. According to those who arrange surrogacy transactions, some women who have acted as surrogates do report altruistic motivations. See Noel P. Keane and Dennis L. Breo, *The Surrogate Mother* (1981); compare "Surrogate Motherhood: A Practice That's Still Undergoing Birth Pangs," §6 at 12, col. 2, reporting the statement of a psychotherapist for a Beverly Hills surrogacy center that the majority of surrogates say that "they enjoy being pregnant, are attracted by the money . . . and feel deep sympathy for women who are unable to have children."

22. To prevent women from benefiting financially from reproductive services, some states have passed criminal statutes prohibiting women who relinquish children for adoption from receiving expenses. Others require a full accounting of fees received. See Comment, "Surrogacy Contracts in the 1990s: The Controversy and Debate Continues," 33 *Duquesne Law Review*

903, 922–926 (1995); Avi Katz, "Surrogate Motherhood and the Baby-Selling Laws," 20 *Columbia Journal of Law and Social Problems* 1, 8–10, nn. 34–37 (1986).

23. The same worry applies, of course, to ordinary commissioned adoption in jurisdictions in which paying the mother's expenses is allowed.

24. A solution of this kind has been proposed by Martha Field in *Surrogate Motherhood* (1988). For other regulatory suggestions, see Michael J. Trebilcock, *The Limits of Freedom of Contract* 48–57 (1993); Richard Arneson, "Commodification and Commercial Surrogacy," 21 *Philosophy and Public Affairs* 621 (1992).

25. If she changes her mind before birth, she could choose abortion, just as other pregnant women are free to do. A contractual provision waiving this constitutional right would be void. See, for example, In the Matter of Baby "M," 525 A.2d 1128, 1157.

26. See, for example, Surrogate Parenting Assn. v. Kentucky ex rel. Armstrong, 707 S.W.2d 209, 213 (Ky. 1986), holding that the five-day waiting period in Kentucky's termination of parental-rights statute and consent-to-adoption statute "take[s] precedence over the parties' contractual commitments, meaning that the surrogate mother is free to change her mind."

27. See, for example, id., stating that if a surrogate decides to keep her child, "[s]he would be in the same position vis-à-vis the child and the biological father as any other mother with a child born out of wedlock" and that the "parental rights and obligations between the biological father and mother, and the obligations they owe the child," would be those imposed by the statutes applicable to this situation.

28. See Note, "Developing a Concept of the Modern 'Family': A Proposed Uniform Surrogate Parenthood Act," 73 *Georgetown Law Journal* 1283, 1304 (1985). But compare Hollinger, "From Coitus to Commerce" at 911, n. 174, arguing that financial requirements for surrogate parents are unwarranted because the state does not require that "children generated by coital means be similarly protected."

29. See Margaret Jane Radin, "Market-Inalienability," 100 *Harvard Law Review* 1849, 1930 (1987) (explaining the double bind in the context of surrogacy); Mary Becker, "Four Feminist Theoretical Approaches and the Double Bind of Surrogacy," 69 *Chicago-Kent Law Review* 303 (1993); Debra Satz, "Markets in Women's Reproductive Labor," 21 *Philosophy and Public Affairs* 107 (1992).

30. As this argument seems structurally similar to an important strand of the prochoice position on abortion, feminists who are prochoice on abortion but not on commissioned adoption must distinguish the two. See, for example, Cass R. Sunstein, "Neutrality and Constitutional Law (With Special Reference to Abortion, Pornography, and Surrogacy)," 92 *Columbia Law Review* 1 (1992).

31. See Carmel Shalev, *Birth Power* (1989); see also Marjorie M. Shultz, "Reproductive Technology and Intent-Based Parenthood: An Opportunity for Gender Neutrality," 1990 *Wisconsin Law Review* 297, arguing that courts should apply principles of contract law to agreements to create children through new reproductive technologies.

32. See Margaret Jane Radin, "Reflections on Objectification," 65 *Southern California Law Review* 341 (1991); see also Elizabeth S. Anderson, *Value in Ethics and Economics* 170–175 (1993).

33. For a discussion of what information we currently have on this point, see Lori B. Andrews and Lisa Douglass, "Alternative Reproduction," 65 *Southern California Law Review* 623 (1991). See also Janet L. Dolgin, "Just a Gene: Judicial Assumptions about Parenthood," 40 *UCLA Law Review* 637 (1993).

34. See Allen, "Surrogacy, Slavery, and the Ownership of Life" at 139.

35. See Anita L. Allen, "The Black Surrogate Mother," 8 *Harvard Blackletter Journal* 17 (1991).

36. Johnson v. Calvert, 851 P.2d 776 (Cal. 1993).

11. Commodification, Objectification, and Subordination

1. See Margaret Jane Radin and Frank I. Michelman, "Pragmatist and Poststructuralist Critical Legal Practice," 13 *University of Pennsylvania Law Review* 1019 (1991). See also Michel Foucault, *The History of Sexuality,* vol. 1: *An Introduction* 11 (trans. Robert Hurley 1990); idem, *Discipline and Punish: The Birth of the Prison* 25–29 (trans. Alan Sheridan 1979); idem, "Two Lectures," in *Power/Knowledge: Selected Interviews and Other Writings* (trans. Colin Gordon 1980); Fredrick Jameson, *Postmodernism, or, The Cultural Logic of Late Capitalism* 14–16, 20, 74–76 (1992); Pierre Schlag, "The Problem of the Subject," 69 *Texas Law Review* 1627 (1991).

2. Evans v. Romer, 882 P.2d 1335 (1994), *cert. granted,* 115 S.Ct. 1092 (1995) (No. 94-1039 1995 Term).

3. John Rawls, *Political Liberalism* 265–271 (1993). Joseph Raz, *The Morality of Freedom* (1986). Martha C. Nussbaum, "Human Functioning and Social Justice: In Defense of Aristotelian Essentialism," 20 *Political Theory* 202, 205–207 (1992); idem, "Aristotelian Social Democracy," in *Liberalism and the Good* 217–226 (ed. R. Bruce Douglas et al. 1990); idem, "Nature, Function, and Capability: Aristotle on Political Distribution," in *Oxford Studies in Ancient Philosophy* 145 (ed. Julia Annas and Robert H. Grimm 1988); idem, "Non-Relative Virtues: An Aristotelian Approach," in *Midwest Studies in Philosophy* 32 (ed. Peter A. French et al. 1988). See discussion in Chapter 5.

4. See Gary S. Becker, *The Economics of Discrimination* 14 (2d. ed. 1971): "If an individual has a 'taste for discrimination,' he must act as if he

were willing to pay something, either directly or in the form of a reduced income, to be associated with some persons instead of others." See also Michael J. Trebilcock, *The Limits of Freedom of Contract,* 188–240 (1993); Richard A. Epstein, *Forbidden Grounds: The Case against Employment Discrimination Law* (1992); John J. Donohue III and Peter Siegelman, "The Changing Nature of Employment Discrimination Litigation," 43 *Stanford Law Review* 983 (1991); and Cass R. Sunstein, "Why Markets Don't Stop Discrimination," 8 *Social Philosophy and Policy* 22 (1991).

5. At this point a serious argument would have to be made by those who wish to uphold women's choice of abortion but preclude their choice to sell babies. See Cass R. Sunstein, "Neutrality in Constitutional Law (With Special Reference to Pornography, Abortion, and Surrogacy)," 92 *Columbia Law Review* 1, 44–48 (1992).

12. Free Expression

1. C. Edwin Baker, *Advertising and a Democratic Press* (1994), describes the manner in which commercial interests leverage their purchases of advertising in newspapers into influence over the newspaper content. In Margaret Jane Radin, "Property Evolving in Cyberspace," *University of Pittsburgh Journal of Law and Commerce* (forthcoming) I discuss the evolution of intellectual property in the networked digital environment and examine the thesis that advertising and content will be fused. On candidates and campaigns, see, for example, Rodney A. Smolla, "Report of the Coalition for a New America: Platform Section on Communications Policy," 1993 *University of Chicago Legal Forum* 149 (arguing that the use by political candidates of paid advertising in electronic mass media be prohibited to "end the 'thirty-second spot' political advertising common today, in which candidates are essentially 'sold' to the public like commercial commodities"); Gary Minda, "Interest Groups, Political Freedom, and Antitrust: A Modern Reassessment of the Noerr-Pennington Doctrine," 41 *Hastings Law Journal* 905, 957 (1990) (noting that Supreme Court precedents have permitted "deregulation of campaign financing because market ordering is assumed to be the proper mechanism for both commodities and ideas").

2. An overview can be gleaned by comparing Catharine MacKinnon, "Pornography: Left and Right," and Joshua Cohen, "Pornography: Left," in *Laws and Nature: Shaping Sex, Preference, and the Family* (ed. Martha C. Nussbaum and David Estlund forthcoming).

3. John Stuart Mill, "Of Liberty of Thought and Discussion," in *On Liberty,* in *Three Essays* 79 (1975): "If the opinion is right, we are deprived of the opportunity of exchanging error for truth; if wrong, we lose, what is

almost as great a benefit, the clearer perception and livelier impression of truth, produced by its collision with error."

4. Abrams v. United States, 250 U.S. 616, 630 (1919) (Holmes, J., joined by Brandeis, J., dissenting) ("the best test of truth is the power of the thought to get itself accepted in the competition of the market").

5. Some liberals do argue that the marketplace of ideas should indeed become more analogous to the marketplace of goods. Cass R. Sunstein, for example, argues for a "New Deal" for speech. Cass R. Sunstein, "Free Speech Now," 59 *University of Chicago Law Review* 255 (1992). See also Owen Fiss, "Why the State?" in *Democracy and the Mass Media* (ed. Judith Lichtenberg 1990).

6. See, for example, Turner Broadcasting Sys. v. FCC, 113 S. Ct. 1806, 1808 (1993) (quoting Red Lion Broadcasting Co. v. FCC, 395 U.S. 367, 390 [1969]: "it is the purpose of the First Amendment to preserve an uninhibited marketplace of ideas in which truth will ultimately prevail"); Hustler Magazine, Inc. v. Falwell, 485 U.S. 46, 52 (1988) (stating that "[f]alse statements of fact are particularly valueless; they interfere with the truth-seeking function of the marketplace of ideas"); Lane v. Random House, Inc., 23 *Media Law Reporter* 1385 (1995), No. 93-2564 (RCL), 1995 U.S. Dist. LEXIS 1332 at *20–21 (D.D.C. January 26, 1995) (quoting with approval the defendants' reference to "our tradition of arriving at truth through a robust exchange of views in the marketplace of ideas"); Bernard v. United Twp. High Sch. Dist. No. 30, 804 F. Supp. 1074, 1079 (C.D. Ill. 1992) (quoting Red Lion Broadcasting, supra). See also Donna R. Euben, Comment, "An Argument for an Absolute Privilege for Letters to the Editor after Immuno AG v. Moor Jankowski," 58 *Brooklyn Law Review* 1439, 1445 (1993) (arguing for a privilege under the First Amendment for letters to the editor because "letters to the editor embody the notion of the marketplace of ideas because through the exchange of letters to the editor truth will emerge"); J. Skelly Wright, "Money and the Pollution of Political Equality?" 82 *Columbia Law Review* 609, 636 (1982) (arguing that "the truth-producing capacity of the marketplace of ideas is not enhanced if some are allowed to monopolize the marketplace by wielding excessive financial resources").

7. Indeed, I would say we cannot do without it, for the reasons argued by Hilary Putnam in *Reason, Truth, and History* (1981).

8. See, for example, C. Edwin Baker, *Human Liberty and Freedom of Speech* 22–25 (1989). As Baker points out, the marketplace of ideas does not capture the dialogic ideal. The dialogic ideal posits that each *person* should contribute to the conversation, whereas the marketplace of ideas posits that each *idea* should be represented in the debate.

9. The notion that the government is just as free as anyone else to push

its own ideas, but may not suppress others', gives rise to the unsatisfactory doctrine of unconstitutional conditions. See Kathleen M. Sullivan, "Unconstitutional Conditions," 102 *Harvard Law Review* 1413 (1989).

10. For evidence of this phenomenon, see Baker, *Advertising and a Democratic Press.*

11. See, for example, Geoffrey Stone, "Content Regulation and the First Amendment," 25 *William and Mary Law Review* 189 (1983).

12. See, for example, Laurence Tribe, *American Constitutional Law* 789–794 (2d ed. 1988), discussing two tracks in First Amendment law.

13. Even in the realm of "conduct," it is of course possible to try to account for all regulation on the basis of market failure. Even the universal commodifier sees some role for regulation. Academic lawyers often advocate analogous market-failure arguments as a way of justifying regulation of the marketplace of ideas, but so far they have failed to carry much weight. See, for example, Sunstein, "Free Speech Now."

14. Academic constitutional lawyers—those who have not abandoned the commitment to a laissez-faire marketplace of ideas—have struggled with cases such as flag-burning in which the speech/conduct distinction did not seem clear-cut. See, for example, John Hart Ely, "Flag Desecration: A Case Study in the Roles of Categorization and Balancing in First Amendment Analysis," 88 *Harvard Law Review* 1482 (1975). Ely purports to abandon the speech/conduct distinction entirely (at least for some categories of cases), but then reiterates it by suggesting that the proper question is "whether the harm that the state is seeking to avert grows out of the fact that the defendant is communicating, and more particularly out of the way people can be expected to react to his message, or rather would arise even if the defendant's conduct had no communicative significance whatever." Id. at 1497.

15. In its modern form this conception was elaborated by Alexander Meiklejohn. It still holds force for many liberals who reject laissez-faire ideology; see, for example, Sunstein, "Free Speech Now."

16. See, for example, Robert H. Bork, "Neutral Principles and Some First Amendment Problems," 47 *Indiana Law Journal* 1, 20 (1971).

17. See, for example, John Rawls, *Political Liberalism* 178–195 (1993).

18. See, for example, Frank I. Michelman, "Law's Republic," 97 *Yale Law Journal* 1493 (1988). For example, Janet E. Halley argues that legal regulation of homosexuality restricts the discourse needed both to form personal identity as gay and to engage in political debate about practices that identify one as gay, concluding that such regulation violates a political conception of freedom of expression. Janet E. Halley, "The Politics of the Closet," 36 *UCLA Law Review* 915 (1989).

19. In turn, our culture shapes our institutions. Neither is foundational for the other; instead there is a feedback loop.

20. See Lee Bollinger, *The Tolerant Society* (1986).

21. See Steven Shiffrin, *The First Amendment, Democracy, and Romance* (1990).

22. Baker, *Human Liberty and Freedom of Speech.*

23. John Dewey, *The Public and Its Problems* 144, 147, 148 (1927). For studies of Dewey's political thought see Alan Ryan, *John Dewey and the High Tide of American Liberalism* (1995); Robert B. Westbrook, *John Dewey and American Democracy* (1991).

24. John Dewey, *Experience and Nature* (1965).

25. Hilary Putnam, "A Reconsideration of Deweyan Democracy," 63 *Southern California Law Review* 1671 (1990).

26. Dewey, *The Public and Its Problems,* chap. 5.

27. John Dewey, *Freedom and Culture* 133 (1939).

28. Dewey, *The Public and Its Problems* at 166, 167.

29. John Dewey, *Liberalism and Social Action* 79, 71 (1935).

30. Dewey, *Freedom and Culture* at 97–98.

31. The proposed Equal Rights Amendment was primarily a symbolic culture-shaping statement of this kind. From the point of view of women seeking equality, the fact that we could not pass the amendment shows how much we needed it.

32. For a discussion of development of socially constructed meaning of transactions see Michael Hutter, "Communication in Economic Evolution: The Case of Money," in *Evolutionary Concepts in Contemporary Economics* (ed. Richard W. England 1994).

33. See Robert C. Post, "Cultural Heterogeneity and Law: Pornography, Blasphemy, and the First Amendment," 76 *California Law Review* 297 (1988).

34. See MacKinnon, "Pornography: Left and Right," and Cohen, "Pornography: Left."

35. Employment Division v. Smith, 494 U.S. 872 (1990), "overruled" by Congress in the Religious Freedom Restoration Act, Public Law No. 103–141, 107 Statutes 1488 (1993).

36. David I. Williams and Susan H. Williams, "Volitionalism and Religious Liberty," 76 *Cornell Law Review* 769 (1991) (detailing the Supreme Court's recent struggles with religions other than those in the mainstream). A test case for this hypothesis would be to see whether these judges would uphold a law that happened to proscribe ingestion of communion wine as part of a general prohibition of alcoholic beverages. (During Prohibition judges did not face this question because the "neutral" cultural commitment to mainstream religion had the result that Prohibition was constitutionally and legislatively structured to exempt sacramental wine.)

37. See, for example, almost anything written about jurisprudence by Stanley Fish; for instance, "Dennis Martinez and the Uses of Theory," 96 *Yale Law Journal* 1773 (1987). Frederick Schauer also seems sympathetic to

this position; Frederick Schauer, "Rules and the Rule of Law," 14 *Harvard Journal of Law and Public Policy* 645 (1991).

38. See, for example, Steven L. Winter, "Indeterminacy and Incommensurability in Constitutional Law," 78 *California Law Review* 1441 (1990); Joseph William Singer, "The Player and the Cards: Nihilism and Legal Theory," 94 *Yale Law Journal* 1 (1984); Mark V. Tushnet, "Following the Rules Laid Down: A Critique of Interpretivism and Neutral Principles," 96 *Harvard Law Review* 781 (1983).

39. See, for example, Fiss, "Why the State?"

40. See, for example, Duncan Kennedy, "Freedom and Constraint in Adjudication: A Critical Phenomenology," 36 *Journal of Legal Education* 518 (1986). It seems that accepting a psychological premise of this kind prompts some writers to think that it would be better if we didn't tell conservative judges about the death of traditional formalism. Scott Altman, "Beyond Candor," 89 *Michigan Law Review* 296 (1990).

41. A characteristically pragmatic understanding situates freedom of expression in a world of lowered expectations; a nonideal world. If we think the government will always include scoundrels, or at any rate blind partisans, and if we think the maxim "Power corrupts" must characterize even those who attempt to govern in good faith, then a free-expression rule to entrench the "checking value" makes sense. Mistaken or scurrilous attempts to suppress dissent must always be expected, and so must attempts by those in power to paper over suppression with good reasons for it. In this nonideal world we might have reason to precommit ourselves to disbelieve any such reasons. See Frederick Schauer, "The Second-Best First Amendment," 31 *William and Mary Law Review* 1 (1989); Vincent Blasi, "The Checking Value in First Amendment Theory," 1977 *American Bar Foundation Research Journal* 521; idem, "The Pathological Perspective and the First Amendment," 85 *Columbia Law Review* 449 (1985).

42. Wittgenstein remarked: "Disputes do not break out (among mathematicians, say) over the question whether a rule has been obeyed or not. People don't come to blows over it, for example. That is part of the framework on which the working of our language is based (for example, in giving descriptions)." Ludwig Wittgenstein, *Philosophical Investigations* 30–34 (2d ed. 1958). In many of the cases that confront the legal system, disputes break out over how to describe something. In some of them, neither side changes its position even after being confronted by what the other side believes to be completely uncontroversial reasoning.

43. Tinker v. Des Moines Independent School District, 393 U.S. 503 (1969).

44. United States v. O'Brien, 391 U.S. 367 (1968).

45. Texas v. Johnson, 491 U.S. 397 (1989).

46. City Council of Los Angeles v. Taxpayers for Vincent, 466 U.S. 789 (1984).

47. Flemming v. Nestor, 363 U.S. 603 (1960).

48. See Schauer, "Rules and the Rule of Law." There is a caveat, though. The stronger the judges' commitments are to their own positions on the underlying substantive ground, the less constraining are the rules. Margaret Jane Radin, "Presumptive Positivism and Trivial Cases," 14 *Harvard Journal of Law and Public Policy* 823 (1991).

49. See, for example, Stanley Ingber, "The Marketplace of Ideas: A Legitimizing Myth," 1984 *Duke Law Journal* 1.

50. "If there be time to expose through discussion the falsehood and fallacies, to avert the evil by the processes of education, the remedy to be applied is more speech, not enforced silence." Whitney v. California, 274 U.S. 357 (1927) (Brandeis, J., concurring) (*upholding* a conviction for criminal syndicalism).

51. Standards are transparent to their substantive ground; they are rules only in a prima facie sense. They do not constrain decisions in situations in which the rule is over- or underinclusive with respect to its substantive ground. (I am following the terminology of Schauer, "Rules and the Rule of Law," and others.)

13. Compensation

1. See, for example, Sarah L. Brew, "Making Amends for History: Legislative Reparations for Japanese Americans and Other Minority Groups," 8 *Law and Inequality Journal* 179 (1989); Boris I. Bittker, *The Case for Black Reparations* (1973).

2. In a pure deterrence model, it is a further question whether the damages should be paid to the victim. In favor of doing so one can postulate "demoralization" costs that would otherwise accrue, but against doing so one can postulate that more efficient uses can be found for the money. See Guido Calabresi, *The Costs of Accidents: A Legal and Economic Analysis* 88–94 (1970); Peter Cane, *Tort Law and Economic Interests* 492–493 (1991); A. Mitchell Polinsky and Yeon-Koo Che, "Decoupling Liability: Optimal Incentives for Care and Litigation" (National Bureau of Economic Research Working Paper No. 3634, 1991).

3. See Loren E. Lomasky, *Person, Rights, and the Moral Community* 142–144 (1987).

4. See, for example, Stephen D. Sugarman, *Doing Away with Personal Injury Law: New Compensation Mechanisms For Victims, Consumers, and Business* (1989).

5. One leading example is New Zealand's comprehensive social insurance scheme. See Accident Compensation Act, No. 181 (1982) (N.Z.); Geoffrey

W. R. Palmer, *Compensation for Incapacity: A Study of Law and Social Change in New Zealand and Australia* (1979).

6. I do not mean to imply that interpersonal utility comparison is not problematic if utils do reduce to money. For one thing, people may obtain extra utils by lying about how much they value something, and this would make comparison difficult.

7. *Restatement (Second) of Torts,* §903 (1979). In fact the line between pecuniary and nonpecuniary harms is fuzzy. For example, loss of a wife's consortium was historically thought of as an economic harm to her husband, because the law focused on the services she owed him; but in a modern understanding, the emotional component of the loss is more important. See, for example, Diaz v. Eli Lilly & Co., 302 N.E.2d 555 (Mass. 1973). Moreover, if a goal of economic damages is to make the victim functional again as a worker, it becomes difficult to separate items necessary for functioning from items directed toward emotional satisfaction; psychotherapy or going back to school to learn something new can be both. In this chapter I ignore the difficulty of drawing the line between pecuniary and nonpecuniary harms, as well as what we can learn from this difficulty, and focus instead on the arguments for and against compensation for harms that are determined to be nonpecuniary, however that determination is made.

8. McDougal v. Garber, 536 N.E.2d 372, 374–375 (N.Y. 1989) (citing Skelton v. Collins, 115 C.L.R. 94, 130 (Austl. 1966)).

9. Louis L. Jaffe, "Damages for Personal Injury: The Impact of Insurance," 18 *Law and Contemporary Problems* 219, 224 (1953).

10. The courts traditionally were reluctant to grant recovery for such distress. See, for example, Borer v. American Airlines, Inc., 563 P.2d 858 (Cal. 1977) (holding that children have no nonstatutory cause of action in negligence for loss of parental consortium). But see, for example, Weitl v. Moes, 311 N.W.2d 259 (Iowa 1981) (holding that a minor has an independent cause of action for loss of the society and companionship of a parent who is tortiously injured by a third party so as to cause a significant disruption or diminution of the parent-child relationship); David J. Leibson, "Recovery of Damages for Emotional Distress for Physical Injury to Another," 15 *Journal of Family Law* 163 (1977) (criticizing judicial reluctance to award emotional distress damages in instances of injury to another).

11. See Marilyn Minzer et al., *Damages in Tort Actions,* §4.21[3] (1989) (citing cases).

12. See *Restatement (Second) of Torts,* §925; David W. Leebron, "Final Moments: Damages for Pain and Suffering Prior to Death," 64 *New York University Law Review* 256, 260, 278 n. 92 (1989).

13. Tort recoveries in cases of the victim's death are governed by statute because at early common law an action did not survive the death of the plaintiff. Survival statutes allow the decedent's survivors to recover any

damages the decedent could have recovered, including damages for her own conscious pain and suffering before death, but not damages for her own death; wrongful-death statutes allow surviving relatives to recover on account of the death itself. See Fitzgerald v. Hale, 78 N.W.2d 509, 514 (Iowa 1956); *Restatement (Second) of Torts,* §§925–926. Wrongful-death statutes traditionally limited recovery to pecuniary damages associated with the loss, excluding such items as loss of the decedent's companionship; but many states now permit recovery for nonpecuniary loss, especially parents' loss of a child's companionship, and some courts interpret traditional statutes broadly to get a similar result. See, for example, Green v. Bittner, 424 A.2d 210 (N.J. 1980).

14. Jaffe, "Damages for Personal Injury" at 224.

15. Id. at 224, 225.

16. See, for example, Alan Schwartz, "Proposals for Products Liability Reform: A Theoretical Synthesis," 97 *Yale Law Journal* 353, 364–367, 408–411 (1988).

17. See id. at 413–415.

18. That is why economic efficiency is confidently put forward to explain cultures that have never heard of efficient market exchange. See Edmund W. Kitch, "The Intellectual Foundations of 'Law and Economics,' " 33 *Journal of Legal Education* 184, 187–188, 191 (1983); Richard A. Posner, "A Theory of Primitive Society, with Special Reference to Law," 23 *Journal of Legal Education* 1 (1980).

19. See, for example, Randall R. Bovbjerg, Frank A. Sloan, and James F. Blumstein, "Valuing Life and Limb in Tort: Scheduling 'Pain and Suffering,' " 83 *Northwestern University Law Review* 908, 913, 927–928 (1989): "recent empirical research forcefully concludes that intangible harms like the loss of enjoyment of life are economic losses, and proponents apply a disarmingly straightforward calculus to compute the monetary value of such losses. . . . Evidence on the 'value of life' comes from accumulating findings about how people value risks of injury and death, both on the job and at home. . . . The most obvious application of this expertise is in lawsuits for wrongful death and survival actions, but it would also be relevant to pain and suffering, loss of pleasure of life, and other new notions of intangible loss in personal injury cases. These losses would be newly supportable as 'economic' elements of loss, and would have corresponding and specific dollar values, not merely vague verbal descriptions."

20. Kwasny v. United States, 823 F.2d 194, 197 (7th Cir. 1987).

21. Presumably this value would be measured by observing what people are willing to pay to avoid being injured. See W. Kip Viscusi, *Fatal Tradeoffs: Public and Private Responsibilities for Risk* (1992).

22. See James F. Blumstein, Randall R. Bovbjerg, and Frank A. Sloan, "Beyond Tort Reform: Developing Better Tools for Assessing Damages for

Personal Injury," 8 *Yale Journal on Regulation* 171 (1991); Bovbjerg, Sloan, and Bernstein, "Valuing Life and Limb in Tort"; Frederick S. Levin, "Pain and Suffering Guidelines: A Cure for Damages Measurement 'Anomie,' " 22 *University of Michigan Journal of Legal Reform* 303 (1989).

23. Of course, it is necessary to face the serious problem of determining the circumstances under which it would be just simply to force future awards to follow the patterns of the past. For example, in the past, pain and suffering from medical malpractice has seemed to be "worth" more than pain and suffering from auto accidents. Should this pattern be made into a rule, or does it instead require correction? See Bovbjerg, Sloan, and Bernstein, "Valuing Life and Limb in Tort" at 943, n. 166.

24. Id. at 938–942.

25. The National Association of Insurance Commissioners set forth this nine-point severity-of-injury scale with examples: "(1) Emotional only (Fright, no physical damage); (2) Temporary insignificant (Lacerations, contusions, minor scars, rash. No delay); (3) Temporary minor (Infections, misset fracture, fall in hospital. Recovery delayed); (4) Temporary major (Burns, surgical material left, drug side-effect, brain damage. Recovery delayed); (5) Permanent minor (Loss of fingers, loss or damage to organs. Include non-disabling injuries); (6) Permanent significant (Deafness, loss of limb, loss of eye, loss of one kidney or lung); (7) Permanent major (Paraplegia, blindness, loss of two limbs, brain damage); (8) Permanent grave (Quadriplegia, severe brain damage, lifelong care or fatal prognosis); (9) Death." National Association of Insurance Commissioners, *Malpractice Claims: Final Compilation* 10 (ed. M. Patricia Sowka 1980). Bovbjerg, Sloan, and Blumstein, "Valuing Life and Limb in Tort" at 923, think this scale would be useful in preparing an appropriate damages schedule, and they claim that severity of injury, measured by this scale, accounts for two-fifths of the variance in reported damage awards. They find the categories "intuitively appealing," with the possible exception of the "emotional only" category, which encompasses too wide a range. For example, surely there are emotional injuries that are worse than lacerations and contusions. Id. at 920. Others might find the death category just as debatable; some things are worse than death.

Even if the scale strikes us as intuitively capturing a rough sense of increasing severity of injury, why should we assume that pain and suffering vary linearly with the severity of the injury? On the contrary, death, and possibly "severe brain damage," brings an end to suffering.

26. See W. Kip Viscusi, "Pain and Suffering in Product Liability Cases: Systematic Compensation or Capricious Awards?" 8 *International Review of Law and Economics* 203, 207 (1988) (listing amputation, asphyxiation, brain damage, bruise, burn, cancer, concussion, dermatitis, dislocation, dis-

ease–other, electrical shock, fracture, laceration, para/quadriplegia, poison, respiratory, sprain/strain, and other).

27. Id. at 207–208.

28. Richard Abel, "A Critique of Torts," 37 *UCLA Law Review* 785, 804–806 (1990). It may seem ironic that a socialist comes to the same policy recommendation as some proponents of law and economics, just as it may seem ironic that many feminists ally with them on the issue of baby-selling. The intersection of commodification and wrongful subordination upsets expectations.

29. If the observer is a proponent of a comprehensive social insurance scheme, she still might hold that no payments should be made on account of pain and suffering, not primarily because the payments express or foster commodification, but rather because such payments will need to be forgone if there is to be enough money to go around to satisfy everyone's basic needs. See, for example, Sugarman, *Doing Away with Personal Injury Law* at 36–38.

14. Democracy

1. See, for example, Jules L. Coleman, *Risks and Wrongs* (1992).

2. Dennis Mueller, *Public Choice* 1 (1979).

3. For discussions of prisoners' dilemmas and more recent research into cooperative strategies, see, for example, William Poundstone, *Prisoner's Dilemma* (1993); Elinor Ostrom, *Rules, Games, and Common-Pool Resources* (1994); idem, *Governing the Commons* (1990); Drew Fudenberg and Jean Tirole, *Game Theory* (1991); Ian Ayres, "Playing Games with the Law," 42 *Stanford Law Review* 1291 (1990); Eric Rasmusen, *Games and Information: An Introduction to Game Theory* (1989).

4. Robert D. Tollison, "Public Choice and Legislation," 74 *Virginia Law Review* 339, 364 (1988).

5. See Linda Cohen and Matthew Spitzer, "Term Limits," 80 *Georgetown Law Journal* 477 (1992); Frank H. Easterbrook, "What Does Legislative History Tell Us?" 66 *Chicago-Kent Law Review* 441 (1990); Richard A. Epstein, *Takings: Private Property and the Power of Eminent Domain* (1985); W. Mark Crain and Robert D. Tollison, "The Executive Branch in the Interest-Group Theory of Government," 8 *Journal of Legal Studies* 555 (1979); Edward H. Clarke, "Some Aspects of the Demand-Revealing Process," 29 *Public Choice* 37 (1977); William H. Landes and Richard A. Posner, "The Independent Judiciary in an Interest Group Perspective," 18 *Journal of Law and Economics* 875 (1975). A legal overview of public choice theory is found in Daniel A. Farber and Philip P. Frickey, *Public Choice in Practice and Theory: Law and Public Choice* (1991).

6. See, for example, Nollan v. California Coastal Commission, 483 U.S. 825, 837 (1987), in which Scalia sees his role as using strict judicial review to guard against "leveraging the police power" into an "out-and-out plan of extortion." See also Margaret Jane Radin, "Government Interests and Takings: Cultural Commitments of Property and the Role of Political Theory," in *Reinterpreting Property* 166–190 (1993); Chicago Bd. of Realtors, Inc. v. City of Chicago, 819 F.2d 732, 742 (7th Cir. 1987) (Posner, J., concurring); Hall v. City of Santa Barbara, 813 F.2d 198 (9th Cir. 1987) (Kozinski, J.); Richard A. Epstein, "Rent Control and the Theory of Efficient Regulation," 54 *Brooklyn Law Review* 741 (1988).

7. Robert Bork, "Neutral Principles and Some First Amendment Problems," 47 *Indiana Law Journal* 1, 10 (1971). Compare the skeptical view (discussed in Chapter 2) of Guido Calabresi and A. Douglas Melamed, "Property Rules, Liability Rules, and Inalienability: One View of the Cathedral," 85 *Harvard Law Review* 1089, 1111–15 (1972), in which value commitments are "moralisms."

8. "If in the long run the beliefs expressed in proletarian dictatorship are destined to be accepted by the dominant forces of the community, the only meaning of free speech is that they should be given their chance and have their way." Gitlow v. New York, 268 U.S. 652 (1925) (Holmes, J., dissenting). On Holmes's skepticism, see Thomas C. Grey, "Holmes, Pragmatism, and Democracy," 71 *Oregon Law Review* 521 (1992).

9. See, for example, John Rawls, *Political Liberalism* 190–195 (1993); Charles E. Larmore, *Patterns of Moral Complexity* (1987); Thomas Nagel, *Equality and Partiality* (1991); Joseph Raz, "Facing Diversity: The Case of Epistemic Abstinence," 19 *Philosophy and Public Affairs* (1990); Will Kymlicka, *Liberalism, Community, and Culture* (1989). Kymlicka endorses the "principle of neutral concern" but not skepticism about values. He says (and I agree) that his liberalism without skepticism, although it accords with the thought of some important liberal social philosophers, "may not be what people think of as liberalism, for it has become part of the accepted wisdom that liberalism involves abstract individualism and scepticism about the good." Id. at 13.

10. Although it is not my project here to develop a position that could contribute to the debate about liberal neutrality, I should say that my present view is that any political ideal put forward as foundational cannot help but be connected with a category of views about the good life that may not be universally shared. Charles E. Larmore, for example, in *Patterns of Moral Complexity* (1987), suggests that what grounds neutral conversation is a desire for civil peace and (a particular conception of) an obligation of respect for persons. Those who do not accept a view of the good in which civil peace is paramount, and those who do not accept a view of the good in which a Kantian obligation of respect is central, are labeled "fanatics" (id. at 60) or

put in a category with "virulent forms of racism" (id. at 66) and are simply read out of the political conversation. ("Why must a political value be made justifiable to those who are scarcely interested in rational debate about justification anyway?" Id. at 60. "Liberals need not have an argument to convince people of this sort, only safeguards for preventing them from acquiring political power. After all, such people seem little interested in rational argument." Id. at 66.) Reading these people out of the political conversation might or might not be the right thing to do, but I cannot see how doing so remains neutral in the significant sense that Larmore claims for it. At times Larmore suggests that his view is pragmatic: all he means by neutrality, he suggests, is that liberalism can remain neutral for all practical purposes because there are very few, if any, in our polity at this point in our history who do not share the broad views of the good involving civil peace and Kantian respect. If this is Larmore's view, then it starts to coalesce with the nonneutral idea that what maintains liberalism is a broad enough commitment to the specifics of liberal culture. (If this is his view, I am not at all sure he is right about how marginal in our society those who do not accept his two commitments actually are.)

11. See, for example, Joseph Raz, *The Morality of Freedom* (1986); idem, "Facing Diversity."

12. See, for example, Richard Rorty, *Contingency, Irony, and Solidarity* (1989); idem, "The Priority of Democracy to Philosophy," in *Philosophical Papers,* vol. 1: *Objectivity, Relativism, and Truth* 175 (1991); Amy Gutman and Dennis Thompson, "Moral Conflict and Political Consensus," 101 *Ethics* 67 (1990); Raz, *The Morality of Freedom.* See also the discussion of Martha Nussbaum in Chapter 5.

13. See, for example, Onora O'Neill, "Practices of Toleration," in *Democracy and the Mass Media* 155 (ed. Judith Lichtenberg 1990).

14. John Dewey, *Liberalism and Social Action* 44, 46 (1935).

15. John Dewey, *The Public and Its Problems* 166 (1927).

16. Dewey, *Liberalism and Social Action* at 46–47.

17. Because of passages like the following, I can imagine how Dewey would respond to sound bites and Ronald Reagan's style of communication—and its spectacular success (instead of making things better with TV, telephones, computers, and the coming videophones and interactive networks, we have made them worse): "No intelligent observer can deny, I think, that [symbols] are often used in party politics as a substitute for realities instead of as means of contact with them. . . . That which we term education has done a good deal to generate habits that put symbols in the place of realities. The forms of popular government make necessary the elaborate use of words to influence political action. 'Propaganda' is the inevitable consequence of the combination of these influences and it extends to every area of life. Words not only take the place of realities but are

themselves debauched. Decline in the prestige of suffrage and of parliamentary government are intimately associated with the belief, manifest in practice even if not expressed in words, that intelligence is an individual possession to be reached by means of verbal persuasion." Id. at 72.

18. Dewey, *The Public and Its Problems* at 117–118.

19. "It is at least suggestive that the terms of the theory [of the responsibility of elected representatives] are best met in legislation of the 'pork-barrel' type. There a representative may be called to account for failure to meet local desire, or be rewarded for pertinacity and success in fulfilling its wishes. . . . The reason for the lack of personal liability to the electorate is evident. The latter is composed of rather amorphous groups. Their political ideas and beliefs are mostly in abeyance between elections." Id. at 121–122.

20. Id. at 47, 89.

21. Id. at 88, 90.

22. "Regimentation of material and mechanical forces is the only way by which the mass of individuals can be released from regimentation and consequent suppression of their cultural possibilities. . . . Earlier liberalism regarded the separate and competing economic action of individuals as the means to social well-being as the end. We must reverse the perspective and see that socialized economy is the means of free individual development as the end." Dewey, *Liberalism and Social Action* at 90.

23. John Dewey, *Freedom and Culture* 128 (1939).

24. Thus Dewey criticized Marxism. It was a species of wholesale (mis)understanding where only pragmatic retail understanding would do: "Any monolithic theory of social action and social causation tends to have a ready-made answer for problems that present themselves. The wholesale character of this answer prevents critical examination and discrimination of the particular facts involved in the actual problem. In consequence, it dictates a kind of all-or-none practical activity, which in the end introduces new difficulties." Id. at 80.

25. Dewey, *Liberalism and Social Action* at 92–93.

26. On the difficulty engendered by the fact that these behavioral premises are both postulates (presupposed) and also hypotheses (to be proved), see Frank I. Michelman, "Reflections on Professional Education, Legal Scholarship, and the Law and Economics Movement," 33 *Journal of Legal Education* 197 (1983). For an example of how economic analysis is thought to yield results independent of history and culture, see Richard A. Posner, "A Theory of Primitive Society, with Special Reference to Law," 23 *Journal of Legal Education* 1 (1980).

27. This is the main argument of John Dewey, *Reconstruction in Philosophy* (1948). For example: "The actual conditions of life in Greece, particularly in Athens, when classic European philosophy was formulated set up a sharp division between doing and knowing, which was generalized into a

complete separation of theory and 'practice.' It reflected, at the time, the economic organization in which 'useful' work was done for the most part by slaves, leaving free men relieved from labor and 'free' on that account." Id. at ix–x. Philosophers took this separation to be foundational rather than contingent, and presupposed rather than consequential, and so "retained the separation of theory and practice long after tools and processes derived from industrial operations had become indispensable resources in conducting the observations and experiments that are the heart of scientific knowing." Id.

28. Dewey, *The Public and Its Problems* at 86–87.

29. Id. at 87–88; see also Dewey, *Liberalism and Social Action* at 40–41 (criticizing Mill for this premise).

30. Dewey, *Liberalism and Social Action* at 16, 20, 14.

31. Id. at 14.

32. Id. at 15.

33. Id. at 32.

34. Lochner v. New York, 198 U.S. 45 (1905), came to symbolize the constitutionalism of laissez-faire market principles. The *Lochner* Court found that state regulation of working hours for health and safety reasons was unconstitutional because it violated a substantive due process right to freedom of contract.

35. Dewey, *Liberalism and Social Action* at 34.

36. John Dewey, *Experience and Nature* 67–137 (1929).

37. Dewey, *Liberalism and Social Action* at 34.

38. Id. at 34–35.

39. The California Coastal Commission—the organization charged with balancing conflicting interests seeking to make use of the California coast—provides an excellent example of the trouble that such a structure can invite. The commission consists of twelve members, with four each nominated by the governor, the Assembly speaker, and the Senate Rules Committee, and has seen at least its fair share of the predicted results when the nominated commissioners remain beholden to the individual or body that nominated them. See, for example, Paul Jacobs and Mark Gladstone, "Capitol Probe Shifts to Coastal Commissioner," *Los Angeles Times* A1 (December 10, 1991); Armando Acuna and Nancy Ray, "Malcolm's Hard-Charging Road to Success Turns to Controversy," *Los Angeles Times,* Metro, II, 1 (November 2, 1986).

40. The reason for the war chest, of course, is to have the capability to win elections and stay in power. As public choice theory predicts, campaign finance reforms are extremely difficult to implement through the electoral system that would be regulated by them.

One other strategy for removing the incentive to use the power of office merely to stay in power is being implemented in practice these days—term limits. However we should look at her actions, a legislator in her last term cannot be maximizing her chance to remain in office in any straightforward sense. Term limits pose interesting problems for public choice theory, having to do with the effect on earlier periods of a game of knowing what period is the final one. See Linda Cohen and Matthew Spitzer, "Term Limits," 80 *Georgetown Law Journal* 477 (1992); Kathleen M. Sullivan, "Dueling Sovereignties," 109 *Harvard Law Review* (1995). I imagine Dewey might look on term limits as a social experiment; he might approve of them, at least if we had the cooperative intellectual wherewithal to evaluate appropriately their efficacy *(vel non)* in making progress toward ideal democracy.

41. Some public choice adherents seem to consider *all* legislation as rent-seeking, but that premise undermines the Hobbesian justification for government. See, for example, Tollison, "Public Choice and Legislation." According to the modern Hobbesian theory espoused at least implicitly by most economists, government exists only to overcome collective action problems in order to implement welfare gains to society as a whole. This justification is undermined if it is impossible for government ever to implement welfare gains for society as a whole. See Margaret Jane Radin, "Positive Political Theory as Normative Critique: A Piece of a Pragmatist Agenda?" *Southern California Law Review* (1995).

Instead of considering all legislation to be rent-seeking, therefore, most public choice adherents consider only some of it to be rent-seeking. So far no convincing theory is presented that would distinguish rent-seeking legislation from non-rent-seeking legislation, and it seems that public choice adherents consider legislation to be rent-seeking when they ideologically don't like it. See, for example, Mark Kelman, "On Democracy-Bashing: A Skeptical Look at the Theoretical and 'Empirical' Practice of the Public Choice Movement," 74 *Virginia Law Review* 199 (1988).

42. Unless, perhaps, the laissez-faire market doesn't yield the ideological results they prefer; see, for example, Vicki Been, " 'Exit' as a Constraint on Land Use Exactions: Rethinking the Unconstitutional Conditions Doctrine," 91 *Columbia Law Review* 473 (1991).

43. See Margaret Jane Radin, "Government Interests and Takings: Cultural Commitments of Property and the Role of Political Theory," in *Reinterpreting Property* 188–189.

44. Elizabeth Anderson calls to task those who engage in just such analyses with regard to worker safety and environmental protection; "Cost-Benefit Analysis, Safety, and Environmental Quality," in *Value in Ethics and Economics* (1993).

45. See Margaret Jane Radin and Frank I. Michelman, "Pragmatist and Poststructuralist Critical Legal Practice," 13 *University of Pennsylvania Law Review* 1019 (1991).

46. For pieces that hint at the trouble brewing for the neoclassical assumptions (particularly those of linearity and independence of variables), see

Warren J. Samuels, A. Allan Schmid, and James D. Shaffer, "An Evolutionary Approach to Law and Economics," in *Evolutionary Concepts in Contemporary Economics* (ed. Richard W. England 1994); William A. Brock, "Nonlinearity and Complex Dynamics in Economics and Finance," and Mario Henrique Simonsen, "Rational Expectations, Game Theory, and Inflationary Inertia," in *The Economy as an Evolving Complex System* (ed. Philip W. Anderson, Kenneth J. Arrow, and David Pines 1988).

Index

Abel, Richard, 203–204
Adoption: commissioned, vs. sale of unwanted children, 97–98; domino theory and, 97–98; feminism and, 149–151. *See also* Baby-selling; Surrogacy
Affiliation, political, 69–71
Affirmative action, 128–129. *See also* Double bind
Alienability. *See* Market-inalienability
Alienation, double meaning of, 80; and liberalism, 113; and market rhetoric, 93
Allen, Anita L., 151
Altman, Scott, 259n40
Altruism: and domino theory, 96–101; and gift exchange, 96–99; impersonality of, 98, 100; and market-inalienability, 96–97; Titmuss on, 96, 245n45
American Civil Liberties Union (ACLU), 166
Anderson, Elizabeth S., 229n1, 236n1, 245n45, 248n1, 269n44
Arendt, Hannah, 105
Aristotle, 63, 64, 69; on civic relations, 69–70; essentialism of, 63–66. *See also* Nussbaum, Martha

Baby M case, 141, 146, 151; *Johnson v. Calvert* compared, 151. *See also* Surrogacy
Baby-selling: and altruism, effects on, 139, 146; *Baby M* case, 141, 146, 151; Becker on, 7–8, 13, 137, 164–165; commodification of babies,

137–140, 164–165; domino theory and, 100–101, 137–138; double bind and, 137; feminist arguments for and against, 149–151; and incomplete commodification, 136–140; and market rhetoric, 136–140, 164–165; nature of harm, 174–175, 181; paid adoption of "unwanted" children, 136–138; personhood and, 100, 137; Posner on, 4, 7, 164–165; subordination and, 161; surrogacy and, 140–153
Baker, C. Edwin, 236n53, 241n7, 255n1, 256n8
Becker, Gary S., 4, 7–8, 13, 121, 137
Bentham, Jeremy, 8, 32, 72, 216–217
Blasi, Vincent, 259n41
Blocked exchanges, Walzer on, 48–49, 237n5
Blood: commodification of, 21, 96–98; gift exchange of, 96; and incomplete commodification, 107; Titmuss on, 96, 245n50
Blumstein, James F., 262n19, 263n25
Body parts. *See* Organs
Bork, Robert, 209
Bovbjerg, Randall R., 262n19, 263n25

Calabresi, Guido, 22
Calabresi-Melamed theory of property rights: compartmentalization in, 87, 243n27; on "distributional" goals, 24–26; economic justification of inalienability, 22–29; and Epstein, 26–27; failure to distinguish between

271

from, 60–63, 76–77; flexibility and, 61–63, 77–78; and personal property, 58; and pragmatic conception of human flourishing, 76–78; and residential rent control, 108; and stability and self-constitution, 57, 60–63, 77. *See also* Dialectic of contextuality

Context-embeddedness: and human dynamism, 76–78; and thick theory of person, 62

Context-transcendence: commodification and, 77–78; and free contract, 77; and human dynamism, 76–78; and thin theory of person, 62, 77; and traditional liberalism, 77

Contract, free. *See* Laissez-faire market; Negative liberty; Slavery

Corrective justice, 187–188, 191. *See also* Compensation

Cost-benefit analysis. *See* Market rhetoric; Transaction costs model of economic analysis

Cultural relativism, 65–66, 68–69

Culture. *See* Law, culture-shaping function of

Dalton, Clare, 249n13

Damages: for breach of sexual services contract, 135–136; for breach of surrogacy contract, 146–147; for pain and suffering, 191–202; for personal injury, 184–205

Davidson, Donald, 10

Democracy: commodification of, 206–211, 214–223; Deweyan ideal and, 74, 211–214; education and, 74, 212. *See also* Public choice theory

"Desperate exchanges," 48–49, 125–126, 154, 159; Walzer, on, 48, 50, 237n5

Deterrence, as model of tort law, 185–186. *See also* Compensation

Dewey, John: on Bentham, 216–217; and culture-shaping function of law, 171–172, 222–223; education and, 74, 212; *Experience and Nature*, 172; *Freedom and Culture*, 172; human nature and, 74, 218; and ideal

democracy, 74, 211; *Liberalism and Social Action*, 211–212; on Marxism, 267n24; and nonideal democracy, 211–214; and public choice theory, 211–214

Dialectic of contextuality, 54, 56–57, 76–78; and flexibility, 61–63; personal property and, 57–60; and self-constitution, 60–63. *See also* Human flourishing; Personhood; Pragmatism

Discrimination, "taste for," 160. *See also* Objectification; Subordination

Domino theory, of commodification, 95–101, 103; and adoption, 97–98; and altruism, 96–101; and baby-selling, 100–101, 145; and gift exchange, 96–99; as justification of market-inalienability, 95–96; vs. prohibition theory, 96; prostitution and, 100; rejection of, 101, 103. *See also* Incomplete commodification

Donohue, John J. III, 246n6

Double bind: affirmative action and, 128–129; and conceptualization of marriage, 129–130; defined, 123–124; and elitism of market-inalienability, 124–146; and nonideal justice, 123–124; and organ-selling, 125–126; and rape, 129; social justice and, 124–126; and special treatment/equal treatment debate, 128; and "women's issues," 127–130

Economic efficiency. *See* Market rhetoric; Transaction costs

Ellickson, Robert C., 61, 226n13, 231n28

Ely, John Hart, 257n14

Epstein, Richard: common-pool argument, 26; conceptualist view of property, 32; on inalienability, 26; "rent-seeking" view of politics, 27; on voting rights, 26–27, 231n27; on water rights, 26–28. *See also* Law and economics; Libertarianism; Market rhetoric

Equal Rights Amendment, 258n31

commensurability and, 2; commensurability and fungibility of human attributes, 6; compartmentalization and,
30–32; defined, 2–6; examples of, 23;
fungibility of commodities in, 3; ideal
of efficiency, 5; ideal of individual freedom, 5; objectification in, 6; Posner on,
3; "rent-seeking" view of political and
social interactions, 5; and translation
of values, 120–122. *See also* Market
rhetoric
Utilitarianism: and commensurability of
value, 190–191; and deterrence, 85;
reductionism, 6, 10–11

Viscusi, W. Kip, 263n26

Walzer, Michael: on blocked exchanges,
48–49, 237n5; on "desperate exchanges," 48–49, 237n5; as liberal
compartmentalizer, 46–49, 112; on

market liberty vs. personal liberty,
46–49; on problem of coercion, 48–49;
on "spheres of justice," 46–49
Water rights, 26–28
Weitzman, Lenore J., 250n5
West, Robin L., 129
Wittgenstein, Ludwig, 12, 89
"Women's issues," double bind and,
127–130. *See also* Baby-selling; Double bind; Feminism; Prostitution;
Sexuality; Surrogacy
Words: and facts and values, 89–91;
and the world, 80–84, 88–91, 92–93.
See also Market rhetoric
Work: incomplete commodification of,
104–108; as pure object, 37–38; regulation of, 108–110; vs. labor,
105–106. *See also* Incomplete com-
modification

Zelizer, Viviana, 245n51